Midwestern
Folk Humor

Midwestern
Folk Humor

Compiled and edited by
James P. Leary

With an introduction by W. K. McNeil

THIS VOLUME IS A PART OF
The American Folklore Series
W.K. McNeil, General Editor

August House Publishers, Inc.
LITTLE ROCK

Published by August House, Inc.,
P.O. Box 3223, Little Rock, Arkansas 72203,
501/372-5450

Printed in the United States of America

10 9 8 7 6 5 4 3 2 1

LIBRARY OF CONGRESS CATALOGING-IN-PUBLICATION DATA
Midwestern Folk Humor / compiled and edited by James P. Leary :
with an introduction by W.K. McNeil.— 1st ed.
        p.   cm. — (The American folklore series)
Includes bibliographical references and indexes.
ISBN 0-87483-108-3 (hb : acid free) : $24.95
ISBN 0-87483-107-5 (tpb : acid free) : $11.95
1. Folklore—Middle West. 2. Tales—Middle West.
3. Middle West—Social life and customs. I. Title II. Series.
GR107.L42   1991   91-11948
398'.0977—dc20

First edition, 1991

Executive: Liz Parkhurst
Design director: Ted Parkhurst
Project Editor: Judith Faust
Cover design and illustration: Kitty Harvill
Typography: Lettergraphics, Little Rock

This book is printed on archival-quality paper which meets
the guidelines for performance and durability of the
Committee on Production Guidelines for Book Longevity of the
Council on Library Resources.

AUGUST HOUSE, INC.   PUBLISHERS   LITTLE ROCK

To the memories of
Frank Berigan, Sr., George Russell,
and Warren D. Leary, Sr.—
a trio of Irish-American raconteurs
whose legacy persists.

Acknowledgments

Humorous tales are not told in isolation. They are collaborations. A teller tells, an audience responds. And one who responds to a joke or funny story in one context may tell it in another. This anthology likewise emerges from a long process of listening and telling, by many participants and over several decades. As compiler and editor, I have many people and even a few institutions to thank.

John Meggers, Dean of the University of Wisconsin's two-year branch in my hometown, Rice Lake, gave me my first teaching job in the summer of 1975. In order to enliven evening lectures on Wisconsin Folklore, my daily fieldwork included tape recording a trove of jokes from my old neighbor George Russell. The University of Kentucky granted me a research fellowship to document joke telling in central Wisconsin in the summer of 1978. That summer I also recorded humorous narratives while documenting the folklore of miners on Minnesota's iron ranges for the Minnesota Folklife Program. While documenting traditional music along Lake Superior's south shore for Northland College, with support from the Folk Arts Program of the National Endowment for the Arts, I encountered or heard about numerous fine raconteurs. Although I was too involved at the time with recording musicians to pay much attention to joke tellers, I was able to track down some of the best a few years later. Fieldwork for the Office of Folklife Programs at the Smithsonian Institution and for the Traditional Arts Program at Michigan State University likewise led me to exemplary talkers—as did research for filmmaker Michael Loukinen of Northern Michigan University.

The Folklore Program at the University of Wisconsin, for which I have taught "Folklore of Wisconsin" on an intermittent basis since 1984, brought me into contact with students who both collected and told fine regional jokes. Similarly, my work since 1985 for the Wisconsin Folk Museum of Mount Horeb, formerly the Wisconsin Folklife Center, has occasionally led me to raconteurs.

Besides including the results of my own fieldwork and that of students, this anthology draws upon the labors of a handful of other folklorists and joke collectors: Thomas Barden, John Berquist, Charles Brown, Larry Danielson, James Michael Krotzman, Michael Loukinen, Emily Osborn, Kay Pavlik, Helene Stratman–Thomas, Mark Wagler, and Ward Winton of the Washburn County Historical Society. Barden, Loukinen, and Wagler were especially generous.

For general advice, assistance, and good conversation, I am grateful to Jim Bailey, Archie Green, Niels Ingwersen, Sandy Ives, Richard March, Phil Martin, Elliott Oring, Ellen Stekert, and Tom Vennum. My parents, Patricia and Warren Leary, put me up on many a field excursion and even told some fine jokes. And Janet Gilmore, my wife and fellow folklorist, was a steadfast supporter and critic.

It has been a pleasure to work with the people at August House. Publishers Ted and Liz Parkhurst have been cheerful and savvy. Bill McNeil, general editor of the American Folklore Series, who lured me to this project in the first place, augmented several annotations and wrote a fine introduction. Lou Ann Norman's editorial work was highly competent and committed.

My greatest debt, however, is to the joke tellers themselves. I hope I have done justice to them and to their traditional artistry.

Contents

Introduction

In their folklore studies, Americans have, at least until very recent times, often followed the lead of European scholars. This influence has perhaps been more pronounced in folk narrative publications than elsewhere. Greatest emphasis has been placed on investigation of the *Märchen,* that form of marvelous tale publicized by the Grimm Brothers in their 1812 volume *Kinder und Hausmärchen.* Thus, this aspect of folk narrative was the main concern of Stith Thompson (1885–1976), the major American folk narrative scholar of the twentieth century and the founder of the first graduate folklore program in the United States. Throughout his long association with Indiana University, Thompson promoted the so-called historic-geographic method of folktale study formulated primarily by the Scandinavian folklorists. Under Thompson's tutelage a large number of type and motif indexes, mainly concerned with *Märchen,* were produced.[1] The irony of all this activity was that *Märchen* were in a state of decline and in many parts of the United States were difficult to find in folk tradition. At the same time, the joke, a form of folk narrative found everywhere in the United States, was virtually ignored.[2]

As a result of the bias of folklorists, the earliest collections of jokes were made by joke book compilers whose motivations were anything but scholarly. Among the earliest of these is the two-volume *The American Jest Book* (1796–1797) which, according to its subtitle, is "a choice selection of jests, anecdotes, bon mots, stories, etc."[3] These compilers were concerned with selling books and not with being academic or, for that matter, with the folk pedigree of the items they published. Even so, in printing their joke books they were continuing a tradition dating back to the early sixteenth century when *A C. Mery Talys* (A Hundred Merry Tales), the first joke book in English, was printed.[4]

Many other volumes similar to *The American Jest Book* have appeared in the nearly two centuries since 1797. A few of these that have some items of interest to folklorists are Samuel Putnam Avery's *The Book of 1,000 Comical Stories* (1859) and *The Harp of a Thousand Strings, or, Laughter for a Lifetime* (1868); Frances J. Cahill's *Rare Bits of Humor, After-Dinner Stories, Convivial Toasts and Humorous Anecdotes* (1906); Irvin S. Cobb's *A Laugh a Day Keeps the Doctor Away* (1923); and Willard Scott's *Down Home Stories* (1984). What value they have to the folklorist is entirely accidental, for these compilers made no claim to any knowledge of oral traditions. Indeed, they were often chauvinistic in tone, several of the editors echoing sentiments akin to these expressed by Irvin S. Cobb: "Americans did not invent or discover the short humorous story, it is true. Indeed, some short stories still are making their rounds which were old when the Pyramids were young.... But I am quite certain that we, more than any other people, have made it a part of our daily life, using it to point morals, to express situations, to help us solve puzzles. To these extents, at least, it is a national institution with us."[5]

Typically, these joke book compilers presented a collection of texts with no information about where they acquired each joke, or from whom. There is, however, one who is something of an exception to this trend—he too says nothing in his book about sources, but the methods of his collection are known. Perhaps it is fitting that he was also the least likely and most successful joke book editor of them all. Thomas W. Jackson (1867–1934) was a functional illiterate who started adult life as a railroad brakeman. He was also an excellent joke teller who constantly regaled his fellow crew members and passengers with funny stories. This audience also served to replenish his supply of material. Jackson gained some renown for his joke telling, so much in fact that he started thinking of publishing some of the best material in a book. Lacking the writing abilities of most other joke book compilers, he devised a rather unique approach for coming up with his manuscript. He used C. J. "Mickey" Carr, a conductor who worked on the same train as Jackson, as a test audience for jokes to be included in the book. Jackson would try individual stories out on Carr; if the conductor laughed, the text was retained for the eventual manuscript. Any stories that Carr found appealing were then retold to Jackson's wife, who put them in readable form. Perhaps this pre-testing enabled Jackson's book to sell better than any other joke book in American history.[6]

Gaining less public acclaim at the time were a number of collections of bawdy humor. Although these also lacked information on sources and the contextual data folklorists desire, they are worthy of mention here because their contents were largely drawn from oral tradition. Earliest of these is *The Stag Party,* which, according to internal evidence, was published about 1890. It has been characterized as "perhaps the first large-scale collection of the more modern, non-local type of humor, centering on urban life, immigrant dialects, and a club or smoking room atmosphere."[7] It is, of course, not exclusively devoted to jokes but also includes anecdotes, parodies, songs, and riddles.

Of the several similar publications that followed during the next fifty years, the most important by far are two volumes titled *Anecdota Americana.* The first of these was compiled by Joseph Fliesler, an advertising man of Hungarian background, who in 1927, when the first volume was published, was national publicity director of UFA Films. This, and the second volume, which was not edited by Fliesler, contain jokes, anecdotes, and other unexpurgated examples of earthy wit. Many of the items given in the two volumes are from oral tradition, and several of the jokes have found their way, unacknowledged, into both scholarly and other popular collections.[8] Unlike many similar publications, the two *Anecdota Americana* volumes contain good indexes.

Unlike Jackson, Avery, Cahill, Cobb, and others who published "clean" joke books, the two compilers of *Anecdota Americana* not only used a pseudonym—that of J. Mortimer Hall—they also supplied the books with a fictitious publisher (Humphrey Adams) and even changed the place of publication from New York, where the two collections were actually published, to Boston. Fliesler's 1927 volume and its 1934 follow-up by a still unknown compiler spawned a number of imitative collections, of which the first was the most blatant and the biggest commercial success. In 1933, Samuel Roth published an expurgated version of Fliesler's work, which was given the same title. This *Anecdota Americana* was reissued in 1934 and was revised and updated in 1944 as *The New Anecdota Americana.* Roth's two versions are often confused with the Fliesler and the 1934 collections but are of much less value from the standpoint of folklore. Later works inspired by Fliesler's pseudonymous volume, such as J. M. Elgart's multi-volume *Over Sixteen* (the first volume appeared in 1951), contain little traditional, or earthy, material.

It was not until the 1940s that any joke collections were issued by compilers primarily concerned with the folk nature of the material. One is reluctant to put Charles E. Brown's *"Cousin Jack" Stories* (1940) in this category, but this is clearly where it belongs. Brown's texts are obviously "improved" versions of traditional materials, and the sources are not identified. Brown, however, had some knowledge of the material from oral tradition that he provided in this and numerous other slender pamphlets published by the Wisconsin Folklore Society.[9]

Far more important from the folklorist's perspective is James R. Masterson's *Tall Tales of Arkansaw* (1942), a book that grew out of a seminar paper written at Harvard while the author was working on a Ph.D. in English.[10] Masterson's subject is the entire field of humor concerning Arkansas, and he covers it masterfully. He discusses the fiddle tune and dialogue "Arkansas Traveler," legends about Davy Crockett, Thomas Bangs Thorpe's "The Big Bear of Arkansas," and many other examples of literary and folk humor pertaining to Arkansas. A special bonus for those interested in jokelore is the extensive attention given to biographical information on Thomas W. Jackson and Marion Hughes, the latter responsible for a book similar in style to Jackson's, titled *Three Years in Arkansaw* (1904).

Mody C. Boatright's *Folk Laughter on the American Frontier* (1949), like Masterson's book, is made up of materials drawn mainly from published and written sources rather than from oral tradition. In Boatright's case, though, this was absolutely essential because he was dealing with a historical era at least sixty years in the past, leaving him with few other sources except "memory culture." Boatright's book is also akin to Masterson's in that it is devoted to the entire spectrum of humor and not just to jokes, although there are plenty of the latter. Finally, the two books are similar in that the authors are concerned with the cultural significance of the humor and don't just present a collection of texts. Boatright deftly takes the boasts, exaggerations, metaphors, stump and pulpit parables, tenderfoot baitings, and the like and indicates why they are important documents of social history. In other words, his emphasis is as much on interpretation as on text.

Predictably, Boatright offers a theory of frontier humor. He maintains that much of the humor is a sort of reverse bragging about the hardships of settling a frontier, in which natural features of the landscape were greatly exaggerated. Tall tales and the like served not only as a reaction to the wilderness itself but to Eastern versions of life-out-West. Individual traits were exaggerated to the point of absurdity; people who were sometimes referred to as ignorant and crude became in frontier folk humor the most ignorant and crude people of all. In this way, the frontiersmen who were the subject of laughter achieved a superlative state and thereby lessened the negative effects of humor directed against them.

In 1951, two years after Boatright's book appeared, the initial major work on humor by another important American folklorist arrived. Vance Randolph had already published two pamphlets, *Funny Stories*

About Arkansas (1943) and *Funny Stories About Hillbillies* (1944), but they were unanalytical, popular collections. With *We Always Lie To Strangers,* he provided a more scholarly and more detailed work. Entirely devoted to a single genre of jokes collected by Randolph himself, the book presents tall-tale narratives in categories based on subject matter. Characteristics of Ozark yarns are discussed at length in what remains one of the few extensive studies of American tall tales in folk tradition. Randolph followed *We Always Lie To Strangers* fourteen years later with *Hot Springs and Hell and Other Folk Jests and Anecdotes From the Ozarks* (1965). This collection of 460 items collected by Randolph over a period of four decades is distinctive, among other reasons, because it includes detailed scholarly annotations. Some of the jokes are verbatim transcriptions, but most are the result of recall, being originally written in longhand and typed a few hours later "while the details were fresh in my mind."[11] Randolph did not, however, intend to "improve" on the texts but tried to give them in language as close to the informants' words as possible. *Hot Springs and Hell* is an exemplary collection that includes extensive biographical and contextual data on informants and their texts and the already-mentioned annotations that trace the jokes through a wide range of published sources. In addition, type and motif numbers were supplied whenever possible, indicating the jokes are part of international folk tradition.

Estimable though it is, *Hot Springs and Hell* is not Randolph's last important contribution to the scholarship on folk humor, although it is the last manuscript that the author originally intended as a book. Randolph's *Pissing in the Snow and Other Ozark Folktales* (1976) is a volume made up of 101 tales that had been deleted at the publisher's request from four books of folk narratives that appeared from 1952 to 1958.[12] Thus, the volume Randolph referred to as PITS is that relative rarity, a book made up entirely of material rejected for other volumes.[13] Its value is heightened by Randolph's usual excellent biographical notes on informants and comments about the contexts in which the tales are used. Added to these are a lengthy introduction by Rayna Green that traces the history of Randolph's manuscript and explains the collection's significance, and extensive annotations by Frank A. Hoffman. Although made up of material culled from other publications, *Pissing in the Snow* is "one of the outstanding works on American ribald folklore."[14] It is rare that one can honestly make such a claim for a book that its author originally envisioned as merely parts of several other volumes.

One of the pioneering works in both children's folklore and folk humor was published in 1954. Despite its importance, Martha

Wolfenstein's *Children's Humor: A Psychological Analysis* is generally overlooked by folklorists. There are a number of possible explanations for the neglect of this book by most students of oral tradition. Perhaps most important is that Wolfenstein was a psychologist and made no claim to being a folklorist. Although the study of folklore is interdisciplinary, folklorists are often unaware of works in other disciplines, and they are perhaps less conversant with works in psychology than with those in most other fields of intellectual inquiry. Then, although Wolfenstein frequently wrote about folklore topics, it is clear from *Children's Humor* that she was ignorant of much of the literature of folklore. This may have led her work to be dismissed as uninformed dabbling in folklore. Finally, Wolfenstein was strictly Freudian in her approach, and of all psychological approaches to folklore, the Freudian is the one that has met with least favor from folklorists.

Wolfenstein was a well-known and respected practitioner of child therapy and a specialist in clinical child psychology who collected most of the data used in *Children's Humor* while serving as a psychological consultant to several New York City private schools. Some of the material originally appeared in two articles published in a journal, *The Psychoanalytic Study of the Child,* in 1951 and 1953, one of these essays being the important chapter on children's understanding of jokes. The book's five chapters focus on jokes and riddles from children of different ages and contain much biographical and contextual data. What makes it innovative, though, is Wolfenstein's attempt to show how the child's joking pattern changes as he or she grows older. Nearly two decades passed before any folklorist followed Wolfenstein's lead in this regard.[15]

One other important collection appeared in the 1950s, although it does not rank on a par with Wolfenstein's volume. Benjamin A. Borkin was a prolific writer and one-time head of the Archive of American Folksong in the Library of Congress who is now best known for his several folklore "treasuries."[16] His *A Treasury of American Anecdotes* (1957) is one of the later entries in that series and, of course, has the virtues and faults of the other volumes. Intended for a popular audience, the Treasury mixes together texts taken from printed sources with others recorded from oral tradition, with no distinction made between the two. On the positive side, sources are identified and much information is provided in the accompanying notes. Moreover, several of the texts come from some of the best, and most prolific, folklore collectors in America.

The 1960s saw increased scholarly interest in jokelore, an enthusiasm that has continued to the present. Publications issued during the past three decades are still few, but when compared with the attention jokes received from folklorists prior to the 1960s, the number seems quite impressive. The various books and articles on jokelore issued between 1960 and 1990 have been devoted to six areas of humor: ethnic and racial groups, regional humor, psychological approaches to the study of humor, indexes, historical humor, and the folk humor of urban offices.

Dialect stories dealing with ethnic groups, one of the staples of many early joke books and vaudeville comedians, began to interest a number of professional folklorists early in the 1960s. Richard Dorson, one of the most prolific writers among American folklorists active during the years 1946–1981, published a collection of seventy-six "Jewish–American Dialect Stories On Tape," most of them recorded in 1954 from four men.[17] Ed Cray followed this in 1964 with an article on "The Rabbi Trickster." It is interesting that Cray felt it necessary to apologize for publishing the collection of jokes in a scholarly journal.[18] Perhaps other folklorists have had similar reservations about studying jokes. Thinking they would be regarded as non-scholarly dabblers in trivialities, they have shied away from jokes as a topic for study.

Except for the occasional popular volume like Henry D. Spalking's *Encyclopedia of Jewish Humor: From Biblical Times to the Modern Age* (1969), the study and collection of Jewish humor has languished in recent years, most of the post-1960s scholarship on jokelore of ethnic and racial groups has focused on African–Americans.[19] Although certainly not the first work on black folklore, and not even entirely devoted to humor, Roger D. Abraham's *Deep Down in the Jungle* (originally issued in 1964 and revised in 1970) influenced either directly or indirectly much of the later work on Afro–American folk humor.[20] It is a pioneering volume in several respects, not the least being that it is among the earliest volumes by a professional folklorist to deal in any detail with jokes collected from oral tradition. By focusing on urban rather than rural Negro lore, the book paved the way for many later studies of African–American folklore. Finally, Abrahams devotes much space to analysis and interpretation of texts, treatment that was certainly not commonplace in 1964 when the collection was first published. Abrahams also concentrates on informants and how they tell jokes and other lore, and what it means to them.

But, of course, this was not the earliest publication giving significant discussion to the meaning of jokes told by blacks. Indeed, preceding *Deep Down in the Jungle* there are a number of books and articles in a variety of fields that discuss this matter.[21] Even so, Abrahams succeeded better than any of his predecessors who dealt with Afro–

American folk humor. He set the standard by which subsequent examinations of the meanings of jokes should be judged.

Since 1964, several other publications treating the meanings of jokes told by black Americans have appeared, of which a few merit mention here. Philip Sterling's *Laughing on the Outside: The Intelligent White Reader's Guide to Negro Tales and Humor* (1965) makes the valuable point that the significance of much Negro humor is often missed by white audiences, but the book is concerned as much with literary humor as folk jests. Its 264 narratives include both oral and printed selections—the former collected by Sterling during ten years of fieldwork—but specific contributions are not identified. There is a bibliography, but it is impossible to discern the exact source of most texts; internal evidence provides the only clues. Thus, the value of Sterling's book for folklorists is much less than it should be.

Far more important is Paulette Cross's "Jokes and Black Consciousness: A Collection with Interviews." Cross discusses seven jokes told by two informants in an attempt to find out why the jokes are told, how they relate to black–American attitudes about white America, and why the narrators feel these jokes serve their own purposes and those of their audiences. In sometimes "leading" informants and failing to pursue important points, Cross reveals that she is a relatively inexperienced fieldworker (she was an undergraduate student at the time), but the material she elicits is superb and her perceptions are also quite good. Basically she concludes that the jokes function as a "defensive mechanism" replacing wounded pride and anger with joviality. On the other hand, they also "reflect unpleasant social realities," and in so doing "they emphasize the facts of the black experience in America and the unanimity of the black response to an oppressive system."[22]

More recently, Daryl Cumber Dance, a prolific black scholar, published *Shuckin' and Jivin': Folklore from Contemporary Black Americans* (1978), a significant collection of 565 texts mainly recorded in 1974–1975 from urban residents. Organized into sixteen categories, the narratives here are not all humorous, but a large proportion are. Those who think of black folklore in terms of the Uncle Remus fiction will no doubt be shocked by many of the selections Dance provides, for there is nothing quaint, delightful, or darling about any of these tales. Indeed, Dance frankly admits that several are "obscene, crudely bitter, sardonic, and 'sick.'" Still, he argues, they have the sound of reality about them, and to omit them would be dishonest.[23] Among the book's several virtues are accurate transcriptions of texts, data on informants, and introductory comments to each of the sixteen sections that suggest the common themes of the material therein and its significance in black folk tradition. There are also comparative notes on the tales indicating some of the variants already known, but these are not as detailed as they might be. *Shuckin' and Jivin'* is, as the author maintains, an honest presentation of "folklore as it exists among Black Virginians and among Black Americans generally."[24] For that reason alone, it is a valuable book.

Other ethnic and racial groups besides Jews and Afro–Americans have received little attention from scholars dealing with jokes. Two exceptions to this general trend are Linda Degh's "Symbiosis of Joke and Legend: A Case of Conversational Folklore" and James P. Leary's "The 'Polack Joke' in a Polish–American Community."[25] Degh's article examines the narrative style of Steve and Ida Boda, a Hungarian couple living in the Calumet Region of Indiana. While Steve is known as a joke teller, Ida's repertoire consists primarily of supernatural legends. Although the couple have mutually exclusive repertoires, Degh notes that they tend to reinforce each other in the narrative situation. Her essay makes clear the value of studying genres not only in context but in relation to other genres.

Leary's article, based on sixty-two texts about Poles from a collection of 500 made in Portage County, Wisconsin, in 1978 and 1979, treats the history and cultural rules of "Polack joke" telling in an area with a significant Polish population. Interestingly, about half the "Polack jokes" collected were told by persons of Polish extraction, and reputedly there were several more skilled Polish tellers of these tales that Leary was unable to record. Not surprisingly, Leary found that while Poles were free to tell these jokes anytime, the same was not true of non–Poles. Their tellings

> are confined to moments when they are either not among Poles or gathered with Polish friends. In the latter case, further constraints apply. A non–Pole is permitted to slur a Polish friend only in contexts demanding considerable talk, close cooperation, camaraderie, and mutual respect demonstrated through mutual teasing: "bull sessions" during work breaks, in taverns, and amidst hunting trips. Within these settings, non–Polish participants still cannot utter "Polack jokes" unless: 1) they tell ethnic jokes on their own group, 2) the Pole has done the same, and 3) the rapid-fire exchange of jokes has engendered what locals call the "right atmosphere"—a feeling that the event exists on a licentious plane of unreality clearly distinct from the everyday "real" world.[26]

Though brief, Leary's essay convincingly demonstrates that jokes are many-sided and far more complex than is often assumed.

For some reason, folklorists working with regional materials have been more inclined to put samples of folk humor on commercial recordings than have those working in other areas of jokelore. Perhaps the earliest of these is Hector Lee's *J. Golden Kimball Stories* together with the *Brother Petersen Yarns* (Folk–Legacy Records, Inc., FTA-25) which appeared in 1964. Lee, a mixture of scholar and natural storyteller who earned a Ph.D. with a dissertation on the Three Nephites legend, relates a number of humorous stories collected from various Mormon informants about J. Golden Kimball, a Mormon elder who was never quite able to leave the colorful language of his early years behind him. Brother Petersen is a legendary figure whose exploits are popular with Mormons of Scandinavian background. Useful though Lee's album is, the texts are not in the words of the informants but merely given in Lee's approximation of their style.

The same complaint cannot be lodged against *Not Far From Here: Traditional Tales and Songs Recorded in the Arkansas Ozarks* (1981), a two-record album of which the first is devoted to folk narratives recorded from 1979 to 1981. The eight informants provide twenty-three tales, many of them humorous, that were representative of the folk narrative tradition in the Arkansas Ozarks at the time the records were made.[27] One should realize, though, that while the narratives on this album are related by the informants, they are still not performed in a natural context. The recording studio, or even a tape recording made in the informant's home, is at best merely an approximation of the usual performance situation.

Besides the previously mentioned works of Vance Randolph, there are a number of other publications on regional humor worthy of recognition here. James P. Leary's "George Russell: The Repertoire and Personality of a North Country Storyteller" provides an in-depth examination of thirty-six tales, about half of them humorous, told by a Dobie, Wisconsin lumberjack and farmer and how they relate to his region and his personality.[28] In "Recreational Talk Among White Adolescents," Leary shows how a group of adolescent males in Indiana use jokes and other verbal art forms in specific situations to express attitudes, create self images, and gain status and friendship.[29] A more extensive look at Indiana joke traditions is provided in Ronald L. Baker's *Jokelore: Humorous Folktales From Indiana* (1986), a collection of 352 texts taken primarily from the Indiana State University Folklore Archives. Tales are arranged under twenty-three headings, and comparative notes and sources for each item are provided. A bonus is a twenty-seven–page introduction that reviews various approaches to the study of humorous folktales. This discussion also makes a fine point that some folklorists have overlooked, namely that the same jokes are not always used in the same way even in a relatively small region like the state of Indiana. Thus, in northern Indiana, "ethnic jokes generally stereotype Polish–Americans as stupid, inept, poor, dirty, and vulgar" while the same jokes are used in southern Indiana to stereotype Kentuckians."[30]

Although folklorists maintain correctly that folklore exists everywhere, the indisputable fact is that most collections have been concerned with only a few areas that, presumably, have maintained a greater stock of folk traditions than other parts of the United States. A popular conception is that Appalachia and the Ozarks—both mountainous regions that, in stereotype at least, are more isolated than most sections of the fifty states—are the primary places where folklore is to be found. The numerous folklore publications that have emanated from these two regions seem to reinforce this belief. While there are a large number of books and articles dealing with ballads, folksongs, and tales, there are relatively few publications treating Appalachian and Ozark folk humor. Randolph's work has already been noted, and certainly the work of Leonard Roberts, one of the major collectors of Appalachian folklore during the second half of the twentieth century, deserves notice. Although his primary concern was *Märchen*, Roberts did devote a major portion of his *South From Hell-fer-Sartin: Kentucky Mountain Folk Tales* (1955) to jokes and anecdotes.[31] He also included a few of these humorous folktales in his later *Up Cutshin and Down Greasy: Folkways of a Kentucky Mountain Family* (1959) and its subsequent expansion, titled *Sang Branch Settlers: Folksongs and Tales of a Kentucky Mountain Family* (1974).

Appalachian jokelore received its most extensive coverage in two volumes by Loyal Jones and Billy Edd Wheeler. Their *Laughter in Appalachia: A Festival of Southern Mountain Humor* (1987) consists of material they collected over a period of years to which are added jokes and anecdotes contributed by several participants in a 1983 Festival of Appalachian Humor held at Berea College in Kentucky. Intended as much for a popular audience as an academic one, *Laughter in Appalachia* does include introductory articles by both authors on the subject of Appalachian humor and two additional essays, by W. Gordon Ross and Robert J. Higgs, on the interpretation of humor.

In 1989, Jones and Wheeler compiled a second volume, titled *Curing the Cross-Eyed Mule: Appalachian Mountain Humor*, that followed the same general format as its predecessor. A number of tales are arranged in appropriate categories and the exact words of the narrators are given along with their name and place of residence, but no comparative notes are provided. This book also includes a very readable discussion of the "Esoteric-Exoteric Dimensions of Appalachian Folk Humor" by William E. Lightfoot. Because neither of these books is designed primarily for scholars, professional folklorists may find them wanting. For example, folk revival performers are represented here along with the most traditional folk narrators, and no distinction is made between them. Moreover, for most texts there is no indication of how and when the jokes are used. Nevertheless, the two volumes do provide a good cross section of current Appalachian folk humor.

The most recent examination of Ozark jokelore is my own *Ozark Mountain Humor* (1989), a collection of approximately two hundred jokes and humorous folk narratives told in the Ozarks during the past sixty years. The tales are presented in nine categories and given in the exact words of the informants. Comparative notes indicating the relationship of these jokes to worldwide folk tradition are provided, and information on the dates and places of collection are supplied. Considerable biographical data is included, and sometimes there is discussion of how and when the jokes are used. One of the book's flaws is that several of the texts were not collected by me and contain varying degrees of accompanying information. In some cases, there is little more than a text and name of informant while others have a great body of contextual detail. While these two-hundred-plus jokes do not exhaust all the themes used by Ozark joke tellers, they do cover several of the major themes found in humorous yarns popular among the hillfolk; in that sense, they are representative of Ozark jokelore.

For several centuries, clergymen have been the subject of numerous jokes and anecdotes in folk tradition, so it is not surprising that some authors have compiled collections of such yarns as found in America. What is surprising is that it was not until the late 1980s that anyone undertook a book-length compilation of humor about ministers. Then, in 1989, two such volumes appeared, neither by a folklorist, and both were concerned with jokes and anecdotes about clergymen in the southern United States. Of these, Loyal Jones's *The Preacher Joke Book* is the more successful, primarily because it is the least pretentious. An unannotated collection of texts mostly gathered informally by Jones over a long period of years, with a few other yarns taken from public domain printed sources and from commercial recordings, the book names informants and sources and the informant's place of residence. There are no historical references, comparative notes, or use of folklore reference volumes. Some of these omissions are undoubtedly because

The Preacher Joke Book is intended mainly for a popular rather than an academic audience. The book does have a brief essay by Jones on Southern religious humor, a subject he has studied for many years.

Gary Holloway's *Saints, Demons, and Asses: Southern Preacher Anecdotes* is, as the subtitle says, a collection of anecdotes, but the author clearly has aspirations that go beyond merely assembling a body of texts. In addition to providing entertaining fare for general readers, demonstrating the value of oral tradition to scholars of American religion, and providing folklorists more grist for their mills, Holloway also intends to show what happens when oral texts are transformed to written narratives.[32] Holloway's tales are taken from fourteen printed biographies of Church of Christ preachers and from ten interviews he conducted with eight informants in 1985 and 1986. Unfortunately, Holloway has a naïve, incomplete, and frequently mistaken understanding of folklore methodologies and theories. Stories recorded in tape-recorded interviews, and thus not given in their natural context, are used to demonstrate normal oral style. Even Holloway's introductory commentary is filled with misstatements about the nature of folklore and the relationship between folklore and history. Holloway's attempt to show how the text, texture, and context of oral narrative changes when it becomes written is a good idea but one that is poorly carried out. *Saints, Demons, and Asses* thus serves mainly as a negative example of some of the possible scholarly uses to which a collection of jokes about ministers can be subjected.

Psychological approaches to the study of jokelore may not have resulted in the largest number of publications, but scholars working in this area have definitely produced the most massive tomes. The most famous, and most important, of these is a two-part work whose first volume appeared in 1968. Gershon Legman, who is generally acknowledged as the world's foremost authority on erotic folklore and literature, spent over three decades collecting "dirty" jokes. Much of this material is presented in *Rationale of the Dirty Joke: An Analysis of Sexual Humor* (1968) and *No Laughing Matter* (1975), along with an analysis of the items. No one can honestly question that there is much of value in the two volumes, but there is also a great deal that is problematic. Among the former are the numerous jokes—the books also include several legends, folksongs, and other non-joke material—which are easy to spot because they are printed in italics. Legman's extensive commentary on individual jokes is exemplary. He often provides absorbing accounts of the history and diffusion of specific texts, seeming to leave no relevant sources unmentioned, from obscure medieval references to modern joke books. Legman has total command of the bibliography of erotic folklore and literature, and his expertise is clearly shown.

There are, however, problems with Legman's magnum opus, not the least being that he focuses solely on texts and has little to say about contexts, joke tellers, and audiences. Further, he presents jokes not exactly as collected but as retold by Legman. Moreover, his analysis is Freudian to an extreme; Legman out-Freuds Freud. While the Viennese psychiatrist allowed that some jokes serve to alleviate fears and anxieties and others function purely as entertainment, Legman insists that jokes express only repressed sexual and aggressive impulses. Most folklorists would likely argue against such reductionism, maintaining instead that jokes have many different functions and may have entirely different meanings and functions to two members of a single audience. Another weakness is that the two volumes do not contain an index, or even the bibliography Legman promises in the first volume. Of course, there are many other books about which the same charge can be made, but the problem is considerable here since Legman's two volumes are nearly two thousand pages in length. Furthermore, the classification system employed is inconsistent, frequently leading to duplications. In order to understand where items might be located, one must attempt to think exactly like Legman—an effort that often leads to frustration. Finally, Legman uses the term *motif* in a totally idiosyncratic and virtually meaningless way. In spite of their shortcomings, Legman's two volumes are valuable as a monumental collection and one of the most extensive examinations of jokelore by a folklorist.

Tom A. Burns and Inger H. Burns's *Doing the Wash: An Expressive Culture and Personality Study of a Joke and Its Tellers* (1975) follows Legman in applying both folklore and psychological analysis to jokelore but differs in that it deals with only one joke. Based on a six-volume Ph.D. dissertation, *Doing the Wash* is a detailed exploration of the "psycho-sexual development" of two men and two women who are college sophomores. Filled with jargon and much esoteric commentary, the book makes for heavy reading as the authors focus on the use the four people make of a single "dirty" joke. Among the points they seek to discern are differences in versions told by the four narrators, the activity of the joke in each teller's repertoire, and each teller's social use of the joke. Each narrator was subjected to a series of interviews, close friends of each student were interviewed, then the students were given a physical maturation survey form and a modified Thematic Apperception Test. Much work obviously went into the study—indeed, more time was devoted than is available to most researchers—but the authors engaged in some practices that many folklorists find objectionable. For example, as part of their research the authors talked at some length with their informants' close friends about the sex lives of the four students. Even so, *Doing the Wash* is interesting as the most elaborate example to date of the psychological approach to jokelore as utilized by folklorists. Thus far, it is also the last major attempt by American folklorists to apply such techniques to jokelore. More recent efforts along these lines, such as Baird Jones's *Sexual Humor* (1987), are the work of psychologists.[33]

While interpretation and analysis are desirable goals, they are not any more important or essential than good classification systems; in fact, the latter facilitate the former. Two kinds of indexes are commonly used by folklorists: *type,* referring to whole plots, and *motif,* referring to narrative elements. The best known of these are Antti Aarne and Stith Thompson's *The Types of the Folktale* (commonly called the Type-Index) and Thompson's *Motif-Index of Folk Literature* (commonly called the Motif-Index), but neither of these tomes is particularly helpful to scholars dealing with jokes. The *Type-Index* does have a jokes and anecdotes section, but it consists mainly of the older European jests, or merry tales—humorous stories characterized by short and fairly simple plots, and by realistic settings. In other words, it omits most of the jokes told in modern American tradition. For this reason, several folklorists have had to resort to devising their own classification systems for specific types of modern jokes. In 1963, Jan Harold Brunvand provided "A Classification for Shaggy Dog Stories," a joke form of relatively recent vintage that he defined as "a nonsensical joke that employs in the punch line a psychological non sequitur, a punning variation of a familiar saying, or a hoax, to trick the listener who expects conventional wit or humor."[34] Bruvand's classification, which consists of three major groups and some two hundred types and subtypes, is based on seven hundred texts acquired from printed and oral sources. In recent years, shaggy dog stories have declined in popularity, but if they are like many joke forms, they will undergo a revival in the near future.

Another popular joke form received detailed categorization from William M. Clements in *The Types of the Polack Joke* (1969), which appeared as an issue of *Folklore Forum,* a journal organized and run by graduate students at Indiana University's Folklore Institute.[35] While working as an archivist in the Indiana University Folklore Archive, Clements realized that there were several hundred of the very popular ethnic jokes about Poles in the archive. Using as his inspiration the type and motif indexes devised by European scholars and by the American Stith Thompson, he formulated a very useful forty-five-page index that he later supplemented with a ten-page addendum.[36] Although based to a certain extent on Thompson's *Motif-Index,* Clements's work clearly owes a great deal to Brunvand's example. Both men use letters to designate broad categories with numbers for individual types, but Brunvand's letter categories are fewer and more broadly conceived.

Clement's index and the addendum make the "Polack joke" one of the most thoroughly classified of all joke forms. While such aids are indispensable to future research, they should not be interpreted, as they often are, as the scholar's ultimate goal. Clements himself spells out some of the other possible approaches folklorists might take when dealing with ethnic jokes and jokes about ethnic groups. After discussing the reasons for the Index he notes that his purpose is "not to suggest anything about the psychology of the purveyors of Polack jokes. Nor has there been any attempt to connect these materials with other folklore items in a particular informant's or folk group's repertoire."[37] In addition to these considerations, there is also at least one other potentially fruitful area of study concerning "Polack" and other kinds of jokes, namely consideration of the meanings these narratives have for different joke tellers and members of their audiences. Often the same joke may be perceived as funny by a narrator and two listeners for three entirely different reasons. Few collectors, however, have sought out such information, settling instead for texts alone. So, until better collecting is done, matters such as meaning and function can't be adequately addressed.

One other important index of jokelore remains to be considered. It is perhaps unfair to refer to Frank Hoffmann's *Analytical Survey of Anglo–American Traditional Erotica* (1973) as just a type- and motif-index, for although it contains both types of indexes, it includes much more. There are ten succinct chapters on various aspects of erotic lore; detailed bibliographies of relevant formal, ephemeral, and manuscript items; and a filmography of erotic films. It seems clear, though, that Hoffmann's major contribution is filling in much of the missing material in the standard type- and motif-indexes. Typically, the Europeans and Thompson made a studied attempt to avoid anything that would be considered obscene. Erotic tale types are often described in vague terms, given a title without description, or provided a number with the word "Obscene" in parentheses. The *Motif-Index of Folk Literature* is even more blatant in its omissions and Thompson admits that his own approach is biased and completely subjective.

> Thousands of obscene motifs in which there is no point except the obscenity itself might logically come at this point, but they are entirely beyond the scope of the

present work. They form a literature to themselves, with its own periodicals and collections. In view of the possibility that it might become desirable to classify these motifs and place them within the present index, space has been left from X700 to X749 for such motifs.[38]

By supplying a vast amount of data otherwise missing from folklore indexes, Hoffmann gives a truer picture of both folk tradition and folk humor.

With *Folk Laughter on the American Frontier*, Mody C. Boatright tapped a very valuable vein of jokelore, yet despite his success, he has had few followers who have attempted to mine the riches of historical folk humor. There are works like Michael A. Lofaro's *The Tall Tales of Davy Crockett* (1987) that merit the attention of folklorists interested in humor. Lofaro displays numerous tales originally printed from 1839 to 1841, but although many were derived from an influenced folk tradition, these yarns are literary. Far closer to folk tradition are three collections by Paul M. Zall: *Ben Franklin Laughing* (1980), *Abe Lincoln Laughing* (1982), and *Mark Twain Laughing* (1985). These volumes contain approximately two hundred pages each of jokes and anecdotes told by and about Franklin, Lincoln, and Twain. Each book follows the same basic format: texts are given in chronological order by the earliest known recording, extensive notes placing the stories in context are given, other printed references are identified, and subject indexes are provided making location of individual texts relatively easy. Zall also offers introductory essays discussing the joke telling styles of the respective subjects. Zall's bibliographic work is extensive except in one area—he overlooks much of the literature of folklore.

A different type of historical humor is treated in Robert K. Dodge's *Early American Almanac Humor* (1987). Acting on a suggestion by Mody Boatright, Dodge, a professor at the University of Nevada, Las Vegas, examined hundreds of American almanacs published from 1776 to 1800 for humorous items. He discovered two thousand comic items, only a small portion of which appear in his book. Dodge made inclusions based on five principles: 1) he sought to avoid repetition; 2) he tried to include all of the funniest comic items: 3) he tried to include "most of the comic items which had already appeared in an American form";[39] 4) he sought to include comic items with analogues in literary or traditional American humor; and 5) he tried to provide a representative sampling of the subjects of early American almanac humor. Except for modernizing and regularizing quotation marks, individual items are given as they appeared in the almanac from which they were taken. Dodge arranges the material in eight categories based on subject matter. Most but not all of the material is in joke form. Dodge's slender volume certainly demonstrates that eighteenth century almanacs, which pre-dated the comic almanacs of the nineteenth century, are a rich and virtually unexplored source of folk humor.[40]

Another type of jokelore—that circulated by office copiers—has been even less studied than historical jokelore but for entirely different reasons. Whereas the difficulty of locating historic materials has resulted in few collections or studies, the sheer magnitude of office copier lore has probably contributed to its neglect. Folklorists often tend to shy away from subject matter that exists in enormous quantity, possibly because they think there is no urgent need to document such items. There are other reasons, of course, why copier lore has been generally overlooked. One is that it often is, or seems to be, popular culture rather than folklore, and another is that much of it seems, on the surface, to be of recent vintage. Then, it is transmitted primarily by modern technological means, i.e., xerographic copiers, which to some make it automatically suspect.

Many items of copier lore are far more ancient than they appear to be at first notice. For example, one letter frequently encountered in the copier tradition dates back at least one hundred years.[41] Some copier lore obviously is derived at least partially from popular culture, but then so are many of the jokes and other lore found in American folk tradition that folklorists study without question. Copier lore is demonstrably folklore even though transmitted by technological means.

Much copier folklore is not in joke form, as is amply shown in Louis Michael Bell, Cathy Makin Orr, and Michael James Preston's *Urban Folklore from Colorado: Photocopy Cartoons* (1976) and Cathy Makin Orr and Michael James Preston's *Urban Folklore from Colorado: Typescript Broadsides* (1976). To date, the most comprehensive collections of copier lore are contained in two volumes by Alan Dundes and Carl R. Pagter: *Work Hard and You Shall Be Rewarded: Urban Folklore from the Paperwork Empire* (1975) and *When You're Up to Your Ass in Alligators: More Urban Folklore for the Paperwork Empire* (1987). These two collections present 234 examples showing the variety and richness of the copier tradition, only a small part of which consists of jokes in the usual sense. Dundes and Pagter convincingly demonstrate that old-fashioned notions about folklore existing only among the unlettered are patently false. More importantly, they provide persuasive evidence that the belief that machines and technology destroy folklore is in error. They fail to provide much in the way of comparative notes primarily because they pay insufficient attention to pop culture data and there are few previous studies of the material they treat. As a result, they occasionally fail to identify items circulated by mass media, but their overall presentation is sound.[42]

Although jokes are frequently characterized as simple forms of folklore, they are anything but simple. They are complex, many-sided folk narratives that, when properly collected and analyzed, yield important insights about the culture that perpetuates them. They also have one advantage over some other types of folk narratives, such as myths and *Märchen:* they exist in abundant quantity. While everyone doesn't tell jokes, most people know good joke tellers or at least like to listen to jokes. Yet as the preceding pages indicate, American scholars are only now beginning to realize the importance and richness of the joke tradition. Much remains to be done in exploring this very vital form of American folklore. One of the most useful and basic of the many yet-unfinished tasks is the publication of good field-collected texts from various regions of the United States. The present compilation of jokes from the Upper Midwest is offered as a positive step towards realization of that important goal.

W. K. McNeil
THE OZARK FOLK CENTER
MOUNTAIN VIEW, ARKANSAS

Notes

[1] Of the several type- and motif-indexes prepared by students of Thompson, the most important for American folklore is Ernest W. Baughman's *Type and Motif-Index of the Folktales of England and North America* (The Hague: Mouton & Co., 1966) which was originally produced as a Ph.D. dissertation in 1953. Many of the type- and motif-indexes compiled by Thompson's students dealt with areas outside the United States. See, for example, May Augusta Klipple, "African Folk Tales with Foreign Analogues," compiled for the Ph.D. in 1938, and Kenneth Wendell Clarke, "A Motif-Index of the Folktales of Culture-Area 5, West Africa," for which he was awarded the Ph.D. in 1958.

[2] In *Ozark Mountain Humor* (Little Rock: August House, 1989), p. 16, I have discussed some of the reasons why this occurred.

[3] This book was printed "for Matthew Carey" in Harrisburg, Pennsylvania.

[4] One could date it back to the fifth century when Hierocles published the first compilation of jokes.

[5] Irvin S. Cobb, *A Laugh a Day Keeps the Doctor Away: His Favorite Stories as Told by Irvin S. Cobb* (Garden City, New York: Garden City Publishing Co., Inc., 1923), vii.

[6] See W. K. McNeil, ed., Thomas W. Jackson, *On a Slow Train Through Arkansaw* (Lexington: The University Press of Kentucky, 1985). In an introduction to that volume, I discuss some of the sources of information about Jackson.

[7] Frank A. Hoffman, *Analytical Survey of Anglo-American Traditional Erotica* (Bowling Green, Ohio: Bowling Green University Popular Press, 1973), p. 118.

[8]For information about Fliesler, see Gershon Legman, *The Horn Book: Studies in Erotic Folklore and Bibliography* (New Hyde Park, New York: University Books, Inc., 1964), pp. 485-486.

[9]Brown (1872–1946) published a number of pamphlets on folklore from 1922 to 1945 which he intended for teachers to use in enriching their courses. For a biographical sketch of Brown and his activities, see Herbert Halpert, "A Note on Charles E. Brown and Wisconsin Folklore," *Midwestern Journal of Language and Folklore* VIII:1 (Spring, 1982): 57-59, and Herbert Halpert, "Wisconsin Folklore Bibliography: A Supplement," *Midwestern Journal of Language and Folklore* XI:1 (Spring, 1985): 50-52.

[10]Rose Publishing Company, Inc., in Little Rock, reissued Masterson's book in 1974 with the misleading and inaccurate title *Arkansas Folklore.* That edition is now out of print.

[11]Vance Randolph, *Hot Springs and Hell and Other Folk Jests and Anecdotes From the Ozarks* (Hatboro, Pennsylvania: Folklore Associates, Inc., 1965), xxvi.

[12]The four books, all of which were published by Columbia University Press, are *Who Blowed Up the Church House? and Other Ozark Folk Tales* (1952); *The Devil's Pretty Daughter, and Other Ozark Folktales* (1955); *The Talking Turtle, and Other Ozark Folktales* (1957); and *Sticks in the Knapsack, and Other Ozark Folktales* (1958).

[13]This is the way I heard Randolph refer to the book several times between 1976 and 1980.

[14]McNeil, *Ozark Mountain Humor*, p. 36.

[15]Some publications that deal with this point include Meryl Weiner, "The Riddle Repertoire of a Massachusetts Elementary School," *Folklore Forum* 3 (1970): 7-38; Brian Sutton–Smith, "A Developmental Structural Account of Riddles" in Barbara Kirshenblatt–Gimblett, ed., *Speech Play: Research and Resources for the Study of Linguistic Creativity* (Philadelphia: University of Pennsylvania Press, 1976), pp. 111-119; and Rosemary Zumwalt, "Plain and Fancy: A Content Analysis of Children's Jokes Dealing with Adult Sexuality," *Western Folklore* 35:4 (October, 1976): 258-267.

[16]Some representative Botkin titles are *A Treasury of American Folklore* (1944); *A Treasury of Southern Folklore* (1949); *A Treasury of Western Folklore* (1951); *A Treasury of Railroad Folklore* (1953); and *Treasury of Mississippi River Folklore* (1955).

[17]Dorson's article appears in Raphael Patai, Francis Lee Utley, and Dov Noy, eds., *Studies in Biblical and Jewish Folklore* (Bloomington: Indiana University Press, 1960), pp. 111-174.

[18]Ed Cray, "The Rabbi Trickster," Journal of American Folklore 77 (October–December, 1964): 331-345. The apologetic remarks come at the beginning of this article.

[19]There is the notable exception of Sarah Blacher Cohen's *Jewish Wry: Essays on Jewish Humor* (Bloomington: Indiana University Press, 1987), but although it does contain an article by Joseph Boskin specifically referring to folk humor and a few other general essays that are relevant, the main thrust of this book is literary humor.

[20]Among the large number of twentieth-century works on black folklore that preceded *Deep Down in the Jungle*, the several publications of John Mason Brewer, including *Humorous Folk Tales of the South Carolina Negro* (1945), *The Word on the Brazos* (1953), and *Dog Ghosts and Other Texas Negro Folk Tales* (1958), and some works of Zora Neale Hurston, including *Mules and Men* (1935) and the autobiographical *Dust Tracks on a Road* (1942), are especially worthy of mention because they were written by African–Americans.

[21]Langston Hughes contributed an article titled "Jokes Negroes Tell on Themselves" to a 1951 issue of *Negro Digest* that briefly discusses the subject of meaning. Even earlier, sociologist John H. Burma examined meanings of jokes told by blacks in his 1946 essay "Humor as a Technique in Race Conflict." Two psychologists, Arthur J. Prange, Jr., and M. M. Vitols, published a 1963 article, "Jokes Among Southern Negroes: The Revelation of Conflict." All these essays are reprinted in Alan Dundes, ed., *Mother Wit From the Laughing Barrel: Readings in the Interpretation of Afro-American Folklore* (Englewood Cliffs, New Jersey: Prentice-Hall, Inc., 1973).

[22]Dundes, *Mother Wit*, p. 669. Cross's article originally appeared in *Folklore Forum* 2:6 (November, 1969): 140-161.

[23]Daryl Cumber Dance, *Shuckin' and Jivin': Folklore from Contemporary Black Americans* (Bloomington: Indiana University Press, 1978), xix.

[24]Ibid.

[25]Degh's article appears in Linda Degh, Henry Glassie, and Felix J. Oinas, eds., *Folklore Today: A Festschrift for Richard M. Dorson* (Bloomington: Indiana University Research

Center for Language and Semiotic Studies, 1976), pp. 101-122. Leary's essay appears in *Midwestern Journal of Language and Folklore* 6:1-2 (Spring/Fall, 1980): 26-33.

[26]Leary, 29-30.

[27]*Not Far From Here* was produced by Arkansas Traditions Records. I do not mean to imply that these two records exhaust the list of commercial recordings of folk humor. There is, for example, a most interesting record titled *The Unexpurgated Folk Songs of Men* (1960) which presents a 1959 session recorded by Mack McCormick in Texas. No label name or number is given for this album which, despite the title, includes much more than songs.

[28]Leary's essay appears in Nikolai Burlakoff and Carl Lindahl, eds., *Folklore on Two Continents: Essays in Honor of Linda Degh* (Bloomington, Indiana: Trickster Press, 1980), pp. 354-362.

[29]This essay by Leary appears in *Western Folklore* 39:4 (October, 1980): 284-299.

[30]Ronald L. Baker, *Jokelore: Humorous Folktales from Indiana* (Bloomington: Indiana University Press, 1986), xxxvii.

[31]Leonard W. Roberts, *South from Hell-fer-Sartin: Kentucky Mountain Folk Tales* (Lexington: The University of Kentucky Press, 1955). The 105 tales are presented in three sections: Ordinary Tales, Jokes and Anecdotes, and Myths and Local Legends. The Jokes and Anecdotes section is the second longest of the book's three divisions.

[32]Gary Holloway, *Saints, Demons, and Asses* (Bloomington: Indiana University Press, 1989), ix.

[33]Baird Jones, *Sexual Humor* (New York: Philosophical Library, 1987). Although Jones does discuss jokes his main concern is with limericks, cartoons, and other types of humor.

[34]Jan Harold Brunvand, "A Classification for Shaggy Dog Stories," *Journal of American Folklore* 76 (January–March, 1963): 44.

[35]William M. Clements, *The Types of the Polack Joke.* Folklore Forum Bibliographic and Special Series, Number 3, 1969.

[36]William M. Clements, "The Polack Joke in 1970: An Addendum," *Folklore Forum* IV:1-2 (January–March, 1971): 19-29.

[37]Clements, *Types of the Polack Joke*, p. 3.

[38]Stith Thompson, *The Motif-Index of Folk Literature* (Bloomington: Indiana University Press, 1955–1958), V, p. 514.

[39]Robert K. Dodge, *Early American Almanac Humor* (Bowling Green, Ohio: Bowling Green State University Popular Press, 1987), p. 5.

[40]The book is not without its problems. Perhaps space, or the lack of it, dictated leaving out comparative notes, but other matters are not so easily explained. For example, determination of the "funniest comic items" seems to be somewhat arbitrary. What is "funniest" in the late twentieth century is not necessarily what was considered "funniest" in the late eighteenth century. To be fair, some subjectivity is unavoidable here for, as with all historical research, there is no one from that era who can be asked for opinions. Such difficulties, coupled with the sheer obscurity of most relevant sources, probably account for the small number of studies dealing with jokes from past historic eras.

[41]Alan Dundes and Carl R. Pagter, *Work Hard and You Shall Be Rewarded: Urban Folklore from the Paperwork Empire* (Bloomington: Indiana University Press, 1975), pp. 21-22. Dundes and Pagter title the letter "Full of Corn," but it dates back at least a century; essentially the same letter appeared on a 1901 cylinder recording by Frank Kennedy titled Schultz's Letter from the Klondike. For another version of this letter, see Jackson, *On a Slow Train Through Arkansaw*, p. 69.

[42]See the three texts given under the title "I Had Twelve Bottles" in Alan Dundes and Carl R. Pagter, *When You're Up To Your Ass in Alligators: More Urban Folklore From the Paperwork Empire* (Detroit: Wayne State University Press, 1987), pp. 69-71. The third text is a verbatim transcript of Johnny Bond's 1964 country hit "Ten Little Bottles." Bond can be heard performing the number on *Johnny Bond's Best* (Harmony HL 7308). The two earlier texts given by Dundes and Pagter demonstrate that the recitation has a folk tradition of at least fifty years.

CHAPTER ONE

Yah, Hey!

The first joke I remember hearing as a kid growing up in Rice Lake, Wisconsin, concerned a boasting contest between three Norwegian farmers over who had dug the deepest pit under the outhouse. While the scatological content doubtless appealed to my six-year-old mind, what I remember best is the description of overalled farmers and the rendering of their speech in a lilting "Norsky" dialect. This simple humorous telling was also the first story I recall, whether heard or read, that was peopled with characters who actually looked and talked like my neighbors in an ethnically diverse farming and logging community in northwestern Wisconsin. I have been fascinated ever since by the intersection of folk humor and region, by the funny stories Upper Midwesterners traditionally tell about themselves and their surroundings.

Makis, Kolaches, and Cudahy

Although the exact contours of the Upper Midwest are open to debate, most arbiters apply the term to Minnesota, Wisconsin, and the Upper Peninsula of Michigan (with perhaps a *little* overlap into Ontario, Manitoba, the Dakotas, Iowa, Illinois, and Lower Michigan). The Upper Midwest is the meeting place of Woodland and Plains Indians and the American region with the most entrenched and varied European–American population. It is a territory of woods, waters, fields, and small towns, with a few modest metropolises like Minneapolis/St. Paul and Milwaukee. Its Great Lakes have always been fished commercially and its northern reaches were once mined extensively, while farming, manufacturing, tourism, and logging are the region's economic mainstays. Here in the land of beer, cheese, and sausage—where the polka is danced and winters are unending and where Lutherans and Catholics predominate—everybody is ethnic, the politics are clean, and the humor plentiful.

Like many citizens of the nation or the world, Upper Midwestern men and women might tell jokes—about the president, some current disaster, generic fools, or even talking parrots—that differ little from those told anywhere else. In the main, however, their humorous folk narratives, for roughly a century, have focused on familiar people, activities, and settings. Native– and European–American numskulls, tricksters, and wits (whether Ojibwa, French, Cornish, German, Irish, Scandinavian, Finnish, Polish, Welsh, Dutch, Swiss, Belgian, Italian, or WASP) farm, log, mine, hunt, and fish; they go to town, school, the tavern, and church; and they argue, astound, fool, fight, and love.

This is not to say that such narratives necessarily emerged in the region. Some did, especially those connected with place names like Sheboygan or with aspects of logger's jargon derived from the landscape. Others were brought over from the old country and modified: a landless Finnish farm laborer becomes a wandering logger, a Polish priest's servant becomes a parish janitor. Still others are widely dispersed throughout America and must have been made over: a stubborn Ozark hillman is recast as a Norwegian, giant mosquitoes buzzing through scores of rustic tall tales are situated in a specific "up north" locale. None of these incremental changes makes any one funny story quintessentially Upper Midwestern. Yet collectively, Upper Midwestern folk humor conveys a preoccupation with peoples, places, speech, and events peculiar to the region and sometimes mysterious to outsiders.

Why do Finns commemorate December 7?
   That's the day Pearl Maki got bombed in Two Harbors.

How would you pronounce Cudahy if it wasn't in Wisconsin?
   Cuda.

It was harvest time and an old Norwegian farmer
needed to sharpen, or *slipe,* his scythe, but his
grindstone, or *viev,* wasn't working. So he went to his

Yankee neighbor and asked, "Can I *slipe* with your *viev*? Mine is broken."

Yah, I went over to pick up Wencl for work. Couldn't find find him anywhere. Finally I hear this noise back by the outhouse, and there he is down in the pit.

"What the hell you doing?" I says.

"Dropped my coat," he says.

"That bummy old coat? I wouldn't go down there after it."

"Yah," he says, "me neither, but I had a *kolache* in the pocket."

What's the shortest time in the world?

The time between when the light changes to green and the FIB behind you honks the horn.

A guy walked into a St. Paul bar with his dog. The Vikings were on the tube, first down inside the other team's ten yard line.

Three plays later and they kick a field goal. The dog gives everyone high fives.

An amazed patron asks the dog owner, "Gee, what does he do when they score a touchdown?"

The guy says, "I don't know, I've only had him two years."

Under the right circumstances, each of these jokes might coax wild laughter from Upper Midwesterners, but their telling under any circumstances outside the region would likely invite blank stares or, at best, polite chuckles matched by furrowed brows. Here are widely familiar forms: the "riddle joke" with its paring of plot and character to a question/answer format; the conventional "joke," a brief, fictitious narrative that delivers some incongruity in the final punch line. Here are bits of moderately familiar content: the national observance of December 7 as Pearl Harbor Day; the "Cudahy" name as that of a meatpacking giant (along with Swift, Armour, Hormel, and Oscar Meyer); the homophony between *slipe* and sleep, between *viev* and wife; the plunge in the mire for a valued object; the probably urban

Type-A driver who leans on his horn; and the existence of the Minnesota Vikings as a professional football team. Yet much remains esoteric.

Only those immersed in regional life would know that "Maki" is perhaps the most common Finnish–American name, that Two Harbors on the Minnesota shore of Lake Superior is part of "Finnesota," and that binge drinking is a common northern pastime, especially as winter takes hold. Only Upper Midwesterners would recognize "hey" as a ubiquitous Wisconsin expletive, especially in the greater Milwaukee area (within which Cudahy is a working class suburb) where shouts of "Yah, hey" and "Aina, hey" (isn't that right, hey) drop from every lip. Similarly those within the region would be familiar with dialect jokes, marked by double meanings and misunderstandings that arise from the overlap of several languages, and they would appreciate the improbability of a prudish, probably Lutheran, Norwegian's unwittingly brazen proposition to cuckold his equally strait-laced Yankee neighbor. Any "Bohunk" or bakery eater would associate *kolache* with a prune-, poppyseed-, or apricot-filled Czech pastry as prominent at church dinners and bazaars as *krumkake, kropsu,* or *potica.* Certainly "cheeseheads" from Wisconsin would peg a "FIB" as a cross-state rival, a "Fucking Illinois Bastard" escaping across the border from grimy Chicago, exuding rush-hour freeway manners enroute to dairyland tourist havens. And both Viking fans and hostile Green Bay "Packer-Backers" have made light of the Minnesotans inability to score touchdowns despite the presence of highly touted players and coaches.

Although it would be an overstatement to claim that the cultural worth of these six jokes increases in proportion to their impenetrability by outsiders, it is no exaggeration that the sextet offers insiders a precise glimpse of the familiar. Told about, by, and for Upper Midwesterners, such jokes are valued as fictions that bear essential truths about their shared reality. Together they constitute an important means of creating, acknowledging, and sustaining a rural and small-town world of beer, winter, tavern sociability, religion, and gustatory delights where rival ethnics "talk funny," tease one another, and unite against the breakneck modernity of urban intruders. Elements of this cultural configuration, this world view, are present elsewhere in American life, but its totality exists only in the Upper Midwest.

Talk and Talkers

While work, schools, mass media, travel, government institutions, and an array of other forces may conspire to homogenize all Americans, regional identity lives in everyday conversation. The situations for jocular talk have been manifold in the Upper Midwest. They match the rhythms of life. Weekly occasions for sociable gab might include the following activities: morning gatherings of cafe regulars; lunchtime on the jobsite; afternoon visits to the feedmill or visits by a salesman; evenings at the tavern, around the kitchen table, at the union hall, the softball diamond, the bowling alley, and the fraternal lodge; Saturday auctions, festivals, and dances; and Sunday church suppers and visiting. Life-cycle occurrences, like weddings, funerals, and such seasonal events as Christmas parties, reunions, county fairs, and deer hunting spark the exchange of humorous narratives.

When a number of fine talkers gather with time on their hands, an extended "session," where joke telling exists for its own sake, may well emerge. The lumber camps, where Irish jacks established the tradition of a Saturday evening's entertainment, were legendary for extended story swaps. Here loggers of diverse ethnic backgrounds were thrown together and often compelled, lest they pay a fine, to amuse one another. Roman David "Bimbo" Alexa, a third generation logger of Czech and Italian lineage, fondly remembered sessions in Michigan lumber camps during the early 1950s:

> There were lots of stories years ago. We'd swap stories
> in the evenings. That was one of the pastimes. Some
> couldn't speak English well, or wouldn't talk much as a
> rule, but some of the more happy-go-lucky ones—
> Swedes, Poles, French—they'd be pretty comical.

For Leo Garski, retired from the Army and a maintenance man, recent sessions have come on fishing trips, in hunting camps, at a neighborhood tavern, or following union meetings. Beginning with a single joke, sessions might extend for hours with stories unwinding in skeins. A string of lumber camp jokes, the last of which concerns an Irishman, might lead to Irish stories; an Irishman on the farm might suggest farmer jokes; stories of domestic animals might lead to wild animals, then to hunting, and so on into the night.

Historically such sessions, and even the casual telling of humorous tales, have been dominated by men. Like playing in a dance band, joke telling has been regarded until recently either as something genteel "ladies" did not do because their task was to maintain propriety in the face of male rascality or because the male-dominated society believed that females "just don't know how to tell a joke." Despite such beliefs, Upper Midwestern women have been and continue to be fine storytellers with keen senses of humor. Folklorists and anthropologists may never know for sure just how much women have contributed to the repertoire of jokes generally acknowledged as "male-authored."

Accustomed to exchanging an occasional joke in domestic settings—in mixed company over cards at the kitchen table or with other women gathered for coffee—women began expanding their repertoires and their opportunities for jocular talk when they entered the work force in large numbers in the 1940s. Nowadays society has somewhat relaxed its restraints on women, and as a consequence, women are generally free to tell jokes publicly as often as men.

The late Oljanna Venden Cunneen—photographer, waitress, mother, artist, and tour guide—grew up in rural, heavily Norwegian western Dane County, Wisconsin. Following her immigrant mother, she excelled at Scandinavian handwork, fashioning her own *bunad,* or regional costume replete with intricate Hardanger lace, painting her cupboards in floral *rosemale* style, and crafting elegant trolls, each of them fitted with the garb and tools of different trades, for merchants in nearby Mount Horeb. With a brother named Ole, perhaps it was inevitable that she also heard "Ole and Lena" jokes and was soon telling them in the virtuoso and witty style that characterized her work with needle and brush. By the time she was in her late fifties, she had strung roughly a score of jokes together to form a coherent immigrant saga which she performed for the amusement of busloads of tourists visiting Little Norway, a pioneer farmstead and ethnic shrine.

As a young boy in the 1910s, Jack Foster of Calumet, Michigan, huddled around the woodstove in his grandmother's boarding house to delight in the stories of Cornish miners. Mixing their "Cousin Jack" way of talking with the region's standard English and with the Copper Country's babble of "foreign" tongues (French, Finnish, Swedish, Italian, Ojibwa), these men were what folklorist Richard Dorson called "dialectitians," and Foster became one of them. In the 1980s, marshaling some seventy jests, Foster performed as a featured speaker for local audiences who appreciated his ability to sketch the mining locations, taverns, churches, underground labor, characteristics, and patois of their immigrant ancestors.

The extended monologues of Cunneen and Foster required each to stand and gesticulate, using the conventions of the stage, before a seated audience that clapped and guffawed at appropriate moments. Oljanna Cunneen theatrically donned her Norwegian *bunad* to project a visual image in keeping with her verbal art. "When I wear this, I'm a character, I can get away with things," she told me.

Most tellers, however, prefer dialogues, alternating as performer then audience whenever jokes are told. They never clap or expect applause; they sit when others sit, stand when others stand; and they seldom tell more than two jokes in a sequence. Their egalitarian, everyday mode of performance is not, however, without artistry. Most rely subtly on gesture, pauses, mimicry, and changes in tone to convey action, emphasis, characterization, and mood. And unlike Cunneen and Foster, who had their carefully constructed sequential routines at the ready, most joke tellers depend upon an extended session or "something that just comes up" to spark the recollection of jokes.

For decades, my dad, Warren Leary, has met with cronies for coffee and conversation at Rice Lake cafes. In 1988, talk centered for months around the improbable sighting of cougars, apparently released in the area's woods by some unknown party. One morning, Harold Nelson, co-owner of a soft drink bottling plant, asked if anyone had heard about the kangaroo sighting in nearby Dallas. Incredulous, the assembled reckoned they had not. Harold continued, "Yeah, it turned out to be a Norwegian with his shoelaces tied together." The facts that Nelson is Norwegian, that Dallas is a particularly Norwegian area of rural Barron County, and that Norwegian numskull jokes are rife locally were lost on no one.

George Russell was a master at integrating some tale that not only was appropriate to the topic at hand but also conformed to longstanding patterns of folk humor in the region. Having grown up in a French–Irish–Bohemian Catholic pioneer farming community, logged with Scandinavians and Ojibwas on the Minnesota–Ontario border, and raised sheep, grain, and a social glass in the Rice Lake area, Russell had a story for every occasion. His repertoire mirrored the richness of his world. Sipping brandy at his kitchen table, accompanying him on visits to neighbors, rural haunts, and community festivities, I heard the old Irishman deftly adorn someone else's factual accounts of local figures, locales, or events with pointed twice-told tales of Pat and Mike, Ole and Lena, lumber camp carousers, bear hunters, Bohemian mushroom pickers, French fiddlers, and German priests. Never forcing his role as artful talker, Russell simply cast his gem into the conversational flow, watched it drift away, and awaited the next apt opportunity.

Such incidents allowed George Russell to re-compose a tale, drawing upon its punch line and general plot to improvise a fresh version that built upon what had just happened or been told. Depending on the context, others like Keith Lea might change the ethnicity, "brogue," or location of a character by making a Pole into a Finn, "Stash" into "Eino," and the Tuhquamenon River into the Wisconsin. Leo Garski was fond of linking his tellings with the one before through opening formulas ("You know, that same guy..." or "Yeah, and the next day..."), thus transforming his individual contribution into part of a collective, multi-episodic story.

The skill, stylistic individuality, and sociability of the best racon-teurs have made them valued participants in regional culture. Laborers, tradesmen, farmers, loggers, miners, waitresses, gas station attendants, bartenders, storekeepers, policemen, fire fighters, teachers, students, lawyers, engineers, bankers, businessmen, bureaucrats, social workers, journalists, and clerics, they do not, like the proverbial joke teller of psychoanalytic studies, spew aggression through the mask of humor. Rather they offer a gentle appreciation of the contradictions, conflicts, blunders, witticisms, tricks, eccentricities, and foibles that sometimes render their neighbors and themselves as all too human characters in life's grand jest.

Ethnic Characters, Local Characters

As compressed oral narratives told during the hurly burly of daily conversation, traditional humorous tales contrast significantly with printed novels, or even short stories, that are read in leisured solitude. The printed medium offers the reader chances to turn back a page, to ponder and savor a paragraph. Rather than creating a new world peopled with complex figures, as in novels, folk humor relies on an old world, a world closely resembling the reality of teller and audience—where familiar characters act predictably.

Wiseacres and tricksters, fools and dupes, gluttons and lechers, the pious and the profane, pillars of respectability and rebels, sophisticates and rustics—at root, these characters are found universally in folk humor. In their particular Upper Midwestern guises, however, they might drink Point Beer, fish for walleyes, work in Minneapolis, and go to a Catholic church. Many are ethnic figures and take on such at-tributes associated with their group as eating *lefse, kielbase,* fry bread, pasties, or sauerkraut. They might meet in Ladies Aid groups (Nor-wegians), offer tobacco to elders (Ojibwas), speechify at wakes (Irish), sweat in the sauna (Finns), chomp bratwurst (Germans), or utter blasphemous oaths (French). Ethnic humor is likewise marked by typical names, a few to a group, that often recur to the extent that Pat or Ole or Stash become stock characters whose very name conjures a host of traits.

The fictive Irish duo, Pat and Mike, are perhaps the oldest. Con-ceived in at least the eighteenth century by the British, "Pat," or "Paddy," was the typical bog-Irish bumpkin, illiterate but eloquent, whiskey-soaked, feisty, and superstitious, who left Erin's poverty for Liverpool and, later, America. Ole, the stalwart but thickheaded Scan-dinavian, and his prim yet racy consort, Lena, are the Upper Midwest's most prominent stock characters, doubling as Swedes and Norwegians.

Jan and Bill, a pair of simple Cornishmen, and Jan's adversative wife, Mary Jane, appear in mining country, while Stash is the common Polish character name in folk humor. Eino, Toivo, and Helvi are the most prominent in Finnish jokes, but characters bear other names as well. Where no conventional names exist, some tellers have made them up. Dissatisfied with designations like "this guy" or "an Indian," Ojibwa narrator Earl Nyholm attached "Joe Cloud" to a hunting and fishing guide who amazes and befuddles his white clientele. When I asked Nyholm about an old Joe Cloud I knew, he quickly pointed out that *his* Joe Cloud, a common reservation name, is "just made up," not a real person.

But jokes can be told "on" real people. Indeed some tellers—bent on duping an audience, gaining notoriety, or heightening the absurdity of their tale—spin obvious fictions as their own experiences. In relating a series of tavern jokes, Pete Trzebiatowski enjoyed shifting from third to first person, casting himself as a bawdy, quick-witted barkeep (which was not far from the truth).

To complicate matters further, widespread jokes attributed to particular local characters (like Rice Lake's fearless Norwegian sheriff, Olaus "Red" Norwick, or Richland Center's wily Scottish farmer, Charlie Ferguson) are often told with other funny stories about the same character and are either wholly true or mild fabrications built around a core of truth. After a time, many tellers and their audiences have no clear notion of what old-so-and-so did or did not do or say. Straddling the boundary between fiction and truth, the surreal and the real, these "local character anecdotes," from a scholar's generic perspective, are more legends than jokes. But whatever their formal properties, whether true, made up, or somewhere in between, they are all funny stories to those who tell them, and fact and fiction are freely mixed to suit a given situation.

Enter the Folklorist

Richard Dorson was the first folklorist to chronicle fully the whirl of Upper Midwestern jocular talk, to set down the stories, profile their tellers, sketch their settings, and delve into their origins. A professor at Michigan State University in the 1940s before going on to head the Folklore Institute at Indiana University, Dorson crossed the straits of Mackinac into Michigan's mysterious Upper Peninsula where he sought out raconteurs in boarding houses, taverns, and tarpaper shacks. The brawling loggers, the toughened underground miners, the revels of food and drink, and the babble of tongues inspired him to write metaphorically in *Bloodstoppers and Bearwalkers* of "harvesting" stories, of rich narrative "lodes," of "yeasty" jokes, of the verbal prowess of "dialectitians."

Elsewhere in the region, the "discovery" of folk humor by scholars has, until the mid-1970s, been sporadic. From 1935 to 1939, field workers for the Wisconsin Folklore division of the Federal Writers' Project, under Charles Brown, director of the State Historical Society Museum, captured jokes and anecdotes concerning Cornish life in southwestern Wisconsin, lumberjacks in northwestern Wisconsin's Chippewa Valley, and a few ethnic groups. Because of their literary training and the fact that portable sound recording equipment was not readily available, the fieldworkers recast the oral narratives they heard in a style that, while fairly unadorned, lacks the authenticity of real speech.

In the summers of 1940, 1941, and 1946, Helene Stratman-Thomas of the University of Wisconsin, armed with disc-recording equipment from the Library of Congress Archive of American Folksong, traveled Wisconsin in search of traditional music. Her trove of more than 700 songs and tunes was further enriched by occupational reminiscences, poetic recitations, and a pair of jocular tales concerning, respectively, Cornish miners and a German farmer. The availability of tape recorders in the 1950s and the burgeoning subdiscipline of oral history yielded a few more tellings as community historians taped "old timers," then transcribed their reminiscences, factual and fictive, for local publications.

Since the mid-1970s, a handful of scholars interested in folklore have been active in the Upper Midwest. A few have recorded humorous narratives: John Berquist, Larry Danielson, Kay Pavlik, James Michael Krotzman, and Michael Loukinen. Sometimes working separately, sometimes collaboratively, Mark Wagler, Tom Barden, and Emily Osborn recorded several hundred jokes in southwestern Wisconsin and throughout the state under Pine River Valley and Wisconsin Humor projects. Students in my "Folklore of Wisconsin" course at the University of Wisconsin have also gleaned humorous narratives from tellers around the state and region, the most interesting of which has been a series of "Plattdeutsch" tales that Lois Buss heard from her extended family in the Shawano area and lumber camp stories recorded by Dawn Brunner and Shelly Wolf. My own efforts have turned up more than 1,000 humorous narratives.

Abundant though they are, funny stories are not the simplest phenomenon to document. Since the telling of individual jokes and prolonged sessions are spontaneous events and since there is no infallible way of predicting where and when they will happen, researchers in search of folk humor have resorted to various strategies. They have lurked about hoping to recognize and experience natural joke-telling situations as they emerged, then engaged in documentation after the fact. They have inquired after good joke tellers, then set up meetings with several of them to create an approximation of a naturally occurring sessio, or they have sought out noted tellers individually.

When doing prolonged fieldwork in Portage County, Wisconsin, in the summer of 1978, I would walk each morning from my rented room in Stevens Point to a cafe on the main street where a crowd gathered for coffee and sociable talk that always included a few jokes. Once a day—sometimes in mid-afternoon, sometimes in the evening— I would stop in at Dominic Slusarski's Ritz Tavern where "old timers" thronged or at the Unique Bar which catered to a younger set. After overhearing jokes exchanged in these settings, I would introduce myself and my interest to the talkers, take some notes, then write down what I could recall once back in my room.

While useful for its insights into the ebb and flow of jocular talk in everyday life, this serendipitous method did not provide an abundance of stories, and I was not able to capture the tellers' own words. Consequently, I began asking about people with local reputations as raconteurs with a broad repertoire of humorous narratives. They were well known and easy to find: Keith Lea, Ed Grabowski, Jon Mason, Emery Olson, Leo Garski, Pete Trzebiatowski, and Max Trzebiatowski.

Lea, a librarian, and Grabowski, an administrator, both worked in the Learning Resource Center of the University of Wisconsin–Stevens Point (UWSP). Grabowski informed me that morning coffee breaks in a basement common room featured joke telling nearly every day. I began turning up with my tape recorder. On the second session, Mason, an electrician, joined us. He reckoned that I ought to hear his buddies, Olson, a carpenter, and Garski, a maintenance man, both of whom also worked at UWSP. Soon we were gathering for an evening at a local tavern. The coffee room sessions yielded from twenty to forty jokes at a stretch, while a trio of tavern meetings averaged more than 100 tellings each. Remarkable as extended, even epic, storytelling events, the sessions in coffee room and tavern still had to be augmented with follow-up interviews during which I could ask questions that would have disrupted a skein of performances.

In the case of the Trzebiatowski cousins, I met with each on several occasions in the kitchens of their respective homes. I recorded their biographies, then asked topical questions—do you know any jokes about farmers? about Pat and Mike? about Poles? about tavernkeepers?

about priests?—that seemed to fit their experiences. They told me scores of jokes. I followed up the tellings with questions regarding the source of a given joke, the context in which it might be performed, their notions regarding its significance, and the like. Useful as a means of deciphering the historical, cultural, and personal dimensions of a particular joke from a particular teller, this approach was also awkward. Neither of the Trzebiatowski cousins were accustomed to one-man shows, and although they were good-natured about proceeding, they also occasionally had trouble thinking of jokes without the stimulus of another performer. I soon learned that rather than ask for a joke along topical lines, it was better to tell one in the expectation that it would be matched.

Since this initial work in Portage County, I have kept alert. When Alice Kania told a joke at a house party in the family basement that she had learned in Polish from her dad back in the early 1930s, I made a mental note and recorded it from her later in the evening. When my dad mentioned exchanging jokes and anecdotes with Joe Doyle, a rural Irish–American acquaintance, I arranged a session with the two. And in the course of conversations with Harry Chaudoir about farming, with Lauri "Tuggers" Koski about mining, and with Roman David "Bimbo" Alexa about logging, I threw in occupational jokes heard elsewhere and was rewarded with several new ones.

Working spatially outward from Portage County, the rough geographical center of the Upper Midwest, I have, like a geologist making test drills, sampled humorous narratives throughout the region. In doing so, I have acquired a sense of continuities and boundaries, of what it is about the performers and their jocular repertoires that holds them together and sets them apart from the talkers and tales of other places.

On This Anthology

This anthology reveals those continuities and boundaries. Out in the world, of course, jocular tales are seldom performed along discrete topical lines for more than a few tellings, nor are these tellings generally arranged in any particular order, nor are they named. But Upper Midwestern raconteurs do use rough categories like "farmer jokes" or "Finnish jokes"; they are aware that Pat and Mike's saga begins in the old country, is played out in America, and ends in the afterlife; and they often recall a certain joke with a catch phrase. I have taken the liberty of extending such tendencies. All 305 jokes are aligned topically, arranged with calculation, and individually named.

The first nine chapters concern ethnicity and follow an approximate "who came first" order, from Indians to French, Cornish, Germans, Irish, Scandinavians (Norwegians and Swedes), Finns, Poles, and others (Welsh, Dutch, Swiss, Belgians, and Italians). Doubtless the traditional humor of African–, Asian–, and Hispanic–Americans, relative newcomers, will eventually absorb Upper-Midwestern features. But the groups included here have been active participants in a broad span of regional life for more than a century, and their folk humor has shed much of its Old World skin. A trio of subsequent chapters offers the occupational humor of loggers, miners, and farmers, the region's distinctive industries, while a final pair treats place: the small towns around which the bulk of regional life revolves and the abundant woods and waters where game is stalked and fish are hooked.

Not surprisingly, there is considerable overlap from section to section as Italians mine, Finns farm, Irishmen hunt, Swedes log, and Ojibwas fish. Text 272, for example, might fit in "French" or "Loggers" or "Townsfolk" chapters, but I placed it in the latter because it emphasized tavern repartee more than ethnicity or occupation. Given the nature of individual raconteurs and oral tradition, it is also possible for the same basic story to be offered with considerable differences of detail and emphasis. In five such instances (Texts 60 & 134, 61 & 156, 72 & 247, 114 & 260, 150 & 294), I have placed the contrasting versions in separate chapters.

Introductions to each chapter sketch historical and thematic matters while offering speculations on tantalizing questions. How have Ojibwa jokes drawn upon sacred mythology? Why are Irish jokes, even those told currently, invariably set in the nineteenth century while Scandinavian jokes, especially those involving Ole and Lena, may be set any time from the mid-nineteenth century to the present? Why the dearth of German jokes relative to their numbers, and why have Polish jokes only erupted recently? For what reasons do the bygone eras of underground mining and lumber camps still command artful talk? And how do farmer jokes address the shift from agriculture to agribusiness?

The humorous texts following chapter introductions have, with a few exceptions, been transcribed verbatim from field recordings. The printed page is a poor medium for conveying the skills of raconteurs better heard and seen. When possible, nevertheless, I have tried to do just that through paragraphing, non-standard orthography (especially in the case of "foreign" dialects), explanations in brackets, and commentary.

The commentary provides succinct contextual and interpretive information, especially in the case of esoteric regional tales. It also offers occasional references to standard classification systems of narrative elements (motifs) and plot forms (types) compiled by folkforists: Ernest W. Baughman, *Type and Motif Index of the Folktales of England and North America* (The Hague: Mouton & Co., 1966); Stith Thompson, *Motif-Index of Folk Literature*, 6 volumes, revised edition (Bloomington: Indiana University Press, 1955); Stith Thompson, *The Types of the Folktale* (Helsinki: Suomalainen Tiedakatemia, 1961); and Frank Hoffman, "Motif Index of Erotic Literature" in *Analytical Survery of Anglo–American Traditional Erotica* (Bowling Green, Ohio: Bowling Green University Popular Press, 1973). In the citation of the motifs, Baughman and Hoffman additions to the Thompson canon are preceded by the authors' names. The citation of types are preceded by the letters "AT" designating both Antti Aarne and Stith Thompson, thus acknowledging that Thompson's *The Types of the Folktale* is a revision of an earlier effort by Aarne.

In addition, an appendix of notes provides more complete comparative information regarding individual tales, along with data on who recorded the telling, from whom, when, and where. The notes also sketch, when possible, the life histories and narrative proclivities of the tellers.

One Wintry Evening

The best glimpse, the deepest sense, of tellers and their tales is, of course, found in life not books. I recall one wintry evening in late December some thirty years ago. Friends of my parents were gathered for drinks in the living room of our Rice Lake, Wisconsin, home. We kids were playing on the fringes, but I was listening. My dad was telling a story.

> You know, the Irish over in St. Paul needed a new
> bishop and they recruited one from Ireland, Father
> Hooley. He was to arrive to say midnight mass at
> Christmas. But his train was early and there was no one
> to meet him. So he said to himself, "A cold night like
> this, a wee drop would do me good."

A smirk rippled through the audience. Assorted Learys, Gannons, Conleys, and O'Brians (Irish and Catholic, Upper Midwesterners) recognized the setting, the season, and the genre. They knew that the Irish dominated St. Paul, wresting church control from more populous Germans; they knew the solemnity and pomp of midnight mass, the biting cold around Christmas; they knew, cradling their own "wee drops," of the Irish fondness for strong drink.

Well, Father Hooley had a few too many and lost his
way. He staggered into Minneapolis. It was late and
dark, but he saw the lights of a great church. It was a
Lutheran Church. Full of Norwegians.

Another chuckle of recognition. Wasn't Minneapolis, like Rice
Lake, a Scandinavian town, a place where the Gothic spires of substan-
tial Lutheran churches poked heavenward, a territory where coffee, not
whiskey, was the social drink?

Father Hooley made his way around the back of the
church and went in just off the sacristy. He was just
over from Ireland, and the Lutheran churches look
enough like the Catholic that he figured this is what a
church is like in America.

The minister hadn't showed up yet, the people were
just filing in and the choir was singing a few hymns. Father
Hooley put on some vestments and weaved to the pulpit.
He thought he would greet his new flock before mass
started and he raised his arms in benediction.

Just then the choir rang out, "Hoooly, Hoooly,
Hoooly, Lord God Almighty."

Howls of laughter. Dad had raised his arms shakily in imitation of
priestly buffoonery, then stretched and lilted vowels in the Scandinavian manner we had all heard among the old Norwegian women
buying *lutefisk* and *lefse* at Gamalgard's Grocery or from the snoose-
chewing wool-clad former lumberjacks outside the Buckhorn Tavern.
I heard echoes, too, of a mock high-school cheer that some of my
buddies learned from older brothers: "Rice Lake once, Rice Lake twice,
hoooly yumpin' Yesus Christ!" No one had to tell us about bilingual
dialect jokes, that "Hoooly" as a Norsky rendition of "holy" might be
mistaken for "Hooley." We had heard the like daily in Rice Lake where
Lutherans and Catholics, Scandinavians and everybody else, battled
good-humoredly every day. Before the laughter died, dad finished up.

Father Hooley was flattered and shocked all at once.
"'Tis a foine thing to be welcome, but aren't you going
a little too far?"

Heads nodded in agreement. "I'll have to remember that at coffee
tomorrow, that was a good one," someone said. "Yah," said another.
Yah, hey!

CHAPTER TWO

The Indians

The Ojibwas or Chippewas are the most numerous of the Upper Midwest's native peoples, with reservations scattered throughout Michigan's Upper Peninsula, northern Wisconsin, and northern Minnesota. Their sacred mythological narratives, not presented here, are told neither randomly nor frivolously. They have been reserved traditionally for winter evenings, times when elders might school their charges with extended tales conveying fundamental cultural knowledge and values. Ultimately serious, such tales have nonetheless brimmed over with wordplay and broad humor.

Not surprisingly, the secular jokes of contemporary Ojibwas likewise combine reverent eloquence and minute detail with puns and silliness. Performed amidst informal doings or at summer pow wows (intertribal social gatherings at which tourists are also welcome), they offer a native view of Indians in a white man's world. The erstwhile mythological being, Wenabozho, travels from the world's beginning to "these modern times." Ojibwa men and women alternately confound or are confounded by European–Americans. And much is made of homophonic Ojibwa and English words with wildly different meanings.

The white jocular view of native peoples is narrow. Ojibwa, Winnebago, Menominee, Potowatomi, Oneida are melded together as generic Indians. Whether comic buffoons or sly tricksters, these Indians are invariably somber and laconic—a parody of polite behavior toward strangers generally practiced by the region's native peoples, and a decided contrast to their behavior among themselves. Although lacking the bilingualism of their Indian neighbors, whites nonetheless find enough points of intersection between English and native tongues to attach fanciful narratives to the region's ubiquitous Indian place names.

Wenabozho and the Padlock

I'll tell you one about Wenabozho. Wenabozho is a sacred person, too, but there're certain stories you can tell about him that are not in the other category.

This story is about back up home there. Oh, it takes place about the time the first traders came into the north woods up there.

Aa, Wenabozho he had a *waaginiigaan* on the lake. *Waaginiigaan* is a wigwam. Well, Wenabozho he lived in the old traditional way, you know. He had that bark wigwam there, birchbark on the top, cedar bark on the side, you know, and everything.

Aa, Wenabozho he was a good trapper, hunter. Oh gee, he could get all them animals, fur-bearing animals. He was good. Knew all their, all their ways. Was able to get them. So one morning he woke up. He saw this *chimookomaan*. This white man across the lake over there, chopping trees down like a beaver.

Aa, Wenabozho he hops in his *wiigwaasi-jiimaan*, his birchbark canoe. Paddles over there. *He, he, aataayaa hai, wemitigoozhi*, a Frenchman. Well, that Frenchman come there, and he had all kinds of stuff, you know, stacked up there. He had a big canoe. So Wenabozho went over there and talked to him. Talked to him in Indian, you see. Wenabozho he says to that *wemitigoozhi*, he says *"Aanish ez-hicihigeyan*, what are you doing?"

So this Frenchman he talks back to him in Chippewa, you know, 'cause he has come there to deal, wheel and deal furs. "Oh," he says, "I'm going to make a trading post here, *adaawewigamig.*" He says, "I want to trade these things here that we get from way across the sea over there where they bring that, where the white man comes from."

"Oo," ikido aw Wenabozho. So Wenabozho he sits down there on the ground and watches this *chimookomaan* chopping these trees down with that iron ax, you know. He never seen that before. Oh, just like a beaver he was going at them trees, you know. Oh, day after day that there Frenchman he was laying these logs, kind of a square, rectangular shape. That was new to Wenabozho, too, because they always made everything round. Oh, by-and-by that Frenchman finally got them logs up there and put a roof on there, you know. And every day Wenabozho would hop in his *wiigwassi-jiimaan* and paddle across the lake to watch that guy work. He'd sit there right on the ground. *Namadabi aw* Wenabozho. Finally he got all finished. Put all that stuff in there and everything. Pretty soon some Indians, *bebezhig*, one-by-one, they come by, you know. So that Frenchman he got across the idea what he wanted to the Chippeways there. So they started bringing in these furs.

One guy come there, brought in these furs, and he's got a nice red blanket out of it. Black stripe on the bottom. Guy went away laughing at that old Frenchman, you know. "Gee, that was—I go out there and get them animals' furs and bring them in there and look at the nice things

I get for them. That guy must be crazy: *giiwanaadizi aw,* that Frenchman."

An old woman come there. She had some stuff, too. That Frenchman traded a nice big, what we call a *akik,* kettle. She went off laughing at that Frenchman: *"giiwanaadizi aw wemitigoozhi,* he's crazy, that guy."

Aa, Wenabozho he goes in that store, too, you know. Looks everything over. Well, he really didn't have a need for any of that stuff, 'til he noticed that every time that Frenchman would go away, he'd close that door and he'd put that big padlock on there. Well, that fascinated him. Because the Indian, you know, he never had no use for a lock, because when he'd leave his wigwam to go visit relatives, or go fishing, or berry picking, or whatever, he'd just put that flap down, that skin, you know, and put a little stick in front of there across the door. And that would mean to anybody going by that there was no one home. And nobody would go in and steal anything. A lot of trust.

Well, anyway, he thought he would like to have one of these big padlocks for his wigwam. So one day he got up. Had a little cup of *aniibiish, aniibiishaaboo,* tea. He got to thinking. Oh, I sure would like to have a padlock like that for my wigwam. I think I'll throw a bunch of these furs together, *adaawaagan,* they call them. I'm going to go over there and trade these furs for that padlock, just like them other people did. See if I can get that thing. Well, he hops in his *wiigwassi-jimaan,* paddles across that lake over there and goes up, walks through that door, you know. Frenchman's all set up for business that day. He says, *"Aniin niijii."* That Frenchman he greeted him, too. So Wenabozho, by-and-by—he didn't just march right in there because Indians, you know, don't rush into things—he just kind of sat around, smoked on his pipe a little bit. Finally [he] got around to telling that Frenchman what he was up to.

"Well, I want to trade my furs for something you got."

So that Frenchman says, "All right. See all this nice stuff here: blankets, axes, kettles, beads. We got a whole bunch of stuff here," he says, *"anooj igo gegoo."*

"Aa," Wenabozho says, "I'm not going to bother with that," he says. "What I want is that lock you got on your door, that big padlock. I want that for my wigwam."

"Aa," the Frenchman says, "I don't know. I'll have a hard time before I get another one from Montreal." Anyway he looked at Wenabozho's furs. Oh, they were really nice. "All right, we'll trade then."

So Wenabozho he got that padlock for them furs. So he marched out that door, going down to that beach, laughing at that Frenchman, too. Hopped in that canoe, got back to his wigwam, it was getting dark. So he thought, well, maybe next day I'll go do a little hunting, get some more furs and stuff, trapping.

Ahh, next morning he gets up, puts on his moccasins and leggings, *midaasan*. Puts on his coat, *babiinzikawaagan*. Gets his bow and arrow. Goes out. Puts that flap down. Puts that big lock on the door. Locks it up. Puts the key in his pocket there—he had a little pocket on that leather coat. He was gone all day long out there in the woods. Jeez, he didn't get a thing, didn't see nothing, nothing.

Jeez, that night he come back. Sun was just starting to go down. Struts up to his wigwam, big as life. That big padlock on that skin door there, on that flap. Starts looking for his key, open up that lock. *Aataayaa hai!*

Couldn't find it no place. Looked every place. Looked in that pocket, looked in his quiver, looked in his moccasins. No place. He lost that key. Couldn't get in his wigwam. Oh gee, he was really, really down in the dumps. So he sits down in front of his wigwam, on the ground there.

By-and-by Waabooz come by, his friend the rabbit come by, *Waabooz. Waabooz gwaashkwani*, jumping along on that trail there. He got up to Wenabozho. "*Aanish naa, aaniin ezhiwebiziyan?*" he says. "What's the matter with you?" He could see something was wrong, you know.

Aa, Wenabozho explained to him how he traded that bunch of furs for that padlock and key. "Out hunting today and must have lost that key out in the woods someplace, out in the bush there."

"*Aa, hai, ikido aw Waabooz*, too bad," he says. He left Wenabozho sitting right there on the ground. Went on down this rabbit trail.

Aa, Wenabozho was sitting there, couldn't get into his wigwam, locked out. Aa, he sat there for the longest time. First thing you know, Waabooz come back up the trail. He was going back home again. It was almost dark. Waabooz he looks up on top of the wigwam, there was smoke coming out. Hey, that guy got in there, he thought to himself, you know. And I thought he was locked out of that wigwam. So Waabooz he gets by the door and he hollers in to Wenabozho. "Wenabozho," he says, "I thought you were locked out. How did you get in there?"

Aa, Wenabozho says, "Yeah, I was, but," he says, "I got in."

Well, by this time that curiosity, you know, got that rabbit, the best of him, see. He says, "Come on, Wenabozho, tell me. Wenabozho, tell me how did you get in here?"

Aa, Wenabozho says, "I was sitting there. Finally it hit me, dawned on me how I could get in there."

"Well, come on, tell me, how did you get in there?"

"Well, I got up and I ran around and around until I was all in."[1]

Narrator Earl Nyholm provided Ojibwa transcriptions of his own tellings and proved to be especially adept at bilingual performances. Wenabozho is the trickster/culture hero of the Ojibwa. *Chimookomaan* ("big knife man") is a common term for white man among the Upper Midwest's various Woodland Indians. The plot is an artful precis of the effects of European contact on native peoples that dissolves into the silly double entendre of modern "shaggy dog" stories. Though departing from traditional mythology, the story maintains Wenabozho's character as a crafty, greedy fellow and brother of animals (aptly described by Nyholm as "non-person people") and as one whose misadventures introduce new elements of culture to his people.

Wenabozho in These Modern Times

Here's another one.

Well, you know in the old days, the old days, you know, the Indians they took things—how would you say?—easy, in an easy pace. They were in no hurry. They didn't have high blood pressure, heart disease, and all that stuff. If they were going to have a big meeting, you know, well, "We're going to meet so and so at the new moon. And we'll be there. At the new moon we'll have our gathering." So over the time, over the days, Indians would come by trail or by canoe. There was no hurry. So when they all got there—sooner or later, around new moon time—they'd have their, whatever they were going to do, you know.

Aa, Wenabozho, you know, that guy he's something else. He lived in the old days. A long time ago.

Aa, Wenabozho he was never in a hurry. And them old Indian people, they weren't in no hurry either. But Wenabozho he lived in the past and he lives now, too, for the people—he's still alive. So, anyway, this is about Wenabozho right now. Wenabozho living in these modern times. Can't take the pressure. So he says, "I can't get my life straightened out. I think I'll have to go see Doc Yak."

So, Wenabozho he goes to see a psychiatrist. So on that day of his appointment he goes over to see a psychiatrist. Aa, Wenabozho he lays down on the couch.

"Doctor," he says.

"Well, you tell me all about it. I'll listen here and we'll see what's what."

Aa, Wenabozho laid on the couch. He says, "You know, Doc," he says, "one time I wake up, I think I'm a tipi. Next day I wake up, I think I'm a wigwam."

And the psychiatrist says, "Ah, I see your problem. You're too tense." [Verbal pun—"two tents."]

See some people say, "that's not an Indian story," but these are modern Indian stories. They're told at powwows.[2]

The irony of Wenabozho going to a psychiatrist rather than to a traditional healer underscores the confusions of modern life.

Ducks

Here's another one.

Here's how you say duck in Indian: "*zhiishiib.*" [Pronounced "shesheeb."]

That's how you say duck in the Chippeway language. And as a generic term, that's fine. But how would you say a male duck?

"*Hiihiib.*" [Pronounced "heheeb."][3]

This joke depends on the English-language distinction between male and female animals: bear and she-bear, wolf and she-wolf. The homophony between "she" and *zhii* in *zhiishiib* suggests a "he" counterpart in Ojibwa.

Porcupines

How do you say porcupine in Indian?

"*Gaag.*"

How do you say female porcupine?

"*Zhigaag*" [Pronounced "shegaag"; *zhigaag* is a skunk.][4]

Finndians

Like this one Indian guy walked up to this other Indian guy. "How do you say all these different nationalities in Indian language? How do you say a Finnlander, a Finn? How do you say a Finn in Chippeway language?"

"*Naanwaabik.*"

"*Naanwaabik*" means five bucks. See, a "fin" is five bucks.[5]

The offspring of Finns and Indians in parts of the Upper Peninsula of Michigan are called "Finndians." Of course, "fin," from the Yiddish *finnif*, is slang for a five dollar bill.

The Talking Cat

I got a little short one now. Here I'm getting warmed up now. I'll tell this one in Indian first and then I'll put it in English.

This is like a little children's story because in Indian when you want to say something is enough, or that's it, or even if you're pouring a cup of tea and that's enough in there, you say, *"Mii iw"*—that's it. So whenever you want to be done with something or enough or whatever, you say, *"Mii iw."*

Ingoding nishiime oggi-ayaawaan gaazhagensan nitaa-anishinaabemonid. Babaamose aw gaazhagens enwed "mii iw, mii iw."

My little brother has a cat that knows how to talk Indian. It runs around saying, *"mii iw* [meow], *mii iw* [meow], *mii iw* [meow]."[6]

Stories about the resemblance of animal sounds to human speech are common in European–American folklore while tales of communication with animals abound in Woodland Indian mythology. This trilingual telling playfully embraces both traditions.

At the Trading Post

Here's another story. This guy had this little store there on the reservation. He sold general merchandise. Like a trading post, you've seen them around; like at Mole Lake, you've seen that little store there. Anyway, there was this old Indian lady come in there. She had a daughter, her name was Mary.

You know, they take names in the Chippewa language, and then they corrupt them because some of them old-timers couldn't pronounce. Like you can't say "William" or "Bill" in the Chippewa language, so they say "Wii'am." Well, anyway, they can't say "Mary" because there's no r's in the Chippewa language. So to say "Mary," they say "Manii." In some dialects, they say "Maanii." Either "Maanii" or "Manii." That's how you say "Mary" in Chippewa, see.

One time that old woman she was looking for her daughter. I don't know if she was gone someplace or what happened to her, but she couldn't find her anyway. So she went running to the store, and she couldn't speak English.

So here was this, this guy, store clerk. That old woman come in there, she was all excited. Store clerk was behind the counter, you know. "Manii, Manii," she was hollering. She was really upset, see.

Gee, that store clerk thought there was really something wrong with that woman. Maybe something happened to her? She had that long old dress on they used to wear, them old women. So that old lady, she hollered again, "Manii, Manii." So that store clerk he runs from behind the counter, runs over there and lifts up that woman's skirt like that [arm raised in imitation].

And that old lady, "*Inge, ikogaan omaa,*" get out of here, you know, in Indian.

That store clerk says, "I can't understand you. You have to speak English."

That old lady says, "*Ikogaan omaa—Manii, Manii!*"

That guy goes over there and lifts up her skirt again, kept trying to look at her knees, see. He thought there was something wrong with her knee. "Manii," she was hollering, and here that guy thought there was something wrong with her knee. He thought she was saying "my knee."[7]

The Mole Lake Ojibwa reservation is in northeastern Wisconsin. Set earlier in this century at a time when such trading posts were common on reservations and when young Indian children were placed in government schools, given Christian names, and taught to become "Americans," this story subtly combines humor, outrage, and irony. The elderly woman's rude treatment ironically stems from the fact that her own child has been given a name she cannot pronounce.

Hospitality

This I heard a long time ago from an old friend of mine.

One time this Indian lived out, out of town. Oh, he'd go into town on weekends or whatever. And walking along this road—this was horse and buggy days yet—this farmer, this guy who lived out of town, had a wagon and a team of horses. Going to town for supplies. So one day he was going to town to get some supplies, and he was on his way, he was going to spend all day in town, so he took his lunch along.

And this *chimookomaan* [white man] was going along with his horse, his horse and buggy, his team there. Saw this Indian walking along the road. He didn't know him, but there were Indians living around that town. Anyway, he thought, well, a long ways to town yet, he'll give that Indian a ride into town. So since that farmer, that guy, he was going to spend a whole day in town and get supplies and what-not (those days it was an all-day trip going to town and back), so he took his lunch along. He put it under his seat, under what you call on a wagon a buckboard, he put his luncheon under there, see.

So he whoaed up his horses there and said to the Indian, "Hey, Indian." Indian, he couldn't speak English or anything—this was long time ago. So, anyway, he hollers to the Indian, "Get on," you know, telling him to get on. So the Indian he hops on that wagon. Back there. Farmer takes off with his horses. And the Indian—in the Chippeway language, *gidaan* means eat it all up—well, that old Indian he thought that white guy could talk Indian, see. Indian got on there. That white guy said to him to get on, he thought he was saying eat it all up.

So that Indian hopped on that wagon and saw that lunch box. "Aa!" So he opens up that lunch box, starts eating. Eats that guy's lunch all up.

Jeez, they're going along like that. Almost got to town. The Indian was wiping his face off, you know. Big smile on his face. Looks round at that Indian there. Here his lunch was all gone. That white guy he got mad. "Damn Injun, damn Injun." And the Indian—see in Chippeway language, we say *demiijin,* that means eat sufficiently, eat enough of it, eat it all up, have your fill of it—misunderstood that farmer. He was swearing at the Indian; here that Indian thought he was talking Indian. "*Demiijian.*"

That Indian goes, "*Enh, enh, enh,*" which means "yes, yes, yes." That's the end of the story.[8]

This telling refers both to Indian customs and to white stereotyping. Ojibwas traditionally offered food to guests almost immediately; however, in both the region's oral tradition and literature, native peoples are constantly hungry and begging for food from whites. For example, see the presentation of Indian John in Carolyn Ryrie Brink's children's classic, *Caddie Woodlawn.*)

The Dog Feast

There were these two Sioux Indians, brothers, lived way out on the reservation—somewhere in the Dakotas—and they'd never been off it. But they had another brother who traveled around some. He met an Indian woman from Wisconsin, a Chippewa. And they decided to get married at Odanah.

So these two brothers thought they would go to the wedding. They packed some fry bread and food that they liked to eat and they started driving to Wisconsin.

Well, it's a long drive and they ran out of food. Gee, they were hungry.

So they pulled off the highway. But they weren't used to these fast food places. They didn't know what kind of food was there. They went past a Pizza Hut and a Taco Bell and a Burger King. They didn't know what to do.

Finally they were disgusted and decided to stop at the next place. Dairy Queen. Went in there, looked at the menu. One of them lit up in a big grin. He kinda nudged his brother and pointed. "Hot dog." There was some food they were used to.

So they placed their order, got it in a bag, and went back out to the car. Just as pleased as could be. Then one opens his up and starts frowning. He asks his brother, "Gee, what part did you get?"[9]

The Ojibwa and Sioux peoples are traditional enemies; nevertheless, cultural exchange and intermarriage between the tribes are common. The Ojibwa historically have eaten dog on ritual occasions, but the Sioux have been associated with its regular consumption—a practice that has earned them the epithet of "dog roasters" by scornful Ojibwa.

The Swedish Indian

Henry Otis was a native Chippewa Indian who served in the Civil War. When he returned, he had learned to speak Swedish. Swedish was the most common language spoken around here at that time. It was not uncommon to hear a German, Italian, Yankee, and a Frenchman all talking Swedish together. Whenever a steamboat arrived, usually at Marine, everybody went down to greet them, including Henry Otis. He would welcome the Swedish newcomers and speak to them in their own language. The newcomers were always surprised that an Indian could speak Swedish so well. Henry Otis not only could speak good Swedish, but he also knew a lot about Sweden itself.

One problem that Henry encountered was in the use of the English word "yes." The word "yes" in Swedish means "goose." And Henry was so used to saying "yes" and "no" to questions that he did this even when he was talking to the Swedes. Henry would often answer questions to Swedes with the word "yes." Then the Swede would get mad because he thought he was being called a goose. This sometimes led to fights. Henry, however, usually avoided the fights by asking to arm wrestle instead. The most famous arm wrestle lasted for five weeks and six days—nonstop. Henry won it, probably only because his arms were longer, and as the fight progressed, their arms dug into the ground. The Swede's arms were so far into the ground that he could hardly turn his arms one way or another, and then Henry easily pinned him.[10]

The "Marine" is Marine-on-St. Croix, a former steamboat port and mill town on the Minnesota side of the St. Croix River where it borders with Wisconsin. Henry Otis, who was known as a "river rat," served with the Seventh Minnesota Volunteers from 1862 until 1864 when he was wounded and honorably discharged. This bilingual anecdote combines several motifs: the long fight, the remarkable wrestler, and lies about sinking.

The Lost Canoe

Here's another one. One time these two Indians were out in a canoe, you know, fishing on the river there. Paint River. You know where the Paint River is in the Upper Peninsula? Goes right through Crystal Falls. They were up there. I don't know what they were doing there—fishing, I guess. They weren't setting nets because that's out in the lake, you know. Maybe they were fishing, I don't know.

Jeez. Big storm come, you know. Black clouds coming. Oh, that one Indian says to the other one, "I think we better tie up here until the storm blows over." There were some sticks coming, brushing along the creek bed there. Tie up the canoe with this rope to the tree coming, that brush sticking out from the shore. They tied up. It rained and rained. They had a tarp there or something in the canoe, so they lay down there and they put that tarp over them and they fell asleep. Gee, the river kept rising and rising. And all of a sudden that canoe broke loose. It went down the Paint River there.

That one Indian he wakes up. "*Goshkozi.*" He's gone a long ways. The other Indian says, "Where the heck are we?"

Well, the Indian he looked around. "Oh, we're about two miles from here."[11]

European settlers marveled at how skillfully the Indians managed their canoes while spearing fish in the rapids. This tale is also associated with canoe-paddling French voyageurs in the Upper Midwest.

Bear Grease

There was a little Indian boy, little Indian boy. And his name was Joe Gimiwan. Well, he was about twelve years old. Jeez, you know, that age they start to change, grow up. Voice changes, everything changes. You start to notice girls, things like that.

Well—I'll just call him "Gimiwan" for short, rainy, rainy—one time they went swimming at the river. Him and a bunch of his friends, you know. Indian kids, they go swimming in the buff, you know. No swimsuit. That's the way they did in the old days. Just go skinny dipping, you'd call it now. Well, Gimiwan was starting to look at his buddies, you know. They were all there swimming, all in the nude, you know. He started looking around at their *bajaag. Bajaag*, that's their penis, you know. Boy, they looked big. Then he looked at himself. Oh, just little thing like that [indicates a few inches by holding fingers apart]. Just small, like a shriveled-up little raisin or something. He got embarrassed.

Well, after they swam in the river for a while, that was enough swimming, so they went back to the village. That night he couldn't sleep, couldn't sleep. Next morning he got up, he got to go do something about that. So he went over to see that old medicine man. Old medicine man over there, on the other side of town, the village. So being the good Indian kid he was, he took along some tobacco and a little gift for that old man. So he goes up to that old man's log cabin. Knocks on the door. That old medicine man opens up the door—real dark in there, you know, he just had a kerosene lamp. "*Aa ingos, biindigen,*" he says. "My son, come on in." Gimiwan, he sat down there.

That old medicine man give him a cup of tea there. They were drinking tea. Well, he knew there was something heavy on that kid's mind, you know. Finally that little kid, Gimiwan, gives that old man the tobacco and a gift. Then he knew for sure he come for a request. Well, finally—he had a heck of a time, you know, that little Gimiwan, telling what was wrong. Finally he got it out of him. He says, "Now come on, tell me. You come here for a reason. We may as well get this over with."

Little kid he says, "My *bajaag*, it's so small, and my friends there, they're getting to look like men. I'm just a little, look like a little kid. Can you help me out? I want to make it so its big like theirs."

That old medicine man he looked him over, stroked his chin like this [strokes chin while leaning forward thoughtfully]. "Yeah, I guess so, but you got to do exactly what I tell you."

"All right."

"You go home, and every night when you go to bed, you put a little bear grease right on the end, right on the end there. You do that for a whole year, for a full winter, you know. When spring comes, next year, your *bajaag* will be just like your friends. You'll be just like a real he-man."

Oh, that kid he ran home, he was all excited. Jeez, that night after supper, you know, he was so excited he even wanted to go to bed early. Jeez, he hopped in bed. No bear grease! He couldn't go out and kill a bear this time of night. He couldn't kill one anyway, he was too small. Jeez. Ma and Pa was in bed. He goes in the kitchen. His ma and them, they were all making fry bread all the time. Here was some Crisco up in the cupboard. Goes to get that. That's grease. Gets some, takes it back to his bedroom, puts it on the end of his *bajaag*, see. Every night for a whole year he did that. Oh, his ma... couldn't figure out why that Crisco was going so fast, you know. Didn't make that much fry bread.

Anyway, after a whole year of doing that, putting that Crisco on his *bajaag*, a year later that *bajaag* was still like a little twig, you know. Nothing. Oh, he goes back to see that old medicine man. Knocks on the door. The old man opens up the door. The kid goes in there. Big long face. The old medicine man seen something was wrong. And he knew what it was: something didn't go right. He says, "Well, did you put that grease, that bear grease, on your tip of your *bajaag*, like I told you, every night? Do that a whole year?"

He says, "Yeah," he says—that little kid—he says, "yeah, but I couldn't get any bear grease. The hard part—I couldn't get any bear grease. But I put grease on it every night."

Old man says, "Oh, what'd you use anyway?"

"I put some of my Ma's Crisco on there every night for a whole year, put Crisco on that."

That old medicine man threw up his hands. "*Aatayaa*, that's shortening."[12]

Here, a widespread and generally brief joke is expanded to treat Ojibwa medical practices and decorum toward elders. While the young Gimiwan has learned to approach the medicine man with the traditional gift of tobacco, he has not learned that synthetic storebought grease lacks the efficacy of real stuff rendered from the hunt.

The Tea Drinker

That old Indian liked tea so much. He drank about twenty cups. Next morning he woke up in his tipi [tea pee].[13]

This joke was often told along with a joke about Chief Bowels who refused to move for the railroad and stated adamantly, "Bowels no move." The railroad magnate offers prunes and soon is told, "Bowels move now, tipi full of shit."

Joe Cloud, the Naturalist

Up home we had this guy, Joe Cloud. Anyway, this old Joe Cloud, you know, he worked in the woods and guided them people. Hunters and fishermen coming from the cities, Milwaukee and Chicago, would come up there, vacation around there. So he'd take them out. Cook for them and everything, their meals. Take them through the woods so they wouldn't get lost. He was guiding them along, you know. And he'd tell them: here's a yellow birch here, and this bush here, we use this for that and this for this.

Boy, he was just flabbergasting these here Chicago city folk, you know, how he knew all this stuff. Of course white people are impressed.

Finally that one guy he says, "Boy, that's amazing."

Joe Cloud says, "Yeah, that's the way we learn, we learn all that stuff, you know, handed down." They walk along. "Hey you see that over there? Yeah, that's a dogwood over there."

"Well, how do you know?"

"Oh, by its bark."[14]

Joe Cloud Foretells the Weather

Well, you know the white people have always been flabbergasted by the Indian, how he can forecast things, you know. And the Indian would call that like, it would almost be like a *onwaachige,* foreseeing things.

Gee whiz, this white guy, you know, he saw this Indian one time. (I use this name "Joe Cloud.") "Hey, Joe, how you doing today?"

"Oh, pretty good."

"Well, it's getting along. Leaves are starting to fall now, I see. What do you think our winter's going to be this year?"

Ahh, that old Joe Cloud says, "It's going to be a bad one. We'll get a lot of snow."

"Why? Are the squirrels piling up a lot of nuts or something? How do you know all this stuff all the time?"

"No. I see the *chimookomaan,* the white man, he's piling up a lot of wood there."[15a]

There was an old saying that an Indian can predict the weather. So this old Indian, he's sitting there smoking his peace pipe. So I walked up to him. I says, "How can you predict when we're going to have a cold winter?"

And he says, "When white man lays in much cord wood, cold weather."[15b]

Joe Cloud is a stock character, nominally akin to the Irish "Pat," Scandinavian "Ole," or Polish "Stash," who tricks and confounds white folks.

The Indian Vet

This young Indian guy, you know, he just got out of Vietnam. He was over there. Well, he was raised on the reservation by his grandma, see. Lot of Indian people are raised by their grandma. They lived in an old frame house, like they've got around Odanah, Wisconsin, in old Odanah.

You know how them old houses are laid out. You go up on the porch, and then you got the living room there. And then you got what they call a dining room, or it may be a bedroom or whatever, and then you got the kitchen in back, you know. Well, they never went in the front, they always went in the back there. You know how them kitchens are laid out. Well, you got a table and a sink and a stove and a refrigerator there.

Anyway, this guy, Indian guy, from the res' there, he got honorably discharged. Come back home. He didn't have no place to go. He went to the Cities, Milwaukee, couldn't get no job. Well, he thought he'll go back and spend some time on the reservation with grandma. So he went back home there. He was acting peculiar though. That old lady watched him. Something wrong with that guy. Every time he come in that back, through the kitchen there, he'd salute like that, salute.

So one time he come home, you know. Grandma was sitting there having a cup of tea at the table. Jeez, that guy come in the door. Sure enough he saluted again. Come in that back kitchen door—saluted.

That old lady, she says, "How come every time you come in that door you salute like that?"

He says, "Grandma, there's General Electric."

That's a powwow joke, too. They're bad.[16]

The joke outlines a common pattern among Ojibwa males: military service, the search for urban employment, and a return to the reservation.

How Sheboygan Got Its Name

I know how Sheboygan got its name. A long time ago when the Indians lived around there, there was this Indian chief who was very proud of his tribe and his family, but all the children in his family were boys and he wanted to have a girl. And his wife was pregnant with another child and finally she went into labor. He's just hoping and hoping that it's a girl. And he comes out of the tipi and finally says, "Ugh. She boy 'gain."[17]

Sheboygan, Wisconsin, and Cheboygan, Michigan, are Indian place names probably derived from a word describing an underground river and the noise it produces, but this facetious explanation is a widely known legend.

Oconomowoc

There is also a humorous story that circulates around the town about how Oconomowoc got its name. An Indian from an unknown tribe was trespassing on a settler's land. The settler was upset about this, so he started to run after the Indian to get him off his land. A very long chase ensued, and after a while they both grew very tired. But the chase was still on. Finally the Indian collapsed in the center of what would be Oconomowoc. The settler caught up to the Indian and fell down next to him.

The Indian turned to the settler and said to him, in very poor English, "I can no more walk."[18a]

How Oconomowoc got its name. The two early settlers had come out from Milwaukee, and they had traveled all day by foot.

And as they reached the place that is now Oconomowoc, one said, "I can no mo' walk."[18b]

Oconomowoc means "waterfall," "place where the river falls," "beautiful waters," "beaver dam," and "river of lakes." The second version exchanges Indian/white conflict with the difficulties of frontier settlement.

How to Pronounce Oconomowoc

There are two salesmen in Oconomowoc for the night and they are debating. "Is it O-*CON*-o-mo-woc or Oc-o-*NO*-mo-woc," or whatever, and they've got a little bet on.

They're sitting there and having a sandwich, so they say to the young lad who's serving, "Young man, we've got an important bet on here. We want you to pronounce very slowly and distinctly the name of this place we're in."

And the boy says, "Bur-ger-King."[19]

According to the teller, "this story could be told about any difficult town name."

Reservation Tourists

There was a couple women never saw an Indian reservation. And this one Sunday, this one guy took them over to the Indian reservation. Well, they got there. There was one squaw working in the garden, another squaw washing clothes, and so forth. And the old Indian buck, he's sitting on a chair, smoking a pipe. By gosh, these two women couldn't see it.

So one of them says to the old Indian buck, she says, "My gosh, one squaw's doing that, another's doing this. What do you do for a living?"

Indian says, "Me smoke-um pipe. Me top-um squaw."

And the lady says, "Oh, my dear."

"No, not deer. Him run too fast."[20]

The theme of curious whites visiting reservations is common in the jokes European–Americans tell about native peoples, as is the image of the pipe-smoking "buck" (see Text 15b). This particular version alludes to the occasional but nonetheless established custom of polygamy among Woodland Indians, like Wisconsin's Ojibwa.

City Life

There was an Indian girl, she went to the town, city, to work. And by gol', you know, she was gone for a few months, and all of a sudden she started growing a big belly. So she wrote home to her dad to meet her on the train depot. She's coming home.

So when she got off the train, she's coming towards the old man and she was going to speak Indian to him. She says, "How."

And the old man looked at her. He says, "Yeah, I know how. But I'd like to know who."[21]

There are numerous jokes involving plays on the Indians' supposed use of "how" as an expression of greeting. The Ojibwa and other Alongkian-speaking peoples of the Upper Midwest more commonly greet people with *bazhoo,* derived from the French *bonjour.*

CHAPTER THREE

The French

The French were the earliest Europeans to populate the Upper Midwest in any numbers. They came down from Canada in the seventeenth century and sustained the fur trade through the mid-nineteenth century, when a second wave of peasant farmers or "habitants" from Quebec's St. Lawrence Valley arrived as loggers and homesteaders. Jokes regarding the region's French, heavily reliant on dialect, have diminished as the French–speaking population has declined. Half the jokes presented here were collected in the 1930s. Those told more recently are old tales from the repertoires of old timers or those confined to areas of heavy French–Canadian settlement.

The French in these stories are often noted local characters like Charles Belille, Pete LeGault, and Joe Trepania, loggers and patriarchs of Wisconsin's greater Chippewa River Valley—the heart of the region's nineteenth-century "pinery." Perhaps because these early French settlers were roving bachelors, or married to Indian women (to raise "Bow and Arrow French"), the "Frenchman," not French woman, became the dominant figure in regional humor.

Engaged in bygone or archaic occupations—paddling a *bateau* on rivers, plowing with horses, or cutting timber with an ax—the "Frenchman" is invariably a Catholic fond of blasphemy, an illiterate possessing a peasant's cunning in matters of property, a lusty fellow for whom life and death hold little terror, and a colorful speaker who liberally mixes French words and syntax with English.

A Corpse in a Bateau

Old Man Balille ran a stopping place near Radisson, at Balille Falls. One time he was coming down the river with a corpse in his boat, and two lumberjacks who were sitting on the bank eating their lunch saw him as he rowed by.

One called out, "Hello there, Mr. Balille, what you got there, a corpse?"

Balille shouted back, "No, by Crass, that's a dead Frenchman. That's old French Joe, she's got killed last night; she die this morning, four o'clock."[22]

The Charles Belille ("Balille") of this anecdote lived from 1815 to 1900. He was born in Berchier, Quebec, Canada, and established a fur trading post and eventual "stopping place" (a site for rest and supplies along a route between a lumber company head-quarters and an outlying camp) around 1836 at the confluence of the Couderay and Chippewa Rivers in what has become Sawyer County, Wisconsin. Belille had three Ojibwa wives and nineteen children. The dialect attributed to him is vintage "Frenchyman" talk, complete with blasphemies ("by Crass"/by Christ), lapses in logic, and the use of the feminine pronoun for males and females alike.

An Old Man's Misfortunes

A cyclone once came through the territory where Old Man Balille lived and pulled up his timber by the roots. At the time, Colesh Allen of Chippewa Falls had a mortgage on Balille's cattle. A company man came up the river and stayed all night at Balille's stopping place.

The visitor asked Balille, "Are you going to log this winter, Mr. Balille?"

"By Crass, no," answered the logger, "the God almighty she's take my timber, and the Colesh, she's take my cattle."[23]

Belille's timber was doubtless twisted and tangled, as well as uprooted, and thus almost impossible to log. The "company man" represents a Chippewa Falls logging company for whom Belille cut timber on contract as an independent "jobber."

The News in Montreal

Batiste Trodeau and Jean Legase were two French Canadians who were fishing partners in Montreal. Jean thought there would be much more money in the states, so he came down and became a lumberjack. Here he remained several years, becoming very much a "Yankee Man."

Years later, Jean returned to Montreal for a visit and went to see his former partner Batiste. Arriving, he said, "Hello, Batiste Trodeau."

"Who the hell are you, you know my name so good?" asked Batiste. "I never saw you before in my life. You look just like the Yankee Man. You got the mustache cut off, the swallow-tail coat, and the *chapeau casteau* and the red tie on the throat."

"Why, I'm Jean Legase. I used to be your fishing partner."

When Batiste was convinced it was his old friend, Jean pried him for news on what happened while he was absent.

Batiste said, "Old Pierre Bevine, she's dead. That old Frenchman, you know. She was ninety-eight years old. Joe LaCourtier and Mac Courterier, she's dead, too, and some more old Frenchmen, they ready for die, too."

"Well," said Jean, "so that's all the news?"

"Crass, no, hold on, the Queen is dead."

Jean could hardly believe the news, but Batiste assured him it was true and asked if he never read the papers.

"I don't get much time, Batiste, for to read the papers. Say, who take the Queen's place?"

"Well, by Crass, Jean, I can't remember his name, what take the Queen's place. Let me see, that was 1, 2, 3, 4, 5—I think they was call him Henry the Five. Don't make no difference anyway. He was a Protestant son-of-a-bitch."

"Is that all, Batiste?" asked Jean.

"Oh no, hold on, Jean, the Pope is dead."

"Well, by Crass, Batiste, I am surprised for hear that. Say, Batiste, who take the Pope's place?"

"I don't remember that feller either what took the Pope's place, but I'll guarantee you one thing—that was no Protestant son-of-a-bitch what took the Pope's place."[24]

Many of the French Canadians who came to the lumber camps of the Upper Midwest were originally farming/fishing Quebecois *habitants* and Catholics living along the St. Lawrence River. The reference to the "Yankee Man's" *chapeau castor* (referred to in the story as *chapeau casteau),* a beaver hat fashionable in the nineteenth century, and to his clean-shaven face (without the Frenchyman's status-symbol mustache) suggest a rejection of French–Canadian heritage. The theme of ignorance regarding current events recurs in French anecdotal folklore.

In the Blacksmith Shop

There was this old Frenchyman. He come down to the blacksmith shop. They were talking about Roosevelt getting shot. You know, that other president we had. Teddy. And he was listening quite a while. He said, "Where that man live?"[25]

The blacksmith shop was a common rural hangout where old timers and working farmers might gossip while a horse was being shod or a plowshare sharpened.

Pierre's Plowhorses

Now, I'm told that one time there was a French farmer out in the field plowing with a team of horses. And one of his neighbors came by, leaning on a fence post to watch this spectacle. And the farmer that was plowing, he was using his vocal apparatus as much as possible to encourage his team of horses along.

"Ahhh, Billy. Now, you pull. Goddammit. Pull, pull now. Go left, Billy. Billy, go right now, Billy."

Now, the neighbor noticed something, so he said to his friend, "Hey, Pierre, how come you only yelling at that horse called 'Billy'?"

And the man who was plowing said, "Oh, I yelling at the other one, too. You see, his name Billy also."[26]

While this is apparently an ordinary numskull tale, the Frenchman's use of "Billy" for both horses may indicate a poor grasp of English and a mistaken assumption that "Billy" might be a generic name for all plowhorses.

Two Old French Brothers

Now, my father's cousin Ricky Saari was a Finnish–American of the second generation who was raised in the Sturgeon River Valley over near Chassel, an area that had been settled by a number of French–Canadian families. And Ricky tells some interesting stories about his experiences with the French people.

It seems that one time a couple of old French brothers had driven into the lumberyard there in Chassel with their pickup truck. One of them jumped out of the truck, went indoors, and he said to the man, "My bru-dair and I, we wan' some four-by-two."

And the man said, "You mean some two-by-fours?"

"Ahhhh, I don't know. I'll go ask my bru-dair."

And he went out, and he and his brother had a long involved conversation, waving their hands all over the place. And he came back in.

"My bru-dair say we want four-by-two."

And the lumberyard man said, "Well, I suppose it doesn't really matter how you look at it: four-by-twos, two-by-fours. How long do you want them?"

"Ahhh, I don't know. I'll go ask my bru-dair."

Out he went, and they had another long conversation, waving their hands all around.

He came back in, he said, "My bru-dair say we want them long time. We gonna build a house."[27]

Although widely told about Scandinavian and Polish numskulls, this joke is "Frenchified" by accenting the second syllable of "bru-dair," reversing the sequence of "two-by-four," and the performer's mentioning and imitating hand waving, or "talking with the hands," attributed to the French.

CHAPTER FOUR

The Cornish

Cornish settlers of the Upper Midwest were miners who came to ply their old-country trade in the new world. The skilled workmen and "captains" in the iron and copper mines of Michigan's Upper Peninsula, in the lead mines of southwestern Wisconsin, and on the Mesabi and Vermillion iron ranges of Minnesota were known as "Cousin Jacks." The term's origin is obscure. One explanation proposes that Cornish miners recommended their "Cousin Jack" to fill a vacant job, another suggests the Cornish were prone to "cussin'." In reality and in jokes alike, however, the Cornish are staunch Methodists, although some were not averse to a drop of liquor.

While the "Miners" section places the Cornish underground, the examples here, culled from southwestern Wisconsin and Michigan's "Copper Country," are set in a landscape of scattered "locations" (clusters of homes adjacent to mines) and small farms. Here preachers spew fire and brimstone and maiden ladies uphold propriety, while Cousin Jacks (typified by the fictional Jan and Bill) work out, carouse in taverns, exchange drolleries, and spar with "Cousin Jennies" (epitomized by Jan's wife, Mary Jane) who stay at home to bake ethnic delicacies, like bread or buns flavored with saffron and Cornish meat pies, or pasties.

Their collective antics and those of other Cousin Jacks are enlivened by tellers who replicate Cornish dialectical peculiarities: adding and dropping an "h," elongating vowels, and rendering "you" as "ye."

Cousin Jack and the Dog

A Cornish miner was trudging to town with a bag over his shoulder to buy some supplies. In walking past the home of a settler, he was suddenly set upon by a dog who growled and showed his teeth.

While he was trying to defend himself against Towser by swinging the bag about, the owner of the dog called out. "Jack, that dorg won't bite; e's waggin' 'es tail!"

"I knoaw that," replied Cousin Jack. "E's waggin 'es tail at one hend and barkin' at the hother. I doan't naw which of 'es ends to believe."[28]

The Talking Jug

A Cornishman walked to town one evening to purchase a jug of whiskey. While at the tavern, he found it necessary to sample each of a number of brands of liquor before making his purchase. Then he started on his homeward way in the dark carrying the stoneware jug over his shoulder on the end of a stick thrust through its handle. He was rather unsteady on his legs and his progress was slow and uncertain.

As he did not return after a reasonable length of time, his wife sent their son to find him. When the young man approached the corner of a field, he heard someone talking. Drawing near, he found his father entangled in a barbed wire fence through which he had tried to pass. Lying a few feet behind him was the jug. Its cork had come out and the precious liquor was flowing out of the neck with a "glug! glug! glug!"

The old man was saying in reply, "Yes, I hear 'ee, and I knaw ye're good, but I canna get to 'ee."[29]

Mice in the Tavern

A Cornishman spent a night in the old tavern at Dodgeville. They gave him a room up in the third story. After a while he came down to the office in his nightclothes to register a complaint with the clerk.

"There be two mice a-fightin' in my room," said he, "and I can't sleep!"

To this complaint the irritated clerk replied, "What do you expect for two dollars—a bull fight?"[30]

The three preceding texts are all set in nineteenth-century southwestern Wisconsin, a lead mining district of ridges and valleys dotted with mines, small farms, and villages. The fierce dogs, rough taverns, and seedy hotels give a fair picture of bygone days. The subject matter in these jokes parallels the local legends of drunks meeting ghosts and the devil appearing in dog form.

The Hammer Handle

Mr. Howe a farmer living near Mineral Point, wishing to use his hammer for some purpose, found the handle broken. He told his hired man, a young Cornishman, to make a new one.

The young man took the hammer to the woodshed but soon returned and asked his employer, "Mr. 'owe, Mr. 'owe. Wot's best, hash, hoak, hor helm to make a 'ammer 'andle?"[31]

The Horse on the Highway

A farmer was using his team to haul rocks one spring, and they went lame. So he took them to a Cornish blacksmith. The man looked them over and he told the farmer, "Hit hain't the 'eavy 'auling what 'urts the 'orses' 'ooves, hits the 'ammer, 'ammer, 'ammer on the 'ard 'ighway."[32]

Hawk or Howl?

Hiram and Ida went from Dodgeville to Madison on their honeymoon. Seeing the sights in the old capitol building, they stopped before Old Abe, the historic war eagle. Ida nudged Hiram's arm and said, "'iram, 'iram, look! It is a 'awk or a howl?"

Hiram took another look at the famous bird and replied, "Tis neither, Hida, tis a heagle."[33]

Since the Cornish and the Cockney have a habit of dropping the initial "h" and inserting an "h" prior to a vowel, the two groups share common and closely related jokes.

Jan and Mary Jane

Mary Jane called up the mine one day. Got Jan on the phone. She said, "Jan, just think, mother wants to be cremated." He said, "Get her clothes on, I'll be right home."[34]

This telling and the next five stories concerning Jan and Mary Jane are part of a coherent cycle set in the Upper Peninsula's "Copper Country."

For Richer, for Poorer

Jan said, "Honey, before we were married, you never had a rag on your back."

"Well," she said, "I got plenty of them now."[35]

For Better, for Worse

Jan said, "Honey, I've taken you over the rough spots of life."
She said, "Yes, dammit, and you haven't missed any either."[36]

Saffron Bread

Jan came home one day. Mary Jane was in the kitchen crying. He said, "Honey, what's wrong?"
She said, "Jan, I made a fresh loaf of saffron bread, put it out to cool, and the cat ate it."
"Oh, never mind," he said, "I'll get ye another cat."[37]

The Burglar's Fate

She said, "Jan, wake up. There's a burglar in the kitchen, and he's eating the rest of that there pie we had leftover for supper."
He said, "Go to sleep. I'll bury him in the morning."[38]

In Sickness and in Health

Jan was walking up 5th Street downtown one time. Bill come out of Billy Jones's saloon across the street, and he saw Jan. And he said, "Here Jan, where you going?"
Jan said, "I'm going to the drugstore. My wife isn't looking good."
"Oh," Bill said, "wait a minute, I'll go along with ye. I don't like the looks of the bugger I got 'ome either."[39]

Cousin Jack's Courtship

Well, Jan the Cousin Jack went skating down to Mohawk one Saturday night. And there was a tall Finnish girl there, beautiful-looking girl, long-legged, good skater—Finnish people were. And he struck up an acquaintance with her and asked her if he couldn't skate with her a bit, you know. And while he was skating with her, he asked her if he couldn't walk her home after the rink closed.

Well, you would think he would take the streetcar or horse and cutter or something, but people were strong enough to walk in those days. She was from ten miles to the south.

So after the rink closed, they started to walk. And they took a short cut over by Number 2 Ahmeek Mine. Cold clear night. He thought he'd love her up a bit. But he was so short and she was so tall, he wasn't making out too good. And there was an old anvil there by the machine shop. He kicked the snow off of that and stood on the anvil, and he loved her up a bit there. Then they walked on two miles more to Peterman's store in Allouez. He loved her up a bit there.

Then they walked two more miles to Peterman's store at Wolverine. Loved her up a bit more.

Then they walked on to Albion streetcar station, two miles more. Loved her up a bit more.

Then they walked on to Osceola streetcar station. She was getting close to home. He thought he was going to love her up a bit more.

She said, "That's enough."

"Well," he said, "it's no bloody use carrying this anvil any further."[40]

This telling and the preceding story, presented by the same teller, were well received by old timers because of the reference to bygone landmarks in mining towns of Michigan.

Miss Jones

We had a school teacher down at Centennial one time called Miss Jones. She said, "Don't you dare put that on my headstone, 'Miss Jones.' I haven't missed so much as you think I have."[41]

Miss Jones would appear to be Welsh. Welsh and Cornish people, both of old country mining and Methodist stock, often settled side-by-side in the Upper Midwest.

Methodist Sunday

You know, we had a local preacher here one time called Prevere. He stayed in the Central Hotel, and he used to sell headstones on the side to make a few dollars. He was the local preacher, and he filled in for the Methodist preachers when they were at conference or sick or something.

Well, this Sunday morning, he was preaching at the Centennial Methodist Church. And he was full of hellfire and damnation. The old religious type, you know. The church was full. And Bill and Jan, the two Cousin Jacks, were sitting in the congregation. And Miss Brown, a beautiful blond, was sitting up in the balcony. And she was so engrossed in his speech, she was leaning over the banister.

At one of the high points of his speech, when he bellowed out with this silver tone, she got so excited she fell over the banister. And luckily enough, her dress caught over the chandelier. And there she was hanging over the heads of the congregation.

And the minister, immediately seeing her predicament, bellowed out, "If anybody in this audience dare look up at poor Miss Brown, the good Lord will strike him blind."

Bill give Jan a poke. He said, "Jan, I'm going to take a chance on one eye."[42]

Widely told and often printed, this joke usually involves southern WASPs, the Irish, and African–Americans, but here specific details link the telling to the Cornish mining community.

The Germans

More than half the population of Wisconsin claims some German heritage, while the number of German Minnesotans is exceeded only by the Swedes and Norwegians in combination. From the 1830s through the turn of the century, German immigrants— peasants and tradesmen, Lutherans and Catholics, Mennonites and free thinkers, who were from Mecklenburg and Bavaria, from Saxony and the Rhineland—settled the cities and farmland of the Upper Midwest. Despite, or possibly because of, their numbers and diversity, they do not figure largely in the region's folk humor.

Unlike the Irish (Catholic laborers), the Cornish (Methodist miners), or the Scandinavians (Lutheran loggers and domestics), Germans were not so easily associated with a single religion or occupation. Perhaps as a result, no German "type" emerged strongly as a stock character in jokes. Such a character *is* weakly evident in the "Dutchman," a rotund rube who washes down wurst with beer and speaks in a thick German–English dialect. "Dutch" (from "Deutsch") comic figures were common enough in nineteenth-century tent shows, vaudeville, humor publications, and, doubtless, joke telling, but World War I, with its anti–German images of marauding Huns, appears to have all but obliterated popular notions of gentle, funny Teutons.

The German jokes presented here come entirely from heavily German, mostly rural, settlements where language and ethnic consciousness persist strongly. Some are in-group tellings that play German dialects against "high German" and delight in confused communication between German and English speakers. The rest are anecdotes by non-Germans portraying local characters whose behavior matches pervasive stereotypes of Germans as stolid simpletons (akin to the old country's Bavarian peasants) or stubborn autocrats (of militaristic Prussian ilk).

The Poacher Pursued

There was a man who went fishing at night. His catch was illegal. As he was hurrying home he heard a voice shouting after him: *"Jhifty, jhifty, jhifty."* [Give up, give up, give up.]

The man ran faster, but the faster he ran, the faster the words *"jhifty, jhifty, jhifty"* were shouted. And the person chasing him was keeping up with him.

The man became angry, defensive, and shouted back: *"Ich yav me nicht wen ich me doot loopa mut."* [I won't give up even if I should kill myself running.]

When he reached home, he finally turned around to find no one had been chasing him. The noise he thought was a voice had been his pants legs rubbing together. The faster he had run, the faster the noise or words seemed to be shouted.[43]

The Wood Thief

There was once a man who intended to steal some wood from a neighboring farmer. At night he took his wheelbarrow out and started to the farm. The man's conscience was bothering him. The wheels of the wheelbarrow spoke to him, saying, *"Ye kreeya nicht, ye kreeya nicht."* [You won't get any.] When he got to the woodpile, all the wood was gone.

The man suspected that someone had found him out, and he raced home. The wheelbarrow wheel scolded him all the way home, saying, *"Ich daact me dat, ich daact me dat."* [I thought that, i.e., I told you so.][44]

Everyday noises—bees humming, a clock ticking, or a squeaking wheel—are mistaken for human speech in these traditional "Plattdeutsch" or Low German tales.

Reading Plattdeutsch

To joke about the mixed-up and varied German dialects, my Great-Uncle August would tell his Plattdeutsch joke. He would write these symbols on paper and ask some unsuspecting person if they could read Plattdeutsch. The person would be somewhat embarrassed and admit they did not know how to read it. He then would go on to explain, pointing to each symbol as he told about it.

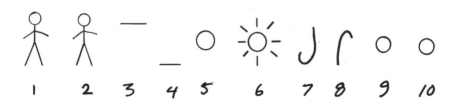

1. *Dit is Franc.* [This is Frank.]
2. *Dit is Fredric.* [This is Frederick.]
3. *Dit is hooch.* [This is high.]
4. *Dit is needric.* [This is low.]
5. *Dit ist maun.* [This is the moon.]
6. *Dit ist zun.* [This is the sun.]
7. *Dit is a hauka.* [This is a hook.]
8. *Dit is a stooka.* [This is a staff.]
9. *Dit is a rund rink.* [This is a round ring.]
10. *Dit is grouz sona dink.* [This is a similar thing.][45]

Wisconsin Germans have been historically trilingual, speaking some English, "High German" (or "sermon German," required in church and in print), and their own regional dialect—in this case, "Plattdeutsch" from the "low" areas of Europe bordering the North and Baltic seas. This telling combines words and pictures, rhymed couplets, and similar and opposite phenomena.

Sockery's Cat

Mine goot friends, I tell you little story 'bout what happened one day last veek. You see Katarina, dat was my *frau,* she go away, she make little picnic.

And she say 'fore she go, "Sockery, you up to barn about, see dat old blue hen don't lay some eggs pretty much already."

So I take the saw and the ax and the hammer, and I goes to work to make the house what was a hen house into a barn what was corn crib. And while I was sawing on a board, dat old blue hen she come out from round through the barn. She say, "Cut-cut, cut-a-cut. Cut-cut, cut-a-cut." I thinks to myself, maybe she lay some eggs pretty much already.

So I creeps down under the barn and way back in the corner. I didn't see any eggs pretty much, but I saw little black and white *kat.* You see Katarina, dat was mine *frau,* she say every day to me we have so many mices in dat house, I think we better get little *kat.* So I creeps up on my hands and knees, and I grabs him by the back of the neck. And oh, my good gracious me, what a schmell. I thought I had stepped on something which was dead. It was worser than a whole barrel of limberger. And I take it in mine arm, and I goes out in the front yard.

And along up the road come old Jake Moser. When he see me with dat *kat* he says, "You old fool, what you doing with dat schkunk?"

"Schkunk!" I say. And I drop him so quick as was half so quick as never was. "Mine goot friend Jake," I say, "what I do make dat schmell go 'way?"

Vell, he say he bury me up to the neck in the ground. Dat make the schmell go away. And he get a schpade, and he bury me up to the neck in the ground. And he say, "Well, I got little business down by the willage. I go there."

So he vent, and pretty soon there was fly light on my nose. And I schpit and think and viggled. Fly he no go way. Pretty soon there was more flies. More than thousand flies. More than a hundred flies light on my nose. And I schpit and viggled, but the fly he no go 'way.

Pretty soon I look down the road, and there was men and vomens and schildrens. And they have schpades and pickaxes and hoes. They have everything. You see dat old fool, Jake, he go by the willage. He tell them there was man buried alive up to Sockery's. Vell, I see I couldn't keep dat schtory schtill any longer. So I tells them the whole business, and those fools, you can hear them laugh more than half mile. I think I not much longer vill schtay in this country. You see, everybody I meet on the road say to me, "Sockery, how you like to buy little *kat?*"[46]

The performance of "Sockery's [or Zachary's] Cat" was offered in an affected "stage Dutch" dialect and appears to be a theatrical piece commonly performed in tent shows, vaudeville, and small town opera houses until World War I.

A Dutchman and an Irishman

I'll tell you one. This is one about a Dutchman. I'm German myself, but that don't make any difference.

There was a Dutchman and an Irishman. They had a weenie. And each one wanted it.

And the Irishman said, "Okay, let's take it in our teeth and pull on it and see who gets the biggest end."

And the Dutchman says, "All right."

They got a hold of it. And the Irishman says [through clenched teeth], "Rrrready?"

And the Dutchman says [opening mouth wide], "Yah."
Irishman got all the weenie.[47]

Much of the success of the joke depends on the performer's characterization of a wiry Irishman's feisty determination and a rotund "Dutchman's" placid attitude through facial and paralingual expressions. The "weenie" in question is, of course, a German sausage.

Heinie Vanishes

Another one. A wife's husband, he went to the barbershop. And then, from the barbershop, he walked away to a tavern. He wasn't coming home, and she kind of went out looking for him. So she come in the barbershop. She was looking around; she couldn't see her husband anywhere. She kind of spoke a little broken. And she didn't see her husband there at all. So she says to the barber, she says, "Vash my Heinie here?"

And the barber says, "No. Just a shave and a haircut." They didn't wash heinies there.[48]

There are two possible ways to interpret "heinie." In the Upper Midwest, "heinie" refers to a person's bottom or "hind end" and to a short or "butch" hair cut. The latter meaning probably derives from an association between the close-cropped hair of Prussian soldiers and the common German name of "Heinrich."

On the Wheels of a Dilemma

This goes way back to when the women had real long skirts to their ankles and the high-wheeled wagons. And this older German lady went into town, walked into town. Farmer next door was giving her a ride home.

So she climbed up this high-wheeled wagon, got onto the seat, rode back to where she was supposed to get off. But meanwhile, in getting off, her long skirt got caught on the high wheel of the wagon.

And so she said to this man, she said, "Don't go ahead. Don't back up. And for God's sake, don't look."[49]

While this may be a purely local anecdote without any known parallels in print, the neat tripartite conclusion suggests a twice told tale.

Raspberry Jam

Then there's another one about this same old German lady. It was back in the summertime when there were wild raspberries. And if anybody has gone picking wild raspberries, there might be a few little worms in things, see.

So she went out, she picked the wild raspberries and came home and was looking them over, and there were all kinds of worms.

So she says, "Ach there's so many vorms, I couldn't get them picked out. I yust dumped them in the kettle. Made jam."[50]

Making jam, as opposed to canning whole fruit or making preserves, is usually an alternative when the berries are overripe and falling apart.

The German's Wives

You know this old German. I won't mention his name. Anyway, they asked him if he was ever married. "Yah," he said, "I vas married two times."

"You were? What happened?"

"Vell," he said, "the first woman, she was a hell of a good woman. But the second one, she was a so-and-so." He said, "She runned away. If she hadn't runned away, I vas going to schoot her."[51]

The teller presents the anecdote, with its stress on stern patriarchy in rural German–American families, as a true story. But the propensity for subtle exaggeration, the tendency to match local characters to traveled stories, and the reliance on a third-party source suggest that the story should be regarded as at least slightly made-over.

Farmer Ritz

Now this farmer Ritz, he had a place near the Mitchell school where V and M meet, and he used to come into town for supplies. And he'd always take a drink, sometimes too many. Next day, he'd be hung over and he wouldn't work.

It was threshing time and it was his turn—time for the neighbors to come to his place and help him. But he wouldn't do any work.

He stood on the porch and told everybody, "The doctor told me to eat vell, sleep vell, do notting."[52]

Although the actual words of Ritz may have been compressed by the teller, this is apparently a true story about an uncharacteristically ne'er-do-well German–American farmer who shirked his neighborly duties.

Lutheran Souls

I was at a retreat not long ago—it was a Lutheran gathering—and they were talking about Lutherans in the southwest—up near Holmen, Wisconsin. It was the centennial of this congregation.

They went back into the church records and went through there. And they come to one particular year: 250 souls and a German. That was the total membership of the congregation.

It was a Norwegian congregation.[53]

The suggestion that members of some occupational or ethnic group are somehow outside the human race is expressed in parallel anecdotes: one from the Pacific northwest in which "three men and a logger were drowned" and another one in which a brewery explosion claims the lives of thirty-eight workers and an Irishman.

A Child's Plaything

I came from a German neighborhood [in Milwaukee], which was on 27th and Cherry when I was a kid. And this was during the Depression. And of course people didn't have much money for anything, and there was a lot of stories going around.

And being in a German neighborhood, there was a story about little Erich, who had just come in very gleefully, into the house. And his dad was reading the paper. And he says to his dad, he says, *"Papa, papa, sie, ich spiele meine yo-yo."* He was playing with his little top.

And the father reading the paper didn't know what was going on. He says, *"Schnell, Erich! Gehen sie sich in bathroom. Waschen sie die hande!"*[54]

This telling parallels another common joke in which masturbation is associated with economic deprivation: "We had hard times. Ma cut the bottoms out of our pockets just so we'd have something to play with."

Milwaukee's A Crazy Old City

This old guy came over from Germany, and he decides to move to Milwaukee because he heard that a lot of people in Milwaukee know how to speak German. He figured he'd get along just fine.

So he gets settled down, and one morning he decides to go to the local restaurant to get some breakfast. He walks in, sits down to the table, and the waiter comes over, and the old guy says, *"Wie gehts."* [Hello.]

Guy yells behind the counter, "Wheat cakes."

And the old guy goes, *"Nein, nein."* [No, no.]

The waiter looks. "The hell with you. You get three like everyone else."

And he goes, "Boy, this Milwaukee's a crazy old city. No one can speak German." He says, "I'm getting the hell out of here."

So he walks down the street to another restaurant. He says, "Maybe I'll have better luck here." He walks in, sits down at the table, and he says to the waiter, *"Wie sachs du?"* [How do you do?]

And he goes, he looks at him, "Well, the White Sox didn't play today."[55]

Milwaukee is considered the "German Athens" of the new world, a place where German culture is still highly visible. The mention of the White Sox, a Chicago baseball team, raises a couple of speculations. Since the joke dates back to the 1930s, a time when Milwaukee had no major league club, some denizens of the beer city might have followed the White Sox, or possibly another version of the joke might have had the disgruntled German traveling from Milwaukee to Chicago in search of a German–speaking community.

The Irish

Driven to America by potato famines and British landlords, some Irish immigrants settled in the Upper Midwest in the 1840s and 1850s. Chiefly uneducated peasants, America's "shanty Irish" worked as miners, loggers, farmers, urban laborers, and domestics, rising gradually to middle class "lace curtain" status.

Evolving from jokes, or "Irish bulls," abroad and in America since the eighteenth century, the Upper Midwest's fictive Irishmen were pugnacious rascals—thirsty and sharp-tongued, and both foolish and cunning. The women were ignorant, stoic, pious, and dependent upon priests. Pat and Mike, a roughly interchangeable pair, figure most prominently in a cycle of humorous tales that chronicle the immigrant generation's socioeconomic journey.

Perhaps because the Irish have been so successful on their journey into the American mainstream, their jocular narratives dwell upon a "golden" past of cheerful struggle. Tellers commonly establish that the youthful Pat and Mike have just "come over to this country" to work as itinerant laborers—hod carriers, rough carpenters—who are continually perplexed by the new world around them. More genteel and savvy in later years, they join fraternal organizations and the Democratic Party, hold grand wakes, and contemplate the afterlife.

Lord of the Dogs

There was an Irishman got on a train. And there happened to be an English lord sitting across from him. The lord was kind of snobby. And he looked out the window, and there was an Irish setter going by. So he said to the Irishman, "There goes one of your relatives." The Irishman looked out and he told the lord, "Bejasus, if he isn't related to both of us."[56]

This represents one of many in the teller's repertoire in which an impoverished Irishman uses his wits to counter an Englishman's presumed superiority.

Pat and Mike Cross the Pond

Pat and Mike, you know, when they was going across the pond—the way it was, when one died the other would throw him overboard. Pat he come across. He threw Mike over, and he come across alone. And then they kind of questioned him. They said, "Where's Mike?"

"I threw him overboard."

"Why? Was he dead?"

"Well, he said he wasn't, but he was such a goddam liar you couldn't believe him anyway."[57]

Another version, traced to Kentucky, substitutes an Anglo–American and African–Americans for Pat and Mike: A truck driver runs over three blacks in Missouri, then tells the sheriff he buried them. "Were they all dead?" "Well, one said he wasn't, but you know how them black bastards lie." (Recorded by James P. Leary, June 8, 1978, at the Northside Bar, Stevens Point, from Leo Garski.)

Pat the Hod Carrier

Pat come over to this country, and he got a job as a hod carrier. So he writes home to Mike. He says, "Mike, you should be in this country. Wonderful, wonderful," he says. "All I have to do is carry the mortar and brick up to the tenth floor, and the other guy does all the work."[58]

This Pat-and-Mike joke and the next four share the new immigrant—"Pat come over to this country…"—opening formula.

An American Fire

This is an old one. This story goes back to the time of about 1910. Maybe some of you remember a time when the fire engines went down the street drawn by some horses, and the smoke and fire came out the top of the engine.

And Pat and Mike had come over to this country. And they went around New York. And they just spent the whole day walking around the city. And when they got through, they went to the hotel. And they were up on one of the high floors, up about the twelfth story, and there was a fire.

Mike looked out at the street. Pat had dropped on the bed sound asleep, he was just so tired. But Mike looked out the window, and there was a fire engine going by with the smoke and the fire coming out the top of the chimney. And he went over, and he says, "Pat, Pat, wake up."

Well, Pat was so tired that he didn't wake up.

And he heard another, he heard *clang, clang, clang.* Looked out the window, and there was another fire engine going by with the smoke and the fire coming out of the chimney. He went over. "Pat, Pat, wake up."

But Pat was so tired that he didn't wake up.

It was a big fire. And he looked out the window, and here was another fire engine going by with the smoke belching out the chimney and the *clang, clang, clang.* And he went over, and he took ahold of Pat, and he shook him, and he says, "Pat, Pat, wake up. They're moving hell. Three loads gone by already."[59]

Pat and Mike Pound Nails

And when they come here once, Pat and Mike, from Europe, they started working on construction.

So by golly, you know, they was sheeting for a building. And Pat pulled out a nail, and the head was facing the board. He said, "Look, Mike, that don't fit here."

"Oh," Mike says, "that goes on the other side."

The other side of the building. They couldn't turn the nail around; they'd have to walk around.[60]

The Crosscut Saw

Pat and Mike come over to this country, and they were very green. There was a lot of tools they used in the United States they didn't know what they were for.

So they were walking out through the country, and there was a father and a son sawing wood with a crosscut saw. And one'd pull it, the other'd pull it. And Mike thought the old man was trying to take it away from the kid.

So he went over and took it away from the old man and handed it to the boy.[61]

Mike Ruts Around

Mike and Pat come over to this country. And Mike got rutting around. And Pat got a pretty good job where he learned quite a lot about America.

And, by God, whatever kind of a deed Mike pulled, they were going to hang him. And they had their trapeze all ready to hang Mike when Pat come along to visit him. And he inquired where Mike was, and they told him, "He's up there on the scaffold."

And Pat come along, and he says, "Well, Mike, what're you doing up there?"

"Oh," he says, "I make a lot of money doing this. And if you want to make it, I'll exchange places with you."

So Pat thought that was all right. So when they tripped the rope, something didn't work right. So Pat fell off the scaffold. And he says, "Some damn fool could get his neck broke doing this stunt."[62]

At the Crossroad

Pat and Mike were walking home. They came to the crossroad, and they didn't know which way they could turn. So Pat shinnied up the pole to see what it said. And he came down. And Mike asked him, "Now, what did the sign say?"

And Pat said, "It says, 'FRESH PAINT, don't touch.'"[63]

Though this telling leaves out the fact that Pat and Mike were probably traveling in a fog or in darkness, similar conditions are standard in other versions of this common anecdote.

The Priest's Advice

Now, Pat was an awful drunk. He used to come home drunk every night. His wife would beat him with a rolling pin.

Finally she went to the priest. "Father, I have this trouble with Pat. Every night he comes home drunk."

And Father said, "What do you do when Pat comes home?"

"Ah, I beat him up with everything."

And Father said, "No, no. Don't do that. Treat Pat nice. When he comes home, lead him to a place by the fire. Sit him down, take his coat off, take off his boots, bring him his slippers, bring him a paper, bring him some tea, bring him his pipe. Treat Pat nice."

She said, "Well, Father, I don't know if it'll work, but I'll try it."

So that night, Pat comes home, he's drunk as usual. So his wife leads him over to his chair, she sits him down, she makes sure he's comfortable. She brings him things and he sits there peacefully for a while. Then she says, "Well, Pat, we might just as well go to bed."

He says, "We might just as well. I'll get hell when I get home anyway."[64]

This telling brings together the stock figures of the drunken Irish husband, the priest as confidant, and the prudish Irish wife.

Drunk as Usual

I remember one where Pat was uptown. And he got gloriously drunk as usual. And he stumbled home in the dark, and he was going to take a short cut through the cemetery.

Well, they had dug a grave the night before, or the afternoon before. They were going to have an early morning funeral. So Pat, he comes stumbling along, and he falls in the grave. And he goes to sleep down there.

In the morning, he wakes up when the sun was hitting him in the eye, and he stands up. And he looks at the dirt heaped around the grave. And he says, "Hallelujah," he says, "here it is resurrection morning, and I'm the first one to be awakened."[65]

This tale closely resembles other versions with similar motifs—a person is made to believe he is dead, and a drunk person falls into an open grave.

Pat's Wake

Pat died and Mike went to his wake, and he was trying to comfort the widow. So he told her, "Ah, Pat was a grand lad."

"That he was, that he was."

"And he was a member of the Democratic Party."

"That he was, that he was."

"And he was a member of the Ancient Order of Hibernians."

"That he was, that he was."

"And he was a member of the Ku Klux Klan."

"What's that?"

"'Tis the divil under the sheets."

"That he was, that he was."[66]

Pat's reputed membership in the Ku Klux Klan is ironic because the Klan is anti–Catholic.

At the Graveside

Oh, I got to tell you one, too. I just happened to think about this Irishman and the Scotsman were good friends. And they had an agreement. And whoever dies first, the other will put a six-pack of beer on his grave.

So this Irishman died, the Scotsman, he goes out. "Well, I suppose I better do that." And he was standing there looking at the grave for awhile. "Well, I don't suppose he'll mind it, me old buddy, if I pass it through me kidneys first."[67]

Whiskey is more commonly the preferred drink of the two Celts. The tale's typically profligate Irishman is joined by a typically parsimonious Scot.

Pat and Mike in Hell

Seems that Pat and Mike were great friends. And Pat died, and of course, he went to hell.

Pretty soon Mike died, and he went to hell. And he come in there. And, oh, there was all cases of whiskey, all over. "Why," he said, "this ain't a bad place, Pat," he said. "It's not what you read about," he said. "Where's the opener, Pat?"

He said, "That's the hell of it. We ain't got any."[68]

Humor is heightened by the matter-of-fact way in which the teller remarks that Pat died and "of course" went to hell.

CHAPTER SEVEN

The Scandinavians

Long before humorist Garrison Keillor popularized "Norwegian bachelor farmers," Minnesota's Twin Cities were home to barnstorming Scandinavian vaudeville comics, radio personalities commenting on daily events in a thick "Yah, Sure" dialect, and scores of Scandinavian jokes. Swedes and Norwegians, the dominant ethnic groups in Minneapolis and St. Paul, are found abundantly throughout Minnesota, in western and northern Wisconsin, and in Michigan's Upper Peninsula. And Scandinavian folk humor is the most vibrant of any ethnic group in the Upper Midwest.

Some Scandinavian jokes exploit the now-friendly rivalry between Norwegians and the Swedes who once ruled Norway, but most concern the doings of stock characters, especially Ole and Lena, who are interchangeably Swedish or Norwegian. A stalwart, stubborn bumpkin, sometime fisherman/farmer/logger, Ole shares numskull adventures with Lars or Sven when not romantically entangled with Lena. Alternately the lusty coquette and the prim Lutheran, Lena begins life as a single domestic. After marrying Ole, she presides over a spotless home, serves *lutefisk, lefse,* and coffee, and keeps her husband off balance with praise and taunts.

Scandinavian jokes have not diminished over a century of telling. Such ongoing delight in joke telling on an everyday folk level has been complemented by the regional production and purchase of an array of joke books, recordings by dialect comedians, and jocular paraphernalia (buttons, bumperstickers, comic artifacts, mock documents) that have updated old tales and introduced new ones situating Ole and Lena in the late twentieth century.

The Quaker's Cow

My favorite is about the farmer and his cow.

And the cow, he was milking it one night—sitting there with his head leaning against her—when suddenly she switched her dirty tail across his face. He didn't like it.

Now, this man happened to be a Quaker. He was milking away, you know. Pretty soon the cow lifted up her foot, bumped the pail a little. He didn't like it, but he didn't say anything.

Suddenly—sitting there a little while longer, he was milking away—the cow put her foot right in the pail. The Quaker became very angry, and he stood up.

And he said to the cow, "Thou knowest I am a Quaker. And thou knowest I cannot curse thee. And thou knowest that I cannot beat thee. But what thou does not know is that I can sell thee to a Norwegian."[69]

The phrase "stubborn Norwegian" is proverbial in the Upper Midwest. The source for this joke was, perhaps appropriately, a Norwegian Lutheran Pastor, Elmer Hjortlund, at a church meeting in Stoughton, Wisconsin, sometime in the 1950s.

Ole Crosses the Ocean

I'd like to tell you a story about my great-great-grandfather, Ole, who was a Swedish immigrant who came from Sweden in 1896. His boat left Sweden, and they were out in the North Sea. They were out there for four days, and a gigantic storm came up. The wind was blowing; the sails were shaking. The people were scairt. The captain was scairt. Everybody was scairt.

So finally my grandfather, Ole, went up to the captain and he said, "Captain," he said, "we haf to do something about this." He said, "All the people are really scairt down in the holdt of the ship." So he said, "What are we going to do?"

And the captain said, "The only thing I can think we can do is hold a prayer meeting up on deck."

So Ole got all the immigrants up on the deck. And the wind was whistling through the sails. The water was flowing over the deck. And everyone was holding onto the railings. And the captain, he took the Good Book out, and he hooked onto the railings with his hand, and in the other hand he had the Good Book. And he said to the people, he said, "Oh, Father, send thy Son to save us."

And my grandpa, Ole, hollered through the wind. He said, "Father," he said, "you better come yourself. This is no yob for a kid."[70]

Trans–Atlantic sailing ships were long gone by 1896, but the perils of the first immigrant crossings linger in this later setting.

Ellis Island

There was this Norwegian come cover from the old country, and this fellow in front of him in the line happened to have the same name. His name was John Johnson, and the guy ahead of him happened to be John Johnson. They were going through Ellis Island. Immigration.

They asked the first guy his name, and he said, "John Johnson." So they wrote it down.

So when the second John Johnson, who was next in line, comes up there, they say, "What's your name?"

He said, "Sam' t'ang" [same thing].

And they wrote it down "Sam Tang."

They claim that's a true story.[71]

The Chinese sound of a Norwegian's pronunciation of "same thing" rendered as "sam tang" or "sam ting" resulted in another version in which a Chinaman gives his true name, Sam Ting, to an immigration official just after an Albert Olson has gone through. The bungling official sets down Ting's name as Albert Olson.

The Swedish Stowaway

Oh, there's all kinds of jokes. There's always jokes. Oh, some of these Irish used to be kidding the Swedes. "Dumb Swedes," you see.

Montreal, Wisconsin, there was a river they used to cross. And they were trying to smuggle one guy in. He was a Swede, you know. So they put him in a bag with some harnesses.

So they were coming across on the boat, and some immigration officials there said, "What have you got in the bag?"

"Oh, nothing. Just harness and sleigh bells."

So they run over and give it a kick, and the Swede was in there. He said, "Yangle, yangle."[72]

The Norwegian rivalry with Swedes comes out in the teller's reference to "dumb Swedes." Most variants of this joke involve a Scandinavian thief hiding from the police in a bag of bells.

Ole and Lars

You asked about Norwegian stories. I had one about the two Norwegians running down the railroad track in front of a freight train.

Ole said to Lars, "I think we ought to cut out across this plowed field."

Lars says, "Oh no, Ole, if we can't keep ahead of it up here on the track, we'll never keep ahead of it on the plowed field."[73]

The theme of numskull newcomers unfamiliar with American technology is similarly found in Pat-and-Mike stories. And, like the Irish, many Scandinavians in the Upper Midwest were itinerant laborers and hired hands.

Jan and Olaf

Then there's another one.

Jan and Olaf were up on a roof on a barn, repairing it. And a windstorm came along and blew the ladder down. And they said, "Now what shall we do?"

"Yah," he says, "I guess the only t'ing we can do is yump."

So they looked down, and there was a manure pile. They would have to "yump" in that. And it would be a little soft landing.

"Jan, you yump first." So he "yumped." He yelled down. He says, "How iss it?"

"Oh," he says, "it's not bad," he says, "it's yust up to my ankles."

"Yah, t'en here I come." He jumped, Olaf "yumped." And he went right up to his neck. And he struggled out.

He says, "I t'ought you said it was all right, you yust went up to your ankles!"

He says, "Yah, I did," he says, "but I yumped head first."[74]

This is a widely traveled joke: Baughman motif J2499.8*, "Man falls into bog or sand; his companion goes for help, says his friend has fallen in to his ankles. People cannot see why he needs help until the man explains that his friend has fallen in head first."

The Swede in the Hoghouse

This Swede went and got drunk and couldn't find his way into the house. So he got down into the hoghouse and opened the door and lay down in the straw and went to sleep. And he woke up. He thought somebody was sleeping alongside him. It was a big sow.

So he poked it with his elbow and said, "*Ar du Svensk?*"
And the old sow says, "*Norsk, norsk.*"[75]

"*Norsk*" is snorted in imitation of a grunting porker. According to the informant, this joke was popular in Wisconsin during the 1920s.

The Newcomer's Banking

You know, way back when we used to have a lot of newcomers coming into this area, they'd work pretty cheap for the farmers around here. And this one newcomer, he'd work real hard all summer long. Come fall—why, the farmer he wrote him a check.

So he goes up here to Dow's Bank. Going to cash that check. So the gal says, "How do you want it?"

He says, "I want it in dollar bills." So she pulls out two $50 bundles of bills. He says, "Wait a minute, you got to count 'em."

"No," she says, "this is fifty dollars, each one of these bundles is fifty dollars."

He says, "You got to count them."

So she counted: "1-2-3-. . .45-46-47-48-49-40. See, there's fifty here."

He says, "Count the other bunch."

And so she was counting, "51-52-53..." Pretty soon she gets up to, "92-93-94-95-96-97-98-99-100." She says, "Didn't I tell you there was a hundred there?"

He says, "Yah, yust barely."[76]

The bank setting and theme of stubbornness paired with fiscal caution matches Text 96.

Olga the Maid

You know, Olga come over from the old country and got her a job as a maid for a big doctor. And they were cleaning up, and she went in the bathroom, and she looked in the wastebasket.

And she said, "Ma'am, ma'am, come here." She says, "Lookit, lookit what's laying in that wastepaper basket." And there was a rubber laying there.

And the lady says, "That isn't so bad. Didn't you ever have inter-course in Norway?"

"Oh yah, but not so hard it takes all the skin off." [77]

In other versions, the foolish maid is African–American, Irish, Puerto Rican, and a "country girl."

Lena the Maid

Lena got a job as maid with a rich family tied up with one of the sawmills. And the mister was testing her on what she could do.

"How are you at making beds?"

Her English wasn't so good, and she had to think a minute.

"Vell, I'm a humdinger in the grass."[78]

Here, and in the following jokes, Lena is cast as a promiscuous young maid.

Ole Meets Lena

Most people have heard Ole-and-Lena jokes. But they've never known how Ole met Lena in the first place. You see, they're both newcomers. Lena had been here a little longer than Ole, and she worked with a farm family over there. But Ole came and he bought this little forty acres over here.

And he was taking his produce to town. Now, you know what produce is? Let's see now. He had a goose, and he had a pail, and he had a heavy stone, and two schickens. And there was a gate across the road, and he stood there pondering how he could get that gate open when he was so loaded down with all this produce. And he looked up, and here stood this pretty girl.

And he said, "Lady, would you open the gate for me?"

And she said, "No sirree."

And he said, "Well, can't you a see a man can't open a gate when he's got a pail, a heavy stone, a goose, and two schickens? Now, you tell me. Why won't you open the gate?"

"Well," she said, "if I open that gate for you, you will come to this side and make love to me."

"Crazy lady. A man can't make love to a woman when he's got a pail, a heavy stone, a goose, and two schickens."

And she said, "I will tell you yust exactly how you will work it. I will open the gate for you. You will come to this side. You will set that pail down. You will put the goose in the pail. You will put the heavy stone on top of the goose. And I will hold those two schickens."[79]

This example illustrates the teller's skill at combining realistic background details with characterization developed through dialogue.

The First Date

So he asked her for a date. "Yah," she'd go out with him.

He said, "Would you like to have a cigarette?"

She said, "No, I can't have a cigarette. What would I tell my Sunday school class?"

"Well," he said, "would you take a drink?"

"No, I can't have a drink. What would I tell my Sunday school class?"

He said, "Lena, will you go home and spend the night with me?"

She said, "Yah, that I will do."

So the next morning, he said, "Lena, what are you going to tell your Sunday school class now?"

"Well, yust the same thing I've been telling them for years and years: 'you don't have to smoke and drink to have fun.'"[80]

Sunday school attendance and temperance are strongly urged by Norwegian Lutherans in the Upper Midwest.

Ole's Furlough

There was a newcomer girl from Norway. And she come over here to the United States, and she got a position as a housemaid. And she worked for an aristocratic family by the name of Johnson.

And this girl's boyfriend was coming home out of the army on a furlough, and she wanted to get off.

And Mrs. Johnson said, "You know I'm going to entertain my club next week, and I'll have to have you here to help me."

"Well," she says, "my boy friend's home on a furlough, and I'd like to have the week off."

Mrs. Johnson said, "How long is Ole's furlough?"

"Yust as long as Mr. Yonson's, but not so quite t'ick."[81]

Since Johnson is a common Scandinavian name, the "aristocratic family's" standing may be an ironic comment on class distinctions within an ethnic group.

Ole Goes to Church

Lena, of course, had been here just a little bit longer than Ole. And she was trying to take on the customs of this country. So she said to Ole, "You know, in Norway we didn't go to schurch so much. But in

America, they do. And if we're going to be Americans, we must go to schurch."

"Well," he said, "you know, by the time I get my schores done on Sunday morning, there just isn't time."

"Ohhh," she said, "I got that one figured out for you. They have an early service, and they have a late service. Now I always go to early services, because I have to go and fix dinner for the farm family. So you can go to the late service. Hurry up with your schores once."

So the next Sunday, he was hauling the manure. And he saw all these people going in to church. He tied up the horses and run and got in and then went for Sunday dinner.

So Lena says, "Well, how did that work, that business of going to schurch?"

"Well," he says, "it was all right. I was met at the door by the pusher."

She says, "No, in America they use different words. That was not a pusher that met you. That was an usher."

"Oh? Well, pusher, usher, makes no difference. Took me right down the alley."

"No," she says, "they don't call that an alley in this country. They call that an aisle."

"Oh? Well, he took me right up in front and set me on that park bench."

"Yah, but," she said, "they don't call that a park bench here. They call that a pew."

"Well," he said, "now that one I should have been able to figure out, because that's what everyone said when I sat down."[82]

The powerful influence of the Norwegian Lutheran Church in America is evident in this chronicle of a blundering, semipagan immigrant.

The Black Eye

Yah, well, this one Sunday, he came to Lena's for Sunday dinner. And he had a black eye. And Lena says, "Oh, now Ole, tell me what happened that you should have a black eye when you yust go to schurch."

"Well," he say, "it was like this. I was sitting right behind a big fat lady. And when she stood up, her dress was caught in the back. And I just figured she didn't want it that way. So I reached over, and I yust pulled it out for her. And she went at me with that great big purse, and that's how I got that black eye."

"Well," Lena said, "nothing is so bad if you learn a lesson. Now tell me, Ole, did you learn a lesson today?"

"Yah," he said, "a lesson I learned." But the next Sunday, he came for Sunday dinner, and he had another black eye.

"Oh, Olaf, now tell me what went on that you should get a second black eye?"

"Well," he says, "Lena, it was like this. I was sitting right behind the same big fat lady. And when she stood up, her dress was not caught in the back. And I learned last week that that was where she wanted it. And I reached over, and I yust put it in for her."[83]

Other Norwegian versions exist, along with an Anglo–American example.

The Bible and Minneapolis

Ole didn't think much of the Bible. Never read it. And he was from Minneapolis.

And his friend came and said, "Now Ole, if you read the Bible, I think you'll feel a little bit different about it."

So he came back to Ole about a month later and said, "Well, what did you think about the Bible?"

"Well," he said, "it was all right. But," he said, "I can't understand— it says a whole lot about St. Paul, but it doesn't say a thing about Minneapolis."[84]

In addition to the confusion of an apostle with Minnesota's capitol, this telling may allude to the fact that Minneapolis has long been a Scandinavian town, while the Irish and the Germans have dominated in St. Paul.

A Little Party

Lars and Lena was having a little party one night, and Lars said, "Do I hurt you, Lena?"

"Oh yes, you hurt me gude."[85]

"Party" is an old-time euphemism for a sexual tryst.

Ole and Lena in Court

Well, Ole was going with Lena, and Lena got in trouble. She took Ole to court for rape. And when the judge asked Lena how the condition of things were:

"Well, he took his long thing, so he could. And he put it up to me so far, so he could."

And the judge said, "Did you holler, Lena?"

"No, Ole had his mouth open; I thought he was going to holler." That's all of that.[86]

This joke, like the one preceding, concerns the common theme of Scandinavian promiscuity, particularly the stereotyping of Lena as a naïve but over-sexed female character.

Blood Relations

There was a couple went to the judge to get a marriage license. They were both named Olson.

And the judge asked them if they had any blood relationship.

"Yes, vunce in St. Paul and vunce in Minneapolis. Ole couldn't wait."[87]

That Scandinavian couples with the same surname—Olson, Johnson, Peterson, Anderson, Swanson, Carlson, and so on—would marry is not unusual.

A Little Swede

What was that one about Ole and Lena? Oh, they were going to get married.

And they asked Ole, they says, "Are you a... what nationality are you?"

He says, "I'm a Swede."

He asked Lena, "What are you?"

Says, "I'm Norwegian, but I have a little Swede in me, too. Ole couldn't wait."[88]

Here is a variation of the previous joke—with an identical punch line.

Ole and Lena's Honeymoon

Well, they got married. And they went to the big city for the honeymoon. And they walked into this big department store.

And right in the center of this whole great big store was a stairway. And it went up. The steps went up by themselves. They looked over here, and a set of steps came down by themselves over here. Couldn't figure this one out.

Pretty soon a little old lady with a bag in her hand, she walks over and she stands on the first step. And up she goes. And they stood there trying to figure this one out.

And all of a sudden, there was a pretty girl that comes down this one.

And Olaf says, "You know, I don't know what kind of business they got going on up there, but that's sure something. Why don't we just run you through that business once, Lena, and see how you turn out?"[89]

This telling combines stereotypical views husbands have about their wives and the theme of country immigrants confronting big-city modern technology.

Ole Goes Further

This story comes immediately after they [Ole and Lena] were married. On their honeymoon. Now, they were married here in Minneapolis, and they decided for their honeymoon to drive to Duluth.

So they got in the old jalopy, and they drove up towards Duluth. They got to the top of the hill, and it was just getting dark and a full moon was rising over Lake Superior. And all the city lights were coming on. It was all a-twinkle and aglow. And they got to the crest of the hill, and it was such a beautiful, romantic sight that Ole pulled that jalopy over to the side of the road and stopped. And the two of them sat there looking at the view until finally Lena—she snuggled up a little closer to Ole. And Ole—he snuggled up a little closer to Lena. And they, "Aaah," they were just enjoying being together.

And then Ole put his hand on Lena's knee. And Lena giggled. And she cuddled up a little closer.

And Ole moved his hand up a little further on Lena's thigh and squeezed it a little bit. And Lena giggled, "Ha, ha, ha."

She said, "Ole, you could go a little furt'er."

So he started up the car, and they drove to Thunder Bay.[90]

Thunder Bay, Canada, is "furt'er"—about two hundred miles to the north.

The Birthday Present

Ole and Olga, they were married then, and it was, it was Olga's birthday. So she went to the Ladies Aid, you know.

And they says, "Well, Olga, it's your birthday. And what did Ole get you? Did he get you a present?"

"Oh," she says, "you ought to see what he got me. He got me the nicest thing."

And they said, "Well, what was it?"

"It was a nightgown. Yah. Had bluebirds all over it. And Ole would feel that at night," she says, "and you know, when he found the nest he just went wild."[91]

The Ladies Aid, associated with the Norwegian Lutheran Church, provided this teller with plenty of material for a number of similar jokes.

Ours

In the summertime, Ole and Lena and John and Eleanor went out walking to the taverns on the east end. And they went to quite a few until it was closing time, time to go home.

They hadn't gone far when Ole and John had to take a leak. They went behind a billboard—you know how they're raised up off the ground—and the women sneaked a look.

The next day, Lena was talking about it over coffee with some ladies. "Was I ever proud when Ole pulled *ours* out."[92]

The teller situates this in the east end of Ashland, Wisconsin, where Polish, Czech, and Scandinavian taverns were once scattered through working-class neighborhoods.

Lena's House Party

Lena, she no longer works for the farm family. She has a little log cabin over here on the forty acres. And she says, "Olaf, you know what? I'd like to have a house party."

"Well," he says, "have a house party."

"Yeah, well," she says, "I want the kind of house party where they tell stories and they have music and they dance and all that sort of stuff."

"Well," he said, "you can have that. There's no problem. You've got a house. Have a house party."

"Well," she says, "the house is all right. I'm not saying it isn't, Olaf. But," she says, "I'm terribly embarrassed about that t'ree-holer that we got in the back. Now, there's nothing wrong with the t'ree-holer either, except that we don't have decent toilet paper. And you know, that snooty Mrs. Carlson is going to come and see that we don't have decent toilet paper."

"Well," Olaf says, "I'll see if I can find out something to do about that for you, Lena." So he took two dollars and put it in an envelope and sent it to Sears Roebuck and says, "Send me toilet paper."

So, of course, they shot it right back to him and said, "You can order toilet paper on page 365 of our new spring and summer catalogue."

And he shot a letter right back to them. "What makes you think this Norwegian would be so dumb as to order toilet paper if I had your spring and summer catalogue?"[93]

Toilet Paper

So he went to the drugstore. He said, "Do you sell toilet paper in this drugstore?"

"Oh, yah," the man said. "We have a brand that's called Northern, and it's four rolls for eighty-nine cents."

He said, "I wouldn't pay eighty-nine cents for toilet paper, don't be crazy."

"Well, we have Cottonelle, but that's the same price."

"I told you I wouldn't pay that price for toilet paper."

And the druggist says, "Well, we have a generic brand. That means that it has no name. It's a no-name toilet paper, and it's four rolls for forty-nine cents."

"That I will take," he says.

So he came back in half an hour. He said, "You can have your dang no-name toilet paper." He said, "What's more, it's no longer a no-name toilet paper because I have given that toilet paper a new name. It's Yon Wayne toilet paper. It's rough and it's tough and it don't take no crap off of nobody."[94]

Snooty Mrs. Carlson

Well, he was terribly sorry that he couldn't help Lena. So he went to Lena, and he said, "I'm yust terribly sorry that I couldn't solve your problem for you, Lena."

"Well," she says, "that's all right. I think I have solved it myself." She said, "I have that great big box of dress patterns up in the back room. And you know, Olaf, that is good paper that they use in dress patterns. And what I am going to do is cut it into squares and lay it in the little box out in the t'ree-holer. And that's going to have to be good enough for that snooty Mrs. Carlson."

Well, the party started full swing. And the snooty Mrs. Carlson disappeared out back. Came back in looking for Lena. She found her in the kitchen. She says, "Lena, I have to really compliment you. When you throw a party, you do everything yust right. Everything is yust perfect. I have to tell you, Lena, never before in my life have I used toilet paper that says, 'This is for the front and this is for the back.'"[95]

Toilet-paper jokes were widely told in rural areas; the teller delivered these three in succession.

Comparative Banking

Then there was one I heard a while ago that I think is really pretty good, but it's had a lot of circulation in the country already. A Norwegian came in the bank. Well, I'll say a Scandinavian, being I'm a Swede, so I'll include Swedes.

And he went up to the cashier and said, "I want to cash a scheck."

Well, the cashier looked at the check and says, "Well, it's a good check, but you've got to sign it."

He says, "I don't sign anything."

"Well," he says, "I'm sorry then, but we can't cash it."

So he went to the next window to the cashier. And the same thing, wanted to cash his check but he wouldn't sign it. He says, "I won't sign anything."

"Sorry, we can't do anything for you here."

So he went to the bank across the street and went up to the teller there and says, "I want to cash this scheck."

And the cashier looked at it. "Well, it's a good check, but you've got to sign it."

He says, "I don't sign anything."

But this teller was a little different. He grabbed the Norwegian by the hair and pounded his head down on the counter about a dozen times. He says, "Are you going to sign it now?"

"Yah sure, I sign the scheck." So he signed it and got his money, and then he went back over to the first bank he was in. He says, "See I got my money."

And they says, "Well, did you sign the check there?"

"Yah sure, I signed the scheck t'ere."

"Well," he says, "how come that you wouldn't sign it here, and you signed it over there?"

"Vell," he says, "over t'ere they *explained* it to me."

Them Scandinavians, you know, you've got to explain things to them and then you'll get along with them.[96]

Despite the teller's inclusion of Swedes, this joke best fits the Upper Midwest's "stubborn Norwegian" stereotype.

The Norwegian Vacation

I got another one. It's a real good one that was told by a fellow from Richland Center. This Arlie Felton told me about the four Norwegians from Wisconsin that struck it rich.

And they decided—they were getting old—and they thought they ought to do something for enjoyment. So they decided to go to Florida. So two of them flew down in the plane, and they were going to have the other two come later in the car when they got through with the harvest.

So the two went down there, and they enjoyed it so much, they wrote back and they said, "The beaches are beautiful and the food is great and the women are nice." They says, "Get someone, hire someone to finish the harvest and come on down with the car right away."

So a week went by. Two weeks went by. The third week, here they came, in the car. And they said, "What in the world took you so long?"

"Oh," they said, "every time we'd get to a filling station, it says 'Clean Restroom.' We've been cleaning restrooms all the way to Florida."[97]

This telling combines stereotypes of the Norwegian numskull and the foolish farmer. Notably, the pair who clean restrooms take time off from harvesting their crops.

Sons of Norway

As they had gotten older, of course, Olaf was spending all his time rocking in the kitchen. Lena says, "Olaf, you've got to get out of my kitchen. I cannot stand this one more day. I work and I work and here you sit and you rock back and forth and don't do a dang thing."

"Well," he says, "I don't have to work anymore. I get that Social Security, you see."

So she said, "Well, you can get out of the house even if you don't have to work." She said, "Why don't you go join the Sons of Norway?"

So it was no problem. After all, he was born in Norway. They're certainly going to accept him. He could answer all the questions. Sure, no problem. They get to the last one, and the lady said, "Do you have any infirmities?"

"Well," he says, "I'm not so sure I got that, but I do have hemorrhoids."

"Well," she said, "I'm sorry, we can't accept you in the Sons of Norway."

So he goes home to Lena, sits down in the rocking chair, starts rocking back and forth, and he says, "You know what? They drummed me out of that Sons of Norway business yust because I had hemorrhoids."

"Well," she says, "I can hardly believe it. When you think of all the years that we been here. And all you ever hear is 'Sons of Norway, Sons of Norway, Sons of Norway.' No one ever told us that you had to be a perfect ass to join the Sons of Norway."[98]

The Sons of Norway is the leading fraternal organization for Norwegian–Americans. One has to have some percentage of Norwegian heritage or be married to a Norwegian to join.

The Norwegian Divorce

I was going to tell you the one about the Norwegian, Helmer. He was going to divorce his wife, Hilda. He went to see the lawyer.

And the lawyer says, "Well, what grounds have you got?"

He says, "I got about an acre and a half."

Well, then he was kind of flustered. He says, "You got a grudge?"

"Yeah, I got a little garage behind the house. One car."

And then he says, "Well, does she beat you up?"

"No, no, no," he says, "I get up at six, and she's still in bed at seven."

Well, then he really got flustered. He says, "Is she a nagger?"

"No, no, she's not a nigger, she's a Norweegan."[99]

This dialect joke is reminiscent of the best of Groucho Marx's confusing words that sound alike.

A Golden Anniversary

Well, they celebrated their fiftieth wedding anniversary. And Olaf says, "You know, Lena, remember the promise we made when we got married?"

And she said, "Yeah, well, Olaf, I remember that."

He says, "Remember we promised to be true and faithful to each other for ever and ever?"

"Yeah," she says, "I remember that."

He says, "Now we have been married now fifty years, so we have to check those dishes."

"Well," she says, "now, Olaf, you go first."

So Olaf goes to the cupboard and he gets his little dish and he dumps it out and counts out thirteen kernels of corn. Pretty embarrassed.

And Lena says, "No, that's nothing, Olaf, when you think of it. Fifty years, and you've been unfaithful to me only thirteen times." She said, "That's nothing."

"Yah, but," he says, "Lena, you're going to have to get your dish."

So she gets hers, dumps it out. And there's ten kernels of corn. And he's pretty proud of her. "But," he says, "you know, Lena, there's a five-dollar bill in that dish. Now you yust tell me once, where did you get that five-dollar bill?"

"Well," she said, "when the price of corn went up, I sold a bushel."[100]

Rocking and Kicking

Anyway, they were sitting down. They each had a rocking chair by this time, of course. And they were sitting down rocking. And pretty soon Lena gets up, and she walks over, and she kicks him in the shins. And he says, "Lena, why did you do that to me?"

She said, "That, Olaf, is for fifty years of being a poor lover." So he sat there and rocked awhile. And pretty soon, he got up, and he walked over and kicked her in the shins.

She said, "Why did you do that to me?"

He said, "That, Lena, is for knowing the difference."[101]

Jokes regarding fiftieth wedding anniversaries are common in oral tradition, as are instances of sexual accounting. Told immediately following the first example, the second joke continues the themes of fifty-year reminiscences and marital infidelity.

Tombstone Dispositions

Ole and Lena had come to a stage in life where they were getting on in years, and they couldn't really decide what to get each other for their birthdays this year. So they thought it over and thought it over and thought it over and decided—you know, they were kind of practical people—what they really ought to get one another this year was headstones. So then they could really enjoy them beforehand. No sense in having those things lay out there in the ground and they'd never see them.

So it comes Lena's birthday first, and she's all excited. Here the truck drives up and delivers the headstone. Lena goes out and unwraps it, and she's really excited. Gets around in front of it so she can read the inscription. It says, "Here lies Lena, still frigid."

So she's a little upset, but she has her moments coming. So a couple months later it was Ole's birthday. And the headstone comes. And Lena's got her moment of glory coming. And Ole goes out, and he unwraps the headstone. And reads the inscription, and it says, "Here lies Ole, finally stiff."[102]

This Lena-and-Ole joke continues in the tradition of mocking marital intimacy.

A Norwegian Discovers Pizza

When they gave that old Norwegian a pizza, he'd never seen one before. And he says, "Uff da! I vonder who in the world threw up on my *lefse.*"[103]

"Uff da!" is an all-purpose Norwegian exclamation, although it chiefly indicates exasperation. It compares with the German "ach!" or the Yiddish "oi." *Lefse* is a flat potato bread, sort of a Norwegian tortilla.

St. Peter's Opinion of Lefse

I told you the one the other morning about the Norwegian going to heaven. St. Peter meets him at the gate and says, "Well, it's going to create a problem here if we let you in."

And the Norwegian says, "Well, how in the world could that be?"

"Well," he says, "I'll be darned if I'm going to start making *lefse* for just one Norwegian?"[104]

Scandinavian variants more commonly mention *lutefisk*—cod that has been processed into an odoriferous, gelatinous state—instead of *lefse* and quote St. Peter saying, "Do you think I'm going to stink up heaven for one Norwegian."

Psychedelic Norskies

What do you get when you cross *lutefisk* with a hit of LSD?
A trip to Stoughton.[105]

Stoughton is a heavily Norwegian–American community just south of Madison, site of the University of Wisconsin. Madison was notorious from the late 1960s through the 1970s as a center for drug-taking youths, and this joke offers a Madisonian's jocular vision of Stoughton

CHAPTER EIGHT

The Finns

The American shore of Lake Superior—the timber and mining country of Michigan, Wisconsin, and Minnesota—is the Finnish–American homeland. Here late nineteenth-century immigrants labored in extraction industries and on small cutover farms, endured bitter winters, built saunas, hunted, fished, and demonstrated their *sisu*—a gritty ability to triumph over hard times.

Sisu pervades contemporary Finnish–American jokes. Characters, dwelling in the present as well as the past, battle famine, game wardens, and imperious outsiders in the struggle to make a living as farmers, loggers, laborers, and truck drivers, as they drink and fight, and as they revel in the sauna's heat. Eino and Toivo (and often Waino, Heikki, Tauno, and Toisto) are the sometimes craftier Finnish equivalents of the Scandinavians Ole and Lars, while Helvi corresponds to Lena.

Tellers of Finnish–American jokes often fill the mouths of characters with "Finglish," a hybrid regional dialect that evolved from the attempts of first-generation immigrants to speak a language with a different set of phonemes. Although the rules of Finglish are not always consistent, usually combinations like *ch* and *sh* are rendered *s*, certain other double consonants are handled by dropping the first letter (*plank* becomes *lank*, *sleep* becomes *leep*, *drink* becomes *rink*), *p* is substituted for *b*, *v* takes the place of *f* or *w*, and, paradoxically, *j* becomes *ch*.

Eino and Toivo

What was that one about Toivo? He had a farm, and the neighbor came over, you know, to breed the cow, like they used to do years ago. They'd lead the cows over to the neighbors, and probably pay a buck for... to get it bred.

Anyway, after they got done, the neighbor asked the kid there, "Well, how much it was?"

"Well," he says, "three dollars."

"Oh," he says, "by the way," he says, "your Eino," he says, "Tell your dad that his son Eino has knock-ed up my daughter."

"Well," he says, "It's three dollars for the bull. I don't know what he charges for that Eino."[106]

In the Orchard

Well, one time Eino and Toivo were neighbors. And one day some fellow came over to Toivo's place, you know, to visit. And as they walked up to the house there, he looked over there in the orchard. And there was Eino and his wife out there in the orchard. And they were going at it.

And Toivo says, "Look at that, Eino, he thinks he's me." He didn't think nothing of it.[107]

The first Eino-and-Toivo joke was widely known in rural areas according Legman in *Rationale of the Dirty Joke* (p. 67) and in *No Laughing Matter* (pp. 251-252). In this joke, the mention of an orchard and the fool's response to cuckoldry resembles elements of AT Type 1423, motif K1418, "The Enchanted Pear Tree. The wife makes the husband, who has seen her adultery from the tree, believe that the tree is magic (or that he has seen double)."

Time Comes

That's just like this one joke in Finnish, this story about a girl. Her mother always called her *vahamielinen* [simple-minded] and belittled her.

Well, anyway, this mother and this girl were making cheese and bologna, you know, *makaroita* [bolognas]. They were making them. And the girl was asking the mother, "When are we going to eat this? When are we going to eat this?"

Mother says, "You idiot, you can't eat them until the time comes."

So then the old folks left for town one day. And they left her to guard the house, you know. And this traveler came there and asked if there was something to eat.

She says, "Oh, we've got lots of bologna and cheese, but we can't eat it until the time comes."

This guy's name was *Aika*. And that's "time" in Finn. So anyway, this fellow come up there and asked for something.

"Yeah, we got lots of cheese and sausage, you know, but we can't eat it until time comes."

He says, "My name is "time," you know, *Aika*."

"Then we'll eat cheese and bologna." They ate cheese and bologna until hell wouldn't have it.

And he went out to leave water outside. And she went with him and said, "What the hell kind of bags you got over there?" You know, in Finn, *mielipussi*. What the hell would that be [in English]? [Pleasure bags.] Anyway, she says, "Won't you give me a little *mielta* [pleasure]?" 'Cause his, her mother always used to say that she's *vahamielinen*, you know, a little off.

"Oh, sure," he says, "you can have some of that." So anyway, he gave her a little *mielta*, you know.

And the father and mother come home, and the girl run to them. "Mother! Time came and we had cheese and crackers."

She says, "*Oi, sina vahamielinen* [Oh, you simpleton]."

"Don't say that, mother. I got more *mielta* [pleasure] in my ass than you got in your head."[108]

The first part of this tale is AT Type 1541, motif K362.1, "For the Long Winter," in which the fool is told to save sausages for the long winter. A trickster appears, claims to be called "Long Winter," or some such name, and gets the sausages. The girl's seduction and her response to her mother in the second part of this Finnish story turn on the similar sounds of "vaha*mieli*nen [simple-minded] and "*mieli*pussi" [pleasure bags].

Marital Problems

Toivo and Helvi were having marital problems, so they decided to go and talk to a marriage counselor. And the marriage counselor was asking them a lot of personal questions, and they were getting kind of embarrassed. But they were answering because they wanted to work this out. They had twelve kids at home, and they were just having real problems.

And it was just getting so personal that he was asking questions like how many times did they have sex in the last month. And he came to a question that troubled them.

He says, "Do you have mutual orgasm?"

And she looks at Toivo, and she says, "I don't think so. I think we got that Northern Finnish Mutual."[109]

The Northern Finnish Mutual mentioned in this telling is an insurance company that emerged from a nineteenth-century ethnic fraternal organization. Lutheran Brotherhood is mentioned in a Norwegian version printed in Red Stangland, *Uff Da Jokes*, p. 13.

Sleeping Out

Toivo and Waino sleeping in the field. Toivo says—they were sleeping out in the field with the cows—Toivo says to Waino, "Kot tammit, it's cold out there."

So Waino got up and shut the gate.[110]

An Irish freezing numskull can be found in Arthur Fauset, *Folklore of Canada*, pp. 163-164, and a Norwegian counterpart in Charlotte Powers, *The New Uff Da*, p. 23.

The Gorilla Bouncer

This guy ran a bar in kind of a rough neighborhood. So he was so tired of manhandling these drunks when they'd get drunk and throwing them out the door.

So he said, "I got to get some different muscle in here." So he bought a great big gorilla. And he trained that gorilla; he kept him in the back room. So when anyone got out of line, all he had to do was whistle. He just whistled. This gorilla'd come out of the back room, and whoever he'd point at, the gorilla would grab and throw right out the door. His problems were over.

Well, this Finn came in this day. He was quite drunk. He ordered a few more, and he was getting out of hand—getting loud and obnoxious, swearing too much. Finally the bartender thought, well, I'd better get rid of this guy. So he whistled twice and the gorilla came out. And he pointed at the Finn. The gorilla grabbed him, and he threw him right through the swinging doors into the street.

And the Finn got up, dusted himself off, and he said: "That's a Finnlander for you every time. Give him a little hair on his chest, and he thinks he's tough."[111]

Finns have been known historically in the Upper Midwest as tough fighters, especially after a few drinks.

Fish and Cars

Heikki was out by the lake shore fishing when Toivo came up. And Toivo stood there watching him for probably quite a long time.

So after about fifteen or twenty minutes of silent watching, he cleared his throat, and he said, "Well, Heikki, you got your limit?"

To which Heikki gave some serious thought and consideration and finally turned around and said, "No, Eino, I got t'at C'evrolet."[112a]

I heard this one about a Finn that was fishing, too.

And the game warden came there. And first thing he asked him was, "Are you a resident?"

He says, "No, 'ruman is 'resident."

And then he says, "Did you get your limit?"

"No, I got a Pontiac."[112b]

This joke is widely told throughout Finnish-America. Other examples of the *limit/Plymouth* element are unknown, though Paul Anderson in *Scandinavian Yokes*, p. 14, mentions a Finn returning from Canada to the United States who responds to the question of residency with "'ruman is 'resident [Truman is president]."

Chased by the Game Warden

Eino and Toivo were fishing on this stream. They were sitting there on the bank. They both had their rods and they were fishing away.

And Toivo happened to glance up, and he could see the game warden coming. So he jumped up and he telescoped his rod and everything, and he started running through the brush. And the game warden took off right after him. So Toivo is running and the game warden is chasing him. And Toivo runs about three miles. Finally he stopped; he's waiting.

And the game warden came puffing up, and he said, "May I see your fishing license?" Toivo took his billfold out, got out his fishing license, and he showed it to the warden. And the warden looks at it. He says, "Well, Toivo, how come you were running?" He says, "It's all legal. You've got a fishing license and everything." He says, "How come you're running?"

Toivo says, "Eino doesn't."[113]

See Text 263 for a related telling in which a licensed fisherman leads a warden astray.

Tauno Trades Horses

Now, Tauno had a horse that was out in the pasture one day when a horse trader came buy. And he saw the horse and decided that he wanted to buy it. So he went up to Tauno, and he said, "I'll give you fifteen dollars for that horse."

Old Tauno said, "No, no, that horse don't look so good. I ain't going to sell him."

"So I'll give you twenty dollars for him."

"No, no, that horse don't look so good. I think I keep him."

"Well, I'll give you twenty-five dollars."

"No, I keep telling you, that horse, he don't look so good. I don't think so."

But the horse trader was determined. He finally got the price up to thirty-five dollars. He said, "Here's the money. I'm taking the horse. Goodbye." And he left Tauno standing there with the money in his hand, and he led the horse away. Well, the next day the horse trader came back, and he said, "You old thief, you. You old swindler. You sold me a blind horse."

And Tauno said, "I told you that horse don't look so good."[114]

Baughman gives motif K134.5 (a) to this particular tale, under the more general motif K134.5, "Owner trades a blind horse. He gives a description that is literally correct."

RR

Heikki and Toivo were recently riding down US 45, somewhere south of Mass City. And they came to the railroad tracks. And they saw a round sign there which had the two letters "RR," as one usually finds at railroad crossings. And having had a few drinks, they were perhaps a little unsure of what the sign was supposed to mean.

So Heikki turned to Toivo and said, "Toivo, what does that sign mean there that says 'errr, errr?'" [Pronounced with exaggerated rolling r's.]

And after a time, his friend replied, "I not too sure, but maybe it means we coming to 'Ruce's 'Rossing."

"Oh. Yah. I guess that makes sense. I thought maybe it meant 'Rout 'Reek."[115]

This joke replicates the Finglish pronunciation of Bruce Crossing and Trout Creek, two villages in the Upper Peninsula of Michigan.

Toivo's Tail

Toivo and Toisto were rinking peer in a Hancock tavern. Toivo say to Toisto, "Vat you say ve ko to dat lift pridge seeing my friend Tauno?"

Toisto say, "I not care to ko to dat gottamit pridge—anyhow, I not like-it dat guy Tauno."

"Vy not you liking my friend Tauno?"

So Toisto say, "Vell, I pe delling you dat in dat 1929, I pe komming here and puying mine sack and some sickens and vun cow. I pe working on sexon putty hart. Vun tay, I pe komming home from working, and my missis saying dat gottamit cow pe sick. I not knowing vat to do, so I pe calling up dat county agent. Hees not pe home, he's ta pe in 'Ruce's 'Rossing out py 'Rout 'Reek. Dat county agent misses see pe delling me vot to do. See say for me to taking some soapy water and pouring it in cow's ass. Den see saying to using funnel an da rupper hose. So I pe going home and fixing dat soapy water and finding rupper hose too, but tat gottamit funnel I can't fine. Now I got one heck of a vix. Den I tink: my poy Eino he's got ta rumpet from blaying in dat school pand, so I pe daking dat rumpet and sticking in cow's ass an pouring whole pail full of soapy water. Ten seesus mighty! Dat cow go racing and run up ta street to dat lift pridge. See fart and holler like son-o-pits. Now dat fellow Tauno on lift pridge, he's ta pe komming out an lisset, an he's ta koing inside and lifting ta pridge so mine cow run off an trounding. Now, I's delling you, any gottamit tumpell dat don't know tifference petween ore poat vistle and horn plo-ing up cow's ass never ket visit from me."[116]

Bruce Crossing and Trout Creek appear as in the previous tale. The "lift pridge" is a drawbridge between Houghton and Hancock; it spans a canal that joins areas of Lake Superior on opposite sides of the Keeweenaw Peninsula.

Off the Road

Now the story is told that out in the Tapiola/Elo area, Eino and Toivo spent the day drinking wine behind Karvikko's Store. And after they had gotten a skinful, they decided they were going to Eino's place, to the sauna, to sweat some of it out.

So they got into Toivo's pickup truck, and they started driving down the road. But Toivo couldn't quite keep his eyes open and, as a result, began to drive the truck right off the road. They crashed through some tag elders. And Toivo, having woken up, managed to wrestle with the wheel and get the truck back on the road.

A little farther on, he started to lose consciousness again, and off the road they went once more, this time plowing through a popple thicket. Well, again, this brought old Toivo back to consciousness, and he wrestled with the wheel so that they got on the road.

Now the third time he started to fall asleep and they started to go off the road, Eino saw what was ahead. So he elbowed Toivo and said, "Toivo, maybe you better put it in second gear. This time we are coming to the hardwoods."

Well, they managed to get it back on the road. And this time they made it to that intersection that there is there, south of Tapiola. And

Toivo put the turn signal indicator on, but he didn't know if it was working. So he said, "Eino, stick it your head out the window. See if that turn signal's working."

And his friend did that, looked out, and he said, "Yah. No. Yah. No."[117]

The details about drinking and sweating it out in the sauna describe a common activity for at least some Finnish–Americans in the Upper Peninsula, especially when winter and "cabin fever" set in. Tag elders, popple (aspen), and hardwoods (especially oak and maple) typify the region's forests where coniferous timber has all been harvested.

The Finnlander Ditch Diggers

The Englishman or whatever was down in the ditch, digging. And the foreman was giving them guys hell for loafing. He says, "You're dumb, Englishman."

"What do you mean, I'm dumb?"

He says, "Watch." He says, "Hit my hand with that shovel." And he holds his hand up like this. [Hand is held up away from the body.] Right behind is a steel wall. So that goddam Englishman, he winds up. He swings with the full force of that shovel. Goddam foreman moves his hand. Boom! He hits that steel wall.

So the Finnlanders are digging. They're watching. Toivo says to Waino, "Hey. Kot tammit. You're an idiot. You're dumb."

"What do you mean, I'm dumb? I'm not dumb."

He says, "You are, too. Kot tam, I'm going to give you a test."

"Well, give me one," he says.

"Okay," he says. "Here. See if you can hit my hand." [Hand is held in front of the face.][118]

Stressing status differences, not to mention different intelligence levels, this joke appears in several variations which include pairings of Pat and Mike, a foreman and a Norwegian dupe, and a foreman and Polish ditch diggers.

Looking for Work

Heikki and Toivo went to the unemployment office to see if there were any jobs. And the lady called Heikki up and said, "Well, Heikki, what can you do?"

"Oh, I used to pile it."

She said, "Oh, you're a pilot. That's wonderful. There are plenty of jobs on the Great Lakes for you. Why don't you go over and sit there under the sign that says 'Group A.'"

Then she called up his friend and said "What can you do?"

"I used to cut it."

And she said, "What do you mean?"

"I go out in the woods with the saw. And where they got the trees, I cut it."

She said, "Oh well," she said, "unskilled labor like that, I'm afraid that we really don't have any work for you."

He looked puzzled, and he scratched his head, and he said, "I s'pose you know best. But if I don't cut it, how is Heikki supposed to pile it?"[119a]

The only lumber camp joke I know was about Eino and Toivo when they went to apply for unemployment. And Eino went in first and asked what he was gonna get a month. He was gonna get $150. And Toivo was only gonna get $75.

So he asked him, "How come you get that much more," he says, "when we're doing the same thing?"

He says, "Well," he says, "I told him I was a pilot."

And he says, "Well, how can you pile it when I didn't even split it yet?"[119b]

Skilled Labor

And another one on that same category. Eino and Toivo went to apply for unemployment. And it's the same thing. One came back with $75, and one came back with $150. They were pipefitters, weren't they? One says that he was a diesel fitter.

He says, "What do you mean, a diesel fitter?"

He says, "All you do is measure it and say 'Dese'll fit her.'"[120]

Truck Driving School

There's that one about Eino and Toivo. They were in the truck driving class, and the boss was, you know, for an example, was telling them that one could be sleeping and the other one would be driving. They come to an intersection. And just as they come there, another truck hits them.

And the teacher asks them, "What's the first thing you would do?" Asks Eino.

He says, "I'd wake up that Toivo; he never saw a big accident."[121]

All three tellings treat the theme of unemployment and the acquisition of new skills frequently experienced in logging areas of the Upper Midwest.

Heikki the Chauffeur

As you know, at one point many of the Upper Peninsula residents went to the Detroit area to look for work. And Heikki was one of them. He left Calumet, and within two weeks he was back again, driving a big Cadillac.

And when he saw his friend, Toivo, Toivo said, "Heikki, where in the heck did you get that car?"

And Heikki said, "Well, I telling you. I went down to that unemployment office. And they sent me to that big rich lady's house at 'rosse Point. And my job there is to drive this Cadillac. She says, 'Heikki, drive me for here,' and, 'Heikki, drive me for there.' And so, that's pretty good. Well, after I been there four and five days, I notice she keep looking at me and kind of smiling. And after I been there a few more days, she starts riding in the front seat and putting her hand on my shoulders and kind of touching my arms all the time. And after I was there about one week, she says, 'Heikki, today you drive me for the country.' And we went out in the country. And while we were out there, she says, 'Heikki, park by that big tree over there.' So I did. And she says, 'Now you close your eyes, Heikki.' And I closed my eyes, so. And she said, 'Okay, now you open your eyes, Heikki.' And I see she had taken off all of her clothes and she was sitting there. And she says, 'Now Heikki, you can have whatever you want.' So I took the car."

And his friend Toivo replied, "Well, that's good thinking, Heikki, 'cause those clothes wouldn't fit you anyway."[122]

This joke is set against a great regional migration from the played-out woods and mines of the Upper Peninsula to the automobile plants and other factories of Detroit. Grosse Point is one of Detroit's wealthiest suburbs.

Finnlander Application for Employment

Hoos poi you?_____

Vere you livit now?_____

Vat kine blais you livit?

    (1) House ___ (2) Partment ___ (3) Hodel ___

    (4) Sauna ___ (5) Reiler ____ (6) Olt sack ___

You koddit tat vamili?

    Vife ___ Pois ___ Curls ___ Toks ___

Vere vas you porn?
    (1) Pooskamp ____ (2) Sauna ____ (3) Sikenkoop ___
    (4) Olt Sack ___ (5) Some nudder blais ___
How you kum tis kuntri?
    (1) Pick sip ___ (2) Lirrol pote ___ (3) Chet blane ___
How olt are you now? ___
Ven you kerrit old aits benson? ___
How you keddit to tis blais?
    (1) Puss ___ (2) Taxi ___ (3) Railrote ___
    (4) Hits-hike ___ (5) Raivit own kar ___
Vat kine kar you koddit?
    (1) Sevvi ___ (2) Fort ___ (3) Tots ____ (4) Limit ___
Vat happen you lass chop?
    (1) Lait-off ___ (2) Kvit ___ (3) Ket vired ___
Vat kine heavi kvipment you can oberate?
    (1) Booltooser ___ (2) Reevarmer ___ (3) Dimberyack ___
    (4) Krater ___ (5) C.M.C. ruk tat hi-pop ___
Can you oberate tat bowerisaw? ___
You like Holly-voot? ___
You koddit tat felt poots vit steel toes for vorkit here? ___
Vat kine money you vent to kerrit here?
    (1) Lotsoo ___ (2) Chust averrits ___ (3) Only lirrol pit ___
Vat kine sickness you hat pebore?
    (1) Mailbox ___ (2) Sickenbox ___ (3) Sooker-taipeetus ___
    (4) Kombensaidon ___ (5) Ploostone boisoning from
    pat moonsine ___ (6) Finn-aireal tisee (from swinging
    in pirch trees) ___
You peen tat chale pefore? List pillow howcum:
    (1) Kame-vorten kats you pote-sing ___
    (2) Mounten bolice kats you make-it tat hoomproo/moonsine ___
    (3) Mounten bolice kats you sellit tat tope ___
    (4) You ket trunk ant raivit you car in ta tits ___
    (5) Too many nife fites at vettinks ___
    (6) You kerrit some Intian curls in rubble ___
    (7) You ket trunk, fall town in no-pank ant bass out ___
    (8) O.B.B. kets you pootlek seep vine ___
    (9) You pit tat rope in pringtime vit out tat bermit ___
    (10) In pringtime you rent out pooslot of pirch trees to nudder
    finlanders vitout tat lie-sens ___
    (O.B.B. tont like tat too mani piple hankink round in ta pring.)
You kot riminal rekort now? ___

Hows you ice-palls?

    Tveni-tveni vision ___ You vere tat lasses ___

Vat kine ports you like-it?

    (1) Huki ___ (2) Paispall ___ (3) Vootpall ___ (4) Kolf ___

    (5) Nooker ___ (6) Pasketpall ___

If you like-it hunting, vat kine kuns you ko it?

    (1) Tree-o-tree ___ How mani you ko it? ___

    (2) Dirty-dirty vinesester ___

    (3) Too-pipe sotkun ___ (vat kaich) ___ (4) Tueni-too ___

Vat you like-it to hunt for?

    (1) Bartrich ___ (2) Rappits ___ (3) Moose ___

    (4) Teer ___ (5) Naibors cows ant piks ___

Vat kine voot you like to eat-it?

    (1) Salt fiss ___ (2) Loot fiss ___ (3) Sarteens ___

    (4) Kala mojaka ___ (5) Melts ___ (6) Harttak ___

    (7) Mooligan stoo ___ (8) Portsops ant raivi ___

Vat kine you like to rinkit?

    (1) Puttermilk ___ (2) Kool-ait ___ (3) Peer ___ (4) Votka ___

    (5) Homeproo ___ (6) Vater ___ (7) Vine ___ (8) Viski ___

How muts you like-it to svare? (Memper tat tee haf curls tat vorkit here too.)

    (1) Lotsoo: Use four lettre verts vit *f*—like you say, "Vuck you ant you hat." ___ (2) Only lirrol pit: You say, "Oh, sit." ___

Vot tos ta vert "Saipuakaupias" mean to you? ___

Vot kine moosik you like-it?

    (1) Lassikall ___ (2) Rocket-roll ___ (3) Pooki-vooki ___

    (4) Noo-vaif ___

Vat time you go leap at nitetime? ___ Vat time you kerrop? ___

How farvest you pin travel?

    (1) Siistonen's Korner ___ (2) Vort Ransis ___ (3) Farter ___

Vat kine nudder lanvits you spik-it?

    (1) Rench ___ (2) Inkliss ___ (3) Cherman ___

Tank you for answer alltees kvestions. Memper ven you kum for tat intervoo, you tress-up soot, vite sirt ant nex-tie ant tat plak soos.

Now you sine tat name on tottet line pillow.

123

The "Finnlander Application for Employment" continues the theme of scarce employment and, like Text 116, is entirely in the Finglish dialect. Besides words in altered English, the application refers to Finnish saunas, to the regional term for the double-barreled shot gun ("too-pipe sotkun"), Scandinavian lutefisk ("loot fiss"), a Finnish fish stew ("kala mojaka"), regional place names (Siistonen's Corner, Fort Francis), and regional occupations and recreational pursuits such as construction, logging, hunting, and fishing.

Waiting for the Doctor

Well, there was a Finnish farmer. He went to town, and he come in the doctor's office, and he said, "I want to see the toctor."

Well, now they have receptionists and everything. So she said, "Give us your name and have a seat, and we'll call you."

So he went and took a seat in the waiting room and sat there for about an hour. And then pretty soon the receptionist come in. "Well, you can see the doctor now. Follow me." And she took him into one of them little rooms, the doctor's room. She says, "And now, take your clothes off and get up on the table and the doctor will be in in a few minutes."

So he stripped down and laid on the table, but, you know, a doctor's few minutes turn out to be a half hour or more. And he was getting goose pimples and blue from the cold. And finally the doctor opens the door and comes in and says, "Well, what can I do for you, my good man?"

He says, "Say, toctor, would you like to buy some potatoes?" He was just selling potatoes.[124]

Though the doctor's office is a common setting for jokes, other versions of this particular Finnish anecdote are unknown.

AM and FM

Urho and Heikki were at home and their goddarn radio broke. And they were arguing what to do. Better go buy one. Goddarn ball games and everything coming on, nothing to listen to. No use us arguing or talking to each other all the time; we've got to have something different here.

So they walked into the radio shop. And they didn't have very many dollars, but they had a few. So they walked in, looking around, and the clerk come. "What you want?"

"We want buy radio."

So the fellow showed them the AM radio. That was $29.95 or similar. They looked at that for awhile. And he says, "Here, here's a better one for $39.95, and it's got FM and AM."

Well, they went in a little huddle there, by themselves, talking. Then they come back, and they told—Urho told the clerk, "We're going to take that $39.95."

Well, his brother started arguing. "What's the matter, this one's cheaper."

"Yah, but," he says, "goddarn it to heck, look at there, you get the American Music and the Finnlander Music."

This joke was when FM started coming out.[125]

This is probably a purely regional joke. "Finnlander Music" can be heard on a number of stations in the Upper Peninsula—especially the accordion tunes of Viola Turpeinin, who was raised near Iron River and recorded prolifically from the 1920s through the early 1950s.

The Cannibals' Sauna

There was a Finnlander and a Cousin Jack traveling through the jungle. They had gone a long way, and they run into man-eating cannibals. Well, they never had a chance to get away. So they [the cannibals] captured them. And they says, "Well, we're going to have a big feast."

They got their big pot out. They put the Finnlander and the Cousin Jack in the big pot, built a big fire, filled it with water. And they were in there a long time—cannibals dancing around, ready for their nice big feast. Then they figured they were all cooked up.

They opened the cover, and the Finnlander popped his head out of there, and he hollered, "Where's the *viita*?"[126]

A *viita* is a switch made from the tips of branches from young cedar trees and bound with bark. Generally a new *viita* is made every Saturday night, "except in the winter, when we just throw them in the snowbank" to preserve for later use. Otherwise the *viitas* dry out and come apart in the sauna. Sauna goers flagellate themselves lightly with the switches, opening their pores and scenting themselves with aromatic cedar.

Bathtub Theology

Toisto and Tauno were walking down the street. And they came on Father Murphy who was on crutches. Now Toisto had met Father Murphy, had done some work for him at the rectory, had done some roofing there I think. And so he knew him.

And so he walked up. He said, "Hey, how you doing, Father? What happened to your leg anyway?"

And Father Murphy said, "Ah, Toisto, don't you know that I slipped in the bathtub, and I broke me leg."

Toisto said, "Oh boy, that's too bad, hey. You take care of yourself, now. We see you around."

And Toisto and Tauno went on down the street. After about four blocks, Tauno tapped Toisto on the shoulder, and he said, "Toisto, what the heck is a bathtub, anyway?"

Toisto thought it over and he said, "I don't know. I ain't Catholic."[127]

The supposed Finnish ignorance of the bathtub does not imply uncleanliness but rather a preference for the sauna.

The Crafty Sauna Maki

Now the fact that the Copper Country of Michigan is one of the centers of Finnish–American settlement and the fact that the Copper Country is also where Michigan Technological University is situated has led to a certain kind of relationship between the natives and the students. For the most part, this relationship has been a friendly and tolerant one. But there have always been a certain number of students that delight in thinking they are in some ways superior to the Finnlanders. And they like to refer to the Finns as "the local Makis" or "the sauna Makis" and to talk about how foolish these people are.

Well, the story is that one day a number of students from Michigan Tech were out riding around in the back country—probably drinking beer, which they shouldn't do. And they've realized that they are lost.

Well, they came to a place where an old Finnish man was leaning against a fence post, watching the world go by. Well, they stopped their car and said, "Hey, sauna Maki, can we take this road to Houghton?"

Well, the old man maybe was a little irked at being called a sauna Maki. I don't know for sure. At any rate, all he said was, "I don't care."

And so the students said, "No, you don't understand, you old bumpkin. We're asking does this road go to Houghton?"

At that point the old man said, "Well, I been living by this road now for almost thirty-five years. It ain't gone no place yet."

And so the students said, "Boy, can't you just please answer our question? Can we take this road to Houghton?"

And the old man said, "You can if you want. I don't know why you would want to. They got plenty roads there already."

The students by now had lost their cool and resorted to name calling. So they said, "Boy, you certainly are a stupid old bumpkin, aren't you?"

And the old man said, "Well, I suppose you college boys must know what's right. So I guess I am stupid. But then again, I ain't lost." And he went into his house.[128]

This telling strings together several motifs widespread in American folklore: Baughman J1649*(e), "Person asks a native where the road goes: Reply, 'No Place'"; and X583(a), the "I am stupid/but I ain't lost" episode. The exchange about "taking" the road is commonly associated with a non-ethnic rural trickster.

Urinalysis

There is the one about the high-toned gentleman from Marquette that wound up in a bar in Baraga. And he said, "Bartender, would you give me a double shot of your finest twelve-year-old Scotch."

So the bartender said to himself, "Twelve-year-old Scotch. I think I've got some back there. But we'll just see if this guy really knows the difference." So he got some four-year-old whiskey, and he poured out a double shot and handed it over to the gentleman.

Fellow took a sip and he spit it out. "That's four-year-old Scotch. I asked for twelve-year-old. Now please give me a drink of what I asked for."

The bartender was impressed, but he still thought he'd give him a test. So he poured out a double shot of eight-year-old Scotch. Handed it over.

The man took a sip; he spit it out. "That's eight-year-old Scotch. Now please, either give me the twelve-year-old stuff, or I'm leaving."

So the bartender finally got out the twelve-year-old Scotch, poured a double shot, the man drank it. "Ah," he said, "twelve-year-old Scotch whiskey. That's what I've wanted, and I'm glad that you finally gave it to me."

Well, old Heikki was down at the end of the bar drinking his beer. And he, he thought that this whole show was rather impressive. So he came down to where the gentleman was, tugged at his sleeve. And he said, "Mister, would you take a sip of this here in this glass and tell me what you think of it?"

And the gentleman from Marquette said, "Well, no. I, I really shouldn't."

But Heikki said, "Oh, I'd really value your opinion. I can see that you have that real discriminating kind taste. I'd like to know what you think."

So the man, his ego properly flattered, took a sip of what it was that Heikki handed him. And he spit it out. "Why, you fool! That's piss!"

And Heikki said, "Yah, I know that. But how old am I?"[129]

This particular battle between sophisticate and apparent rube is one of many barroom contest jokes involving tasting or smelling.

The Traveler's Welcome

Oh, then there was this guy from Oulu that went to Hawaii. And of course when he got there, why the hula girl came and got a lei and put it around his neck and said, "Aloha from Hawaii." He said, "Aho from Oulu."[130]

Aho is a common Finnish surname; *Oulu* is both a province in northern Finland and a northern Wisconsin community.

Michigan Tech

There were three Finnish–American lads that were students over at that Michigan Tech in Houghton. And they were sitting around in the cafeteria one day and drinking coffee as students do. And they were having a discussion about what was the most advanced of all the technological marvels that we have today.

And the first one said, "Well, I don't think there's any doubt that jet airplanes are the most marvelous thing that we have. Why, you can get in an airplane now in Duluth, and six, seven hours later, you can be in Helsinki., Why when my grandpa come over, it took him many months. Just think about that."

And the second boy said, "Well, I don't know. I think that these high-speed computers we have are even greater than that. Why, we can do these incredibly complex computations in just millionths of a second. That's amazing."

The third boy was lost in thought. Finally he looked to the others, and he said, "You know I think maybe the greatest technological innovation of the twentieth century is the thermos bottle."

The other two looked at him. "The thermos bottle! Why would you say that? All it does is keep hot things hot and cold things cold."

He said, "Yah, but how does it *know?*"[131]

In Vance Randolph's *Hot Springs and Hell*, #56, a country boy wonders about the same thing.

The Poles

Clustered today in rural settlements and in cities like Milwaukee, Minneapolis, Stevens Point, and Winona, Polish–Americans first arrived in the Upper Midwest in the mid-nineteenth century from the old Prussian empire (Upper Silesia, Kazubia, Poznan), with immigrants coming from Austrian and Russian Poland by the 1880s. Like many newcomers, Poles maintained their language into the second generation and with it a fund of in-group jokes set in the agrarian old country and filled with peasants and priests and tricksters and fools who battle over food, livestock, and sexual favors.

Poles did not figure significantly in the Upper Midwest's broader joke-telling repertoire until the 1960s, when a wave of "Polack" jokes emerged in industrial cities like Chicago and Cleveland and spread throughout the country. Partially explicable as an attempt by a white middle class (muzzled by civil-rights constraints against openly lampooning blacks) to shift class enmity from African–Americans to working class Slavic–Americans, "Polack" jokes have been rightly criticized by Polish–Americans for their misrepresentation of blue collar conservatism and camaraderie as evidence of stupidity and crudeness.

Nonetheless, Poles in the Upper Midwest tell the jokes avidly, as do their ethnic neighbors. Public joke-telling decorum in the region requires that "only Polish people tell the worst ones." (For example, "How does a Polack put on his underwear? Yellow to the front, brown to the back.") Yet Poles are also known for a skein of jokes in which the quick wit of a supposedly dull "Polack" bests an adversary from some supposedly superior group.

In the Foreign Countries

This was in the foreign countries yet. And they were married for many, many years. And they couldn't have babies. So the mister, he went to work. And the Missis, she stayed home 'cause there was no work for the women. So she stayed home. And the time was lonely.

So then he made her a baby out of wood, a chunk of wood. He hewed it, dressed it just like a baby. They had a cradle and she'd been rocking it.

They had one cow also.

She'd been rocking that baby. She said, *"Bizun Staczku, bizun. Bizun Staczku, bizun."* [Lazy little Staczek.] So the baby was supposed to go to sleep, see? And she was rocking there.

And they had a cow. An old cow that was no good anymore. It was for sale. So the buyers came over there, and they inquired about the cow. But she didn't have no time to go out there to sell the cow, advertise her. She had to be rocking that—the baby's name was Staczek, in Polish—*"Bizun Staczku, bizun."*

And she told them where the cow was. They went and looked at the cow, and they bought her without no deal, no discussion. They just put a few dollars out, and she didn't even have time to take that money from them for that cow. She had to be rocking that *"Bizun Staczku, bizun."*

So they put whatever they wanted—she told them where to put it, to put it under the pillow—and they crapped in a bag and put it under the pillow.

And when he came home, she says, *"Bizun Staczku, bizun."*
She says:

> *Przedlismy buroche* [We gave the animal],
> *Dostalismy peniedzy troche* [We received some money].

He asked her, "Where is it?"

"It's under the pillow."

He went under the pillow, and there was a bag full of crap, full of shit. And he came back and says, "It's full of crap."

And she says:

> *Kupcy sami byli gupcy*
> *Piero u nas srali i*
> *Pod poduszka uskalali.*

I'll translate it if I can: "Them buyers they was nuts themselves that they shit in the bag and hide it under the pillow." In Polish, it sounds good.[132]

With its numskull, cow, and scatological trickery, this tale resembles AT Type 1225A, "How did the cow get on the pole?" A fool hides his purse on a pole extended over a cliff. A rascal substitutes cow dung for money, and the fool wonders how the cow could have reached the pole.

The Polish Fur King

I was going to tell you about this lady who had three daughters. They went out into the world, and finally they came back, you know. One pulls up in a great big Cadillac.

And the mother says, "Well, look at, look at that Cadillac."

And the daughter says, "Well, I married an oil king. We got oil wells and everything."

Mother says, "Well, that's pretty good."

Next daughter pulls in with a big Lincoln.

"Well what about you?"

She says, "Well, I married a lumber king." She says, "We got a lot of wood. We're cutting wood and everything. Making thousands of dollars."

Here come an old rattletrap in with a bunch of kids hanging out, and this gal gets out. Mother says, "My gad, what happened to you?"

And she says, "Oh, I married a fur king."

"Well," she says, "how come you come in an old rattletrap with all these kids?"

She says, "Well, I married a furking Polack from Stevens Point."[133]

The setting of this joke, Stevens Point, is a heavily Polish community where large Catholic families are common.

The Right Nails

There was these two Polacks working on a barn. One Polack was standing on the ground, and the other Polack was up on the barn. The Polack on the ground was watching the Polack on the roof of the barn. He was picking up nails. Looking at it, then pound it in. Pick up another from the pouch, then throw it over his shoulder.

After this was going on for awhile, the other Polack was wondering what in the world he was doing. So he thought, I better go ask him what he's doing. He climbs up the ladder and asks, "What in the hell are you doing?"

The other Polack says, "Well, sometimes I would pick up a nail and put it against the wood and the point was sticking out towards me. So I couldn't use it and threw it away."

The other Polack says, "Why, you idiot, those nails were for the other side of the barn."[134]

For an Irish version and sources regarding this widespread numskull tale, see Text 60 and accompanying note.

Ice Fishing

I find that oftentimes nationalities—they'll tell jokes about their own nationality. Well, this one I heard from a Pole.

He was angry with a neighbor of his, and he said, "You know that dumb Polack went ice fishing yesterday. And he chopped and chopped all day and still couldn't get his boat in."[135]

Ice fishing, or "hard water fishing," is a passionate activity in the Upper Midwest from December into March. Boats, however, only figure in ice fishing on the Mississippi or the Great Lakes where a sudden "break up" might endanger fishers. In another version, Norwegians try to ice fish.

A Norwegian in Poland

This is a combination Norwegian and Polish joke that was told to me by a pastor.

Carl was going to visit Poland. So the Polish people were going to put up something big. "Oh," they said, "something huge." They had to build a suspension bridge. But when they had the bridge ready, they saw they had a mistake made. They put up the bridge on dry land.

So one says, "Well, we can't let Carl see that, a thing like that. So we'd better take it down and put it up over a river."

And the other one says, "We can't do that. There's already sixty Norwegians fishing off of it."[136]

The Fighting Polander

This Polander would go into bars, and he'd get into fights with the Finns. He'd insult the Finns a little. He'd say he could lick any Finn in the place, and how he didn't like them and everything. And they'd beat him up and throw him out. Finally he got tired of this. He thought, I'm going to move to where there aren't any Finns.

So he started moving west. He went into Minnesota, and there were still Finns. Went on to the Dakotas—mostly Swedes, but occasionally you would run into a Finn. So he got way out in Wyoming. He pulled into this town and settled down. He thought, by gosh, you know, he was fairly safe here.

So he got to drinking in this bar, and he said, "All Finlanders screw horses." And boy, a couple of those big rawboned cowboys came over, beat the heck out of him, and threw him out in the street. And he got up. He was brushing himself off. He said, "What the hell? Don't tell me you guys love Finlanders?"

Cowboy said, "No. We're horselovers."[137]

Like the preceding joke, this is an ethnic "combination" joke that demonstrates a command of the relationship between geography and ethnicity in the Upper Midwest.

Stash Visits Texas

Stash was in the service, and he met this Texas boy—Tex. And he says to him, "How big's your ranch?"

"My dad's ranch is so big," he says, "we can get in the car and drive all day, in any direction, and we never come to the end of it."

And Stash thought for a minute. "Yeah," he says, "Pa used to have a car like that, too."[138]

An Irishman and a Texan and a Swede and a Norwegian are paired off in other versions.

The Ignorant Orepuncher

There was an orepuncher on the docks had to work with some Polish people. And he was always putting them down. Dumb Polack this, dumb Polack that. Finally someone got sick of it.

"Can you talk Polish?" they asked him.

"No."

"No? Well then, you're dumber than the Polacks."[139]

Bottom-opening cars from the nearby Gogebic Range would be hauled onto the docks to empty their cargo into "lakers" or ore boats. It was an orepuncher's job to push or "punch" into the boat any ore that hung up in the car.

CHAPTER TEN

Other Ethnics

Long home to Woodland Indians, settled by a myriad of European peoples in the nineteenth century, and haven for African–, Asian–, and Hispanic–Americans in the twentieth century, the Upper Midwest has always been a pluralistic, multi-cultural region, a place where Yankee or WASP elements have been unable to impose a narrow definition of Americanism. While there has certainly been periodic friction between the region's diverse groups, few Upper Midwesterners see a contradiction between being ethnic and being American—and in this atmosphere, ethnic jokes can sustain dual identities.

The groups treated in other sections are most prominent in the region's folk humor, yet they are not alone. The Welsh of Wisconsin joke about the small number of surnames (Williams, Rowlands, Owens, Roberts, Hughes, and especially Jones) shared by most. The economical and efficient Swiss enjoy the foibles of lackadaisical simpletons. And the Dutch, proud of the sobriety of their Reformed faith, nonetheless poke fun at preachers. Belgian farmers dominate the jokelore in the hinterlands around Green Bay, the largest Walloon settlements in the United States, while Italian immigrants figure in the humor of northernmost mining communities from Houghton to Hurley to Hibbing.

The Jones Boys

In the village of Cambria, Wisconsin, lived two brothers, Evan O. Jones and Owen E. Jones. An old English lady with a decided cockney accent, in mentioning these two brothers, explained, "There are two Jones boys, Hee Ho and Ho Hee."[140]

In Cambria, an area heavily settled by the Welsh, Jones is a very common name. The cockney way of speaking coincides with the Cornish dialect exemplified in this anthology.

The Swiss Errand Girl

A joke which is commonly told among the Swiss is the one about the young girl who was sent by her mother to a drug store to get some *karmiller* [tea].

The young girl ran, and as she hurried along she kept saying *"karmiller, karmiller"* to herself so she would not forget it.

A couple of blocks and she was saying *"karmiller, karmiller, rosinli, rosinli, rosinli."*

By the time she reached the store, she had forgotten what she was sent for and asked for *rosinli*, which are raisins.[141]

New Glarus is a Swiss–American community in Green County which in the 1980s still retains a strong ethnic identity. This joke is AT Type 1204, motif J2671.2, "Fool keeps repeating his instructions so as to remember them. He usually forgets."

Pieter Van Der Snooze

The old [Dutch] Reformed minister was about twenty minutes into his hour-long sermon one Sunday when he noticed Pieter Van Der Snooze dozing off in the back pew. Quite upset, the good reverend shouted, "Now everyone who wants to go straight to hell—PLEASE STAND!"

Pieter gives a start and out of habit stands up. Shaking the sleep from his head, he sees everyone else still sitting. "Well, Reverend," he says, "I guess only you and I are going to agree with what you said."[142]

In related variants of this joke, all those wishing to go straight to heaven stand, with the exception of one who reckons that either he does not want to go immediately or he is not a member of the congregation.

The Belgian Brothers

There were two brothers living in Belgium. One brother decided to come to the United States and make his fortune in chicken farming. He settled in Brussels, Wisconsin. He had been raising chickens for two months without much success. All of his chickens were dying. He decided to call his brother in Belgium to ask if he could help.

After hearing his story, the brother said he thought he had the answer to the problem. He said, "Either you're planting them too deep or too close together."[143]

This is a variant of AT Type 1200, "The Sowing of Salt," in which a numbskull sows salt like grain to produce salt (or plants a cow's tail to produce calves). In the Upper

Midwest, this type of joke is often told about ethnic groups as well as about urbanites trying to farm.

The Hygienic Farmer

It's about Jules and John, two farmers. This is years back. Each had a team of horses and were out in the fields plowing. And as they were plowing, one of the horses, John's horse, dropped. And Jules came over to see what was going on, you know, what happened.

"And John," he said, "what happened? Did your horse just drop?"

"Yeah," he said, "we'll have to get a vet and see what's going on."

So they called, the vet came over, and he asked if they had a hose around there. So they found one and they gave it to the doctor. Doc just put it in the horse's hinder, and he started blowing, started blowing. And pretty soon the horse got up, started walking, and was good for the rest of the day.

The following day Jules's horse dropped. John came over, ran over, and, "Whatever you do," he says, "don't call the vet," he says. "We'll save ourselves that money. We don't have to pay the vet. We can do that ourselves."

So they got a hose, and John put the hose up the horse's hinder. And he started blowing, but no way could he get the horse to get up. Jules says, "Give me that thing. You don't know how to blow that thing." So he turns it around. He takes the hose out of the horse's hinder and he puts the other end in.

And John says, "What the heck you doing there?" he says.

"Well," he says, "I'm not going to put my mouth where you put yours."[144]

John and Jules are stock characters in Belgian jokes. Added humor is lent the Walloon version of this telling by the substitution of *guele* (meaning an animal's mouth) for *bouche* (a human's mouth). A circus elephant figures in Legman's *No Laughing Matter*, p. 941.

A Dead Horse

A Belgian farmer and his neighbor were walking out into his field one day and found his horse laying dead. The farmer said, "Dammit. He never did that before."[145]

This is a variant of Baughman motif J1455(a), "Horse drops dead shortly after man trades for it. Former owner explains that it had never done that when he owned it."

The Italian's Naturalization Test

This Italian's been over here for awhile. He goes to be naturalized, and they give him a test. They ask who lives in the White House. There's a big white house on the north side in the Sault.

He says, "Oh, that's where Nelly lives."[146]

The naturalization test is a common setting for old time Italian–American jokes. One plot involves a judge who asks the names of the original thirteen states. An Italian replies, "If you're so smarta, tella me, how many bananas inna da bunch?" (See Jimmy Lyons, *Mirth of a Nation*, p. 5.)

The Organ Grinder's Assistant

This fellow, this Finlander, lived in Sault St. Marie. And of course there's a large concentration of Italians there. Anyhow, the whole town knew that this fellow didn't like Italians. He didn't associate with them; he didn't have a good word to say about Italians. So he and his friend were walking down Ashland Street—that's the Sault's main street. Coming towards him up the street was this elderly Italian man, and he had an organ. He was grinding away. And he had this little monk' in a cute little dress, and a hat on, and the monk' had a tin cup. It was on a leash. The guy came, grinding away.

The two friends walked by, the organ grinder and the monk' going in the other direction. The guy threw a fifty-cent piece. The Finlander, the guy who didn't like Italians, threw a fifty-cent piece into the tin cup. Then his friend looked at him in amazement. He said, "I thought you didn't like Italians, but you threw fifty cents in the guy's cup."

He says, "I hate Italians, but they're so cute when they're little."[147]

This widespread joke has been localized by the teller. Like the preceding joke, this one is set in Sault St. Marie, Michigan.

The Loggers

Logging and woods-related occupations have dominated the northern areas of the Upper Midwest for well over a century, contributing ballads, jargon, legends, and humorous narratives to the region's folklore. Told by loggers or their descendants (Yankees, Canadians, Irish, Ojibwas, French, Finns, Swedes, and Germans), the examples offered here span the industry's major periods: white pine felling and river drives (1870–1910), hardwood logging and transport by rail (1900–1940), and pulp-cutting and trucking (1930–present).

The jokes vividly chronicle changes in the nature of logging, while cataloging common occupational experiences. Through them, we glimpse the trek into the woods, the acquisition of specialized skills and language, and the joys and dangers of the work itself. Their camps are replete with bed bugs, pranks, bad food, and banter, and their talk full of the river drive and revelry in town after.

Noticeably absent are the Paul Bunyan tales favored by popular writer. Loggers in the Upper Midwest didn't tell them, except as a commercially inspired, self-conscious, post–1930s development aimed at broad audiences that might not understand or tolerate the esoteric and bawdy nature of the real stuff.

Lumberjack Lingo

After breakfast, the bull got our crew together. A ground mole, a cross-haul man, a pair of snappy crow-baits, a couple of taileroos, a single line swamp hook, a slash block, a cant hook, and myself as a sky piece. Everything went well until the day after Christmas. My ground mole went down and visited Slewfoot Sally at the crossroads, got pie-eyed, and did not come back. They sent out a punk to take his place, and I got hurt and taken to the hospital.

First they got rid of all my seam spurs, gave me a bath, wrapped my leg with plaster, bound me with tape, and strung me up with block and tackle. Soon a nice nurse came in and asked how I got hurt so bad. I told her the whole story.

My ground mole got pie-eyed at Slewfoot Sally's. A punk misrepresented himself and said he was a ground mole. The first log on the skids was a blue-butted schoolmarm. I told him to sag it, and he St. Croixed it. It swung, canted, and gunned. Broke two slats. That's why I'm here.

I got well and went back up just when they started hot logging. I stayed until the breakup, then came down, blew my stake, and went up on the Flambeau drive.[148]

The main intention of this facetious story is to flaunt esoteric woods talk. See the notes for a detailed explanation of the lingo.

A Green State of Mainer

[Charles Lee] was told to cut skids twelve feet long by four inches thick. He cut what in Maine was called a hornbeam, in Wisconsin, ironwood. One tree he cut lodged against another, and in trying to bring it down, he fell through the ice on the creek when jumping clear of the falling tree. He was sitting on a stump when a lumberjack passing by asked for a match and inquired what happened.

Lee's answer was, "I just cut a hornbeam, and it lodged in a juniper, and I fell into the brook."

The logger asked for another match and asked Lee to repeat his story. That night the logger, Cosgrove, said at supper, "Lee had an awful time today. The green State of Mainer cut a hornbeam, and it lodged in a juniper, and he fell into the brook."

After the laughter of the men had subsided, he learned that in Wisconsin parlance he should have said, "I cut an ironwood, it lodged in a tamarack, and I fell in the creek."[149]

The "skids" Lee had to cut were a pair of saplings used as an incline on which to roll a log from the ground to a sleigh or a railroad car. The term "green," especially appropriate in the woods for its association with unseasoned timber, was applied to an inexperienced hand. Lee's greenness was linguistic because he had not mastered the region's jargon.

The Logger and the Bear

See, when people came here, during the winter months—in fact my grandfather on my mother's side went to the logging camps to make enough money to go to school in Madison to learn how to make cheese and butter. And that's where this one comes from. It's about a guy who was deadly afraid of bears.

He went out up north in the lumber camps. And the guy was going to show him what to do and this and that. He says, "You know, I'm afraid of the bears. Should I have a gun or something?"

"No, don't worry about that," the other guy says. "You always do what the bear does, and he won't bother you."

So they sent him out, and he was cutting wood; he was on his way, that's what it was, he was on his way. He goes over a log and all of a sudden: "*RRRRHHH.*" A bear. He got scared, and he watched the bear. The bear started scratching his head. The bear made a somersault, he made a somersault, too. So after while the bear sits down, and he takes a crap.

"That," he says, "I got you beat. I did that awhile ago when I crossed the log."[150]

Logging as a farmer's winter work was common in the Upper Midwest; so were encounters with threatening animals like bears and wolves.

The Irishman's Cant Hook

Albert Mills had a camp on the Chippewa River, and one day one of his teams got stuck. He sent the Irish shanty boy to get a cant hook to help him out. The boy was gone a long time and finally came back driving camp's "muley ox" (an ox with no horns).

Mills turned to Pat and said, "What the devil you doing with that muley ox? Where is that cant hook?"

The boy replied, "Sure and bejabbers, this is the only thing I could find that can't hook."[151a]

In those days there was a story going around about a logger who asked a farmer if he had a cant hook.

The farmer said, "Ya, I got an old muley cow out in the pasture that can't hook."[151b]

A cant hook is a kind of log wrench—a wooden handle fitted with a hinged metal hook—that was used to manipulate logs when loading or off-loading.

Green Swedes

Bob Smith and Jeff Johnson used to tell stories about the lumberjacks and the logging companies. I remember one they told was about a bunch of green Swedes that Stinson and Gorr imported to break in as lumber-jacks.

They brought them in all the way from Stillwater in tote wagons. When they got to camp on the Clam, they got worried about how they were going to get back to Stillwater in the spring after the winter's work was done.

The boss said, "You boys got nothing to worry about. We are going to drive these logs all the way to Stillwater. We'll take your extra clothes on the wannigan, and you can ride our logs all the way down free of charge!"[152]

The "green Swedes" hired at Stillwater, Minnesota, to log on the St. Croix River were doubtless recent immigrants who had probably come first to nearby Minneapolis.

Fool's Errand

Another story that went around the camps was about the Swede lumberjack that asked the farmer if he had a monkey wrench. Being Swede, "wrench" sounded like "ranch."

The farmer said that he had never heard of a "monkey ranch," but the fellow down the road had a sheep ranch.[153]

This story might be told as easily about a Norwegian, but the Norwegian teller directs it at Swedes.

Chippenazee Creek

I remember every year most of the folks would go up to Chippenazee Creek where the wild raspberries grew in profusion. And once in a while someone would see a bear, but they were friendly. Most people would keep right on picking berries and forget the bears.

It was said that the way the place got its name was a couple of Irish lumberjacks found a big hollow log, and Mike, being inquisitive, crawled into the log but couldn't get out. So it was decided that Pat had to chop him out.

Pat was chopping away and pretty soon Mike hollered, "You're getting pretty close, Pat. Chip-in-aisy!"

But I guess it's an Indian name the same as a lot of places around there.[154]

Either a logger's term or an Ojibwa word, the spelling of the creek's name varies, as does its meaning, but neither has to do with Pat's instructions that Mike chip the log "aisy [easy]."

A Chicago Blacksmith

I have one about a blacksmith. He's shoeing horses. Okay, he—they sent a blacksmith from Chicago—so anyway, he come there late in the evening. And in the morning, the foreman says, "Well, you go out in the barn, there's four horses you can get shod." You know, get shoes on.

He went over there and lifts the front end. "Well, I guess this is about the oldest, more tame horse, so I'll try this first one, the older horse." Picked the front leg up and tried the shoe on. It fit pretty perfect. So he took some horseshoe nails and started nailing. Tried on the sides, that was okay. Not one nail come out the sides. He did the next one, and pretty soon he had that horse shod.

The foreman come in there. He says, "How's everything going?"

He says, "Okay, not one nail showed up on the outside of the hoof."

The foreman says, "Get in the office, get your goddarn time. We don't want them kind of blacksmiths. We want the regular blacksmiths that do the real job"—with the horseshoe nails come out of the hoof on the side and they bend 'em over, naturally.

So that was all of that.[155]

The Peace-Making Foreman

Up in northern Michigan, they sent, they run out of foremen. So they sent a foreman from Chicago. And, well, they got a foreman from there and sent him to the camp. And, well, he got to the camp.

And next morning about six o'clock, he opened the door. He said, "Roll out, boys." Okay, they took off. You know, six in the morning, that was in the fall of the year, December or so; well, it gets pretty dark early in the morning.

So then the foreman went back in the camp office, and he figured, "Well, I'll look in the window. I guess—time to go. It's getting daylight enough. I can see the tracks to where my men's got." Then he took off. And, oh yeah, it snowed that night. There was fresh tracks, fresh tracks this way. "I guess that's the one over there I'll take."

And he run, and first thing he run into was a bunch of sawyers with a crosscut saw. They're sawing. And he looked at 'em. He says, "You know, I don't like this fighting going on in the lumber camp. I want peace here."

So he watched 'em for a while, and they kept on pulling the saw back and forth. The other guy pulled and the *other* guy pulled. And he said, "Well, I'm going to settle this."

He went over there, and he said, "Say, boys," he said, "give me that saw." Then he says, "Give me an ax." He put it on the stump, took an ax, and split that crosscut saw in half. He said, "Now you take this end and you this end. And that settles it. No more fighting."[156]

These two tellings concern the bunglings of urban employees dispatched from Chicago by a distant logging corporation. Although their context is drawn from real life, these tales are traveled fictions.

Deep Snow

I was telling my dad about how deep the snow was up here. He's been in Arizona the last few winters now and kinda got a good life. Well, course he's ninety-two and probably deserves that now.

A few winters ago, I was telling him how deep the snow was up there—in Baraga County. We had fifty-two inches on the level, and we pulled out of there in March. I told him about that when he came home from Arizona.

And he said, "Ah, that's nothing," he said. "Fifty-two inches," he said. "When I was running camp up there in the '30s, I was out checking on the sawyers, and I saw this one big Swede pulling the crosscut all by himself. So I walked over there on my snowshoes, and I hollered to him. I said, 'Where's your partner?' And he said, without losing a stroke, he hollered over his shoulder, he said, 'I'm standing on his shoulders.'"

Dad said, "Now, that's deep snow."[157]

This tale borrows from several narrative elements, including Baughman motif X1653.1*, "Logging in deep snow," wherein loggers must dig down to cut trees. The story is probably related to tales regarding deep mud from England, Arkansas, Missouri, Oregon, and Texas cited by Baughman for motif X1655.1(b), "Traveler floundering in mud picks up a hat in the mud. Man underneath rebukes him. Traveler offers to help submerged man, is told that the man does not wish to leave his horse which is walking on the ground below the mud."

The Deer Dog

Before the game laws limited the number of deer a hunter could kill, many made a business of shipping venison to various markets during the winter season. Sometimes if one of the deer were wounded, a dog capable of tracking it down was used. Such a dog was owned by Old

Man Beliell [sic] of Beliell Falls and was one time borrowed by two strangers who had wounded a buck and were unable to track it down by themselves.

Louis Blanchard was hewing a barn with a broadax nearby when the hunters and the dog came by. He had raised his ax, and just as he let it fall, the dog passed under it and was split in two. The logger swiftly gathered Tige up into a blanket and hastened as fast as he could to an old squaw who was noted for her herb cures. He told her he thought he had killed the best deer dog in the country, but he was still alive when he picked him up.

Seeing the dog, the Indian gasped, "You have made a mistake, Mr. Blanchard, you have put the dog together wrong." Sure enough, in his hurry, he had put the dog together with two feet on the ground and the other two up in the air. However, the herb healer kept the animal for three months, and he miraculously recovered. When he returned to his owner, Tige was the best deer dog to be found anywhere because of his great endurance—he could run all day without becoming tired because after he had run for awhile on two legs, he would flop over and use the other two.

Paul Bunyan offered Beliell $1,000 for Tige to be used in his Lake Superior Camp, but Beliell wouldn't sell.[158]

The elements of market hunting, hewing barn timber, and Ojibwa herbal healing give this telling regional depth. The "Bunyan" element is probably a later addition, as there is little or no evidence of Bunyan tales in Upper Midwest lumber camps before the 1930s.

The Counting Horse

They had horses there. They'd just each have one horse to pull those logs down, skid them out. They weren't big trees, they never got that big. And then they'd put them on a little sled, like. They'd put the front on them; they, they'd tie them down.

And they said that one horse could count. Said he'd take six logs down for you, but if you'd put seven on, he wouldn't move. If you took one off, then he'd go.[159]

The sled-like affair is a *travois* or go-devil, probably used in this case for hardwood and pulp logging. This may well be a true story, but it approaches a tall tale. See Baughman motif X1015(a), "Man is able to tell to a pound what load his mare can draw. Man wagers on ability of his mare to draw a certain log. She is unable to draw it until he removes a pair of wet mittens someone has left on the log."

The Swedish Sawyer

Another story they told was of a green Swede named Ole whom they signed on as a sawyer at twenty dollars per month. In the spring when Ole came to get his pay for his winter's work, the timekeeper asked, "Did you pull the saw alone or did you have help?"

Ole replied, "I pulled one end of the saw, and Hans pulled the other."

The timekeeper shook his head: "I'm sorry. We hired you at twenty dollars a month to saw alone. We can only pay you ten dollars per month because Hans was pulling one end of the saw half the time!"[160]

Attempts to cheat workers were common in some lumber camps.

Ordering a Grindstone

Pete Legault was an old time logger, and though illiterate, he left a good-sized fortune and a great deal of property when he died.

For a while, Pete was employed by the French Lumber Company. The company owned a camp store at Ingram, and Pete ran it though he could neither read nor write. When anyone came into the store and wanted something with which Pete was not well acquainted, such as a certain brand of cough medicine, the customer would have to point to the product and tell Pete the price on the bottle.

One time the company sent word for Pete to order several axes and a grindstone. Legault's ordering letter contained a series of pictures describing his needs. For a broadax, he drew a picture of a large ax of the broadax variety. For the grindstone, his artistic ability was limited to drawing just a plain circle. When the order arrived, it was complete except for the grindstone; in its place was a huge cheese.[161a]

My father [Tom Pratt] used to tell [a story] about Joe Trepania. Mr. Trepania was a French Catholic, very tall and strong, who ran a stopping place at Springbrook for many years and who also ran logging camps. Although he was a very bright man, he had never learned to write.

He was getting his supplies through a firm at Stillwater to whom he sold his logs. He was in need of a grindstone, and being unable to write, he took a piece of paper and drew a picture of a grindstone—a large circle with a smaller circle in the center to represent the hole in the grindstone. He got someone to address the envelope for him and mailed it down to Stillwater.

In due course, he received from headquarters at Stillwater a huge wheel of cheese! He came to father's store and told him his trouble. "Those damn fools," he said, "they don't know nothing." He asked Father to write for him and explain that he wanted a grindstone, which father did.[161b]

See Baughman motif J2685, "Buyer draws picture of grindstone on his order list. The grocer sends him a cheese. The buyer has forgotten to draw the hole."

A Mail Sack from a Turkey

Pete Legault had a camp out of Ingram, and he took a crew of men up with him one fall. They all had their turkeys in the baggage car of the train, and when they got off the train, the baggage master started throwing them off the train. And among them was a small mail bag to be put off there. Old Pete Legault picked up the mail sack and started off with it. He couldn't read nor write and didn't know a mail sack from a turkey.

The depot agent said, "Hey, where are you going with that mail sack?"

Old Pete said, "Crass, that's my sack." The other fellow said that was the mail bag and asked him if he couldn't read "U.S. Mail" on the sack. Old Pete said, "'U' stands for Pete, and 'S' for Legault."[162]

Ingram is in the Chippewa Valley, the heart of Wisconsin's "pinery," and "turkey" is woods talk for a logger's packsack or duffel bag.

Bunk Shack Architect

The bunk shack, or the place where the men slept, it wasn't used very much, only at night. And in fact there was a story that a man built a camp one time and he didn't put any windows in the bunk shack. And the fellows said, "Why don't you put some windows in it?"

"Well," he said, "we never used it in the daytime."[163]

Windowless bunk shacks were common in early camps, as were long hours. Working throughout the winter months, loggers set to work before dawn and returned to camp at dusk.

The Hunter's Dream

One evening in the camps, this jack lay down after dinner. And he dozed off. But we heard him talking like he was in the woods deer hunting. He was saying, "Where's my gun? There goes one deer, and there's another."

And we looked at him. And there were lice running across his eyelids. He thought they were deer.[164]

This story has elements of Baughman motif J1759.2, "Hunter mistakes louse (or other animal) on his eyelash for game. He shoots several times before he notices the trouble."

The Flea Count

One winter, a lumberjack went to a neighboring camp and said he came for some fleas since his weren't doing so well. He said he had never had so few in his clothes. A flea count was suggested between the visitor and a local lumberjack.

Bets were made and the procedure began. The men stripped themselves of nearly all of their clothes, and the count began before all the members of the camp. One man counted sixty-seven while the outsider found seventy-six.[165]

Bets involving vermin were common in lumber camps. In fact, one amusement involved battles between lice, akin to cock or pit bull fighting, with wagers on the outcome.

Crawling Clothes

And then there was one camp where a lumberjack came in the evening looking for work. And he wanted to stay overnight, but they didn't want to let him into the camp till they checked him for bedbugs. And he was just crawling with bedbugs. So they took his clothes off of him and hung them outside, and then took him in and he had to take a real good bath.

And in the morning, he looked outside for his clothes, but he couldn't see them. Then he looked towards the barn. And here the clothes had crawled over to the barn door trying to get in the barn where it was warm.[166]

Removing clothes and cleaning the body before going indoors was a standard routine for the logger returning home from the woods. The crawling clothes motif is similar to Baughman motif X1296.1, "Rag so full of lice it can move."

The Chinese Cook

Good evening, ladies and gentlemen. You are about to hear a recording. This is a story about a—what you would call a "cookee" in a logging camp. We're out here in the brush.

Well, there was a Chinese cook in this camp. And all the, everybody was playing tricks on him. And at one time they started to feel sorry for him—they had played so many dirty tricks on this cookee because he was a Chinaman. So they said to him one day they were going to quit playing these dirty tricks on him.

Oh, the Chinaman, he was happy. "You mean you're not going to tie my shoestrings in knots anymore? You aren't going to tie my bed sheets in knots anymore? You aren't going to put frogs in my bed?"

"No, we're not going to do any of that stuff."

"Good, good, good. I won't pee in your soup anymore either."[167]

Good food was important in lumber camps, and cooks were generally treated with respect. A "cookee," or cook's assistant, had less status. If belittled, he might have responded like the fictitious Chinese "cookee" of this telling.

Canvas Cakes

It came April 1, and the cook thought he would play a joke on Bog Dickey. He cut a piece of soft canvas the size of a pancake, dipped it in pancake batter and fried it. He managed it so Bog got the canvas pancake.

Bog lifted it to his plate, put on some syrup. He sawed with his knife trying to cut the cake and noticed the canvas, so he shoved it to one side of his plate.

The cook noticed this and said, "What's the matter, Bog, don't you like my pancakes this morning?"

Bog said, "Well, sir, I never did like tailor-made pancakes."[168]

Bog Dickey's witticism was in response to a common prank played on loggers by their cooks.

The Cook's Mistake

And that one time that cook quit, the guy, boss, went in and hired a cook for the lumber camp. And so the guy went out. He wanted to make an impression the first day. So he saw these sheep in the barn, so he thought he'd have fresh mutton for the guys, you know. So he butchered that sheep up for supper that night. Boss came back, and here the whole crew is chasing that guy—they were chasing him with axes and everything.

Boy, he caught up with that guy. "Ned," he says, "you screw up the cooking," he says, "the first night?"

"No," he says, "I cooked up the screwing."[169]

Fresh meat and female companionship were lacking in early lumber camps. Some big companies ran farms to supply their hands with beef, and "sporting houses" sprang up in woods towns.

Wild Lettuce

Uncle Glen [Church] had a—he used to cut pulp, and he had a group of guys he stayed with that were lumberjacks. And these guys spend all their life in the woods, pretty near. And, well, one of them broke his chimney—he had a kerosene lamp, and he broke his chimney. So he fixed it, but he used a tin can to fix it. He was pretty proud of that.

Glen used to go in and he'd buy all the groceries, so he'd go into town. This one guy was going to plant a garden, so he ordered five pounds of lettuce seeds. I don't know, that's a lot of lettuce seeds. So he went out and spaded up the ground out, you know, underneath the trees—he never bothered with going out into the open—and the lettuce grew about that tall and that big around. [Hands indicate three feet tall and half an inch thick.]

His comment was, "Everything you bring out here in the woods," he said, "it turns wild."[170]

This anecdote was part of a cycle told about loggers from the Iron River vicinity of Michigan's Upper Peninsula. See Texts 184 and 269.

Bunyan's Prune Pits

We were in the garage looking at the old logging relics. And that brings to my mind a story one of the old timers told. He was with the logging camps when they cut the original pine. And they had a big landing camp on the south shore of Lake Superior.

And from the information, I gather it was one of Paul Bunyan's camps. They would put, pile the logs up on the lakeshore, then raft them away in the winter. But I was walking around the lakeshore a number of times, and I seen a lot of plum trees growing around the shore. And I wondered how they come—till I talked to this old timer.

Ole Johnson told me about that was one of Paul Bunyan's camps. And they fed the loggers a lot of fruit that came shipped in wooden barrels. And the favorite of them was prunes. And they shipped in so many prunes that the prune stones started to be a problem. So Paul Bunyan finally solved the problem by building a prune-stone bridge across Lake Superior. And, uh, this was told by Ole Johnson, the old time lumberjack. So it must be so.[171]

Despite the mock veracity of the closing formula, the teller does not recall Paul Bunyan stories from his youth. The teller claimed, "That's a more recent development." See Baughman motif X1031.7(h), "Paul Bunyan builds a bridge across Lake Superior of prunestones and baling wire."

The Value of Wool

Funnix Grey was always coming up with some joke or bright remark even when all of us were wet and cold. We all wore heavy woolen underwear and thick woolen socks in our caulked boots and woolen outer clothes. All the river men swore by it.

Funnix Grey is credited with the quip, "No matter how cold and wet you are, you're always warm and dry in woolen clothes."[172]

Riding Logs

When we got into the Namekagon, we could ride logs most of the time. I remember on that first drive, I was with Funnix. I wasn't too good yet on riding a log, and Funnix knew it. The round ones could twist and turn under you, especially in the riffles, and it was difficult for a greenhorn to stay on. Sometimes a crotched log would come along. These were logs from trees with a crotch in the top. In order to get a sixteen foot log out of it the saw crew sometimes would have to measure a couple of feet up into the crotched part of the tree, making a crotch in that end of the log. These logs wouldn't roll over in the water, and we greenhorns were always watching for them.

One came along as Funnix and I stood there, and Funnix yelled in his high-pitched voice, "There goes a school ma'm, Jim, grab it." I ran across several logs in the drive and landed on it. Funnix, who was as quick as a cat on his feet, came running across and landed on a big log next to mine.

"Funnix," I said, "why do they call these crotched logs 'school ma'ms'?"

"Because they are easy to ride," he cackled gleefully.[173]

Funnix's mastery of paradox in the previous text is matched here by the sly double entendre.

Cook Overboard

I would like to have your attention, folks. This is another joke. This is about a cookee also, but he worked on the boats. And of course on the boats, they didn't call them cookees because they didn't have to carry wood and water and stuff like they did back in the logging camps. This was on the boats where they just called them cook's helpers.

And this helper, he stuttered. When he got excited, he stuttered to the extent that he could not say one word.

So one day he was up with the cook, and they were unloading the garbage up on the top deck. And it was windy. And a gust of wind came and blew the cook right overboard. So the cookee, he got excited and started running around the deck, and he was yelling for the captain to stop the boat.

"C-C-Captain, C-C-Captain!"

The captain saw him coming, so he figured there was something radically wrong. So he went down there and he met him. And they met there on the deck, and this cookee he tried to say something. He started to stuttering and stuttering: "The c-c-c-c…" He could not say one word.

The captain knew this, and he said, "Well, sing it! Sing it then!" The cookee, he kind of relaxed and he sang [to the tune of "Auld Lang Syne"]:

The old acquaintance be forgotten
And never brought to mind.
The cook has fallen overboard
And he's now ten miles behind.[174]

This is Baughman motif X135.2(b), "Deckhand gets so excited that he stutters so that he cannot be understood. He has to sing the fact that the cook has fallen overboard." Compare to Text 176.

Locomotive Man

Old man Beebe, he's a guy that could bullshit. He was another old-timer, old Beebe, Bill Beebe. Locomotive man for many years. And he always told stories that were really exaggerated. He was telling one time about running a locomotive up by Ely. He was working for a logging company. And, you know, he told the story as if it was true.

He says, "You know, it got so foggy one night. And we didn't know where the hell we were. We just kept plowing along. And you know," he says, "that damn locomotive just kept bogging down. I told the fireman: 'Pour more wood to it.'" They were burning wood. "Pour more wood to it," he says, "we've got to go."

He says, "You know, it started getting light in the morning. We were forty feet off the track. We kept just ploughing through the slush." And he'd tell you with a straight face.[175]

This is Baughman motif X1651.2, "Fog and objects": lying tales about ships and boats traveling on thick fog to end up miles from water.

The Stammering Sawyer

A story they tell about the old mill days had to do with Ardemus (Artie) Crandle. He stammered really bad. Most times he couldn't say anything until he said "damn" first. He was a tail sawyer in the mill. After sawing the end off the lumber, he would drop the boards onto live rollers to go out of the mill onto the grading table. The electric light over him went out, and Frank Slater, the millwright, came over to fix it. He straddled the live rollers with one foot on each side. The lumber was coming along between his legs. He was working with a big screwdriver above his head. He said to Artie, "If a big cant comes along, let me know so I can get out of the way." A little later, a big cant did come along and hit him and carried him along the grading table. Frank finally got off and came back into the mill steaming, ready to plaster Artie with some choice language for not warning him.

When he got back to Artie, Artie was still stuttering "…l-l-look out, Slater!"[176]

A "cant" is a large timber squared off in a sawmill. Compare this joke to Text 174.

An Irishman's Sauna

Now there are hundreds of these jokes, having to do with—one, for example: when the young Finns and Swedes came into this country, before the development of mining, a lot of them went into the logging. They used to be recruited down at Duluth or in the Upper Peninsula of Michigan and brought in.

Well, of course, the Irish had been in the lumber camps, you see, almost a generation before that. So they, a lot of those lumber camps, were owned by Irish. And certainly the foremen and the camp bosses were all Irish. So out of that, you see, there grew up a certain amount of animosity between the working-force foreigner and the English-speaking Irishman—just as there did in the underground mines with the Cornish bosses who were disliked. Because it did take a generation before those foreign people mastered the languages and broke through then into the English-speaking group to take over some of the positions that paid better and gave them better opportunity. So, anyway, they tell this story on an Irish boss.

They said there were a bunch of Finns in this lumber camp. And, of course, they had the washroom in the lumber camp, but they never had a sauna. So anyway there were quite a few Finns in there. One of them said, "Let's go and ask to have this sauna built." So they went and said, "We would like to build a sauna."

So Pat said, "What's that?" They said, "That's a bathhouse. Our kind of bathhouse."

"So what do you need?"

"Oh, just logs and rock, and we'll build it."

So he said, "Go ahead, go ahead."

So they went out and built this log shack. And then they put an old stove, barrel stove in it. And surrounded it with rocks. And put in their benches, as they do, up to the top and each tier gets hotter. And they'd go in there and throw water on and steam themselves. And they'd do that once a week. And sometimes twice a week. And they'd come out and roll in the snow to bring down their temperature rapidly—so they wouldn't be perspiring after this terrifically hot bath.

So, of course, these Irishmen were watching this. And they thought that all these Finns were all crazy. They'd go in the hot bath and then they'd go out and roll in the snow. And you know, that's in the days when it was the custom in the United States that you put your woolies on in the fall of the year and you left them on until spring. You didn't get monkeying around with any of that bath business.

So anyway, there was a young Irishman there that was a teamster. He was about the only Irishman there that wasn't a boss. So these Finns decided that they were going to take him into the sauna. Oh, and he kicked and screamed and hollered. So they took him in, took his clothes off. And then in the sauna, they put him up on the top tier, and they kept throwing cold water on these damn rocks till they had them parboiled. So they went up, they carried him out.

And by god, they found out that, underneath the clothes they had stripped off of him—they found last winter's underwear.[177]

Saunas inspired all sorts of suspicion and speculation among non–Finns who imagined the huts as places of devil worship and sexual wantonness. Another recorded version involved a lice-infested Pat.

The Fragrant Suitor

My dad—I don't know how true, I think he made it up, but he said one time this Finn woman had a date with an Irishman and a Finn.

And anyway, the Irishman had put on lotta cologne. He was really smelling good. And the Finn had crapped his pants. Yeah, he just came from the lumber camp, and he hadn't even taken a bath. He got up there to this girl.

And she says, "What's that smell?" she says.

The Irishman says, "That's me, that's me."

"Well, you get out of here and don't come back." And after he's gone, she says, "You know, it's funny. I can still smell that Irishman."[178]

This telling is partly a wry comment on cologne and partly a reversal of the preceding text's clean Finn/dirty Irishman presentation.

In the Green Garage

There was a big Irishman. He went down to the sporting house. They used to call it the "green garage." He went there with some Finns.

And these Finns were telling me that he went in there, and there was five pretty nice girls there that come out displaying their wares. The big Irishman, he says, "I'm looking for a young Irish lass," he says.

Little red-head piped up. She said, "Well, I'm Irish." So he took her back in the room. She was there. When he pulled out his tool, she looked at it and she says [in a broad Finnish accent], "*Voi, Sataana* [Oh, God damn]!"

She was Irish all right.[179]

Here is yet another telling in the Finnish–Irish cycle. Redheads among the Finns are as scarce as they are common among Celts. "*Voi, Sataana*," a recurrent Finnish expression of surprise or disgust, literally means "Oh, Satan!" and is an oath equivalent to "God damn."

The Swedish Wallflower

We went down to Hatley, Wisconsin, once, you know. And they had an old boarding house across, and the landing was on this side of the railroad tracks. And every time we come down with a load of wood, you know, a big fat girl would come out of the house and stand there, you know. And Mondays, Mondays they always had a dance at the Catholic hall there, you know. So we lumberjacks, three and four of us, we'd go down there. Here was this girl. Dick McCloskey was there, Louis [Lavalier], my loader, and two more guys.

I told Louis, I says, "There's that big girl over there who stands there."

"Oh, is that the one?"

"Yah, that's the one." I says, "I'm going to ask her to dance."

Well, they started to waltzing, you know. I says, "May I have the honor?"

"Hunh?"

"Will you dance with me?"

"Well," she says, "I tell you. When I dance so, I sweat so; when I sweat so, I stink so; so I don't t'ink so."[180a]

When the lumberjacks come to town in the spring, some of the local girls would have a little party for them. And this one lumberjack went up to a Swedish girl. She wasn't bad looking, but she was big. And shy too. So he asked her, "Would you like to dance?"

She told him, "When I dance so, I sweat so; when I sweat so, I stink so; so I don't t'ink so."[180b]

Whether a comment on courtship before deodorants or a disparagement of Scandinavian Lutheran objections to dancing, this story persists because of its lyrical punchline.

Pancake Makeup

A homesteader up in northern Minnesota had a pretty good-looking daughter. And he was talking to a lumberjack one day, talking about how fast his daughter was advancing in school. And she'd graduated and finished.

And the lumberjack says, "Well, I thought she was the cook with all that flour on her face."[181]

An obvious comment on a young lady's cosmetic adornment, this telling also speaks to the rivalry between low-status itinerant and professional loggers and their upwardly mobile and settled agrarian counterparts.

Rainy Lake Honeymoon

A schoolteacher come to Rainy Lake. And he got to where he was friendly with a girl who worked at the hotel, so they decided to get married. But they couldn't go anywhere for the honeymoon because he had to teach school and she had to work in the hotel. So they were going to sleep the night there.

Now what this schoolteacher didn't know was that she'd had relations with some of the men, the lumberjacks, in the town. And that night, they decided to take a ladder and lean it up against the window and listen. And the top one would whisper down what was happening. So he's saying, [whispers] "Now they're getting into bed."

And she told her husband, "You're putting it where no man ever put it before."

And the fellow on the top whispered, "He's putting it in her asshole."[182]

The teller logged in the Rainy Lake area, where he also visited "sportin' houses," experiences that led to the localization of this traveled anecdote.

Brain Food

Funnix Grey was one of the old time loggers in Washburn County. He worked in the woods and on the river drives for many years, and he was always known as a skilled worker and a quick wit.

One story that was told about him had to do with the end of the spring drive. He was working for the O'Brien brothers, and the drive ended up at Stillwater, Minnesota. The O'Briens took some of their best men to a fancy hotel for dinner. Funnix always looked like a woodsman, and he looked a little out of place in the hotel. He'd just come from the drive after all: checked shirt, high-water woolen pants, suspenders, boots, whiskers. Anyway, the waiter came around taking orders, and Funnix ordered fish.

There was a young city fellow from Minneapolis who thought he'd have some fun with the old man. So he said in a loud, kind of smirking voice: "I hear fish is good brain food."

Funnix stopped the waiter, nodded at the fellow. "Waiter, bring that gentleman a whale."[183]

This traveled anecdote has been reported from the Maine woods and the gulf coast of Texas.

Independence Day

Then another one went into town—he used to go to Florence once a year. Fourth of July, they had a big parade up in Florence County. So he'd go in and get all drunk out of shape.

And this one day, one time, Glen [Church] had to go up and bail him out of jail. They put him in jail. He was urinating in the street, and they put him in jail. So Glen bailed him out. Boy, he was mad. He said, "A man don't have the rights of a dog in this town."[184]

One might expect other versions where the logger makes his own protest to the judge. This was part of a cycle told through several generations of the teller's family concerning loggers from Iron River, Michigan. See Texts 170 and 269.

His First Power Saw

Logging used to be a big business in this area [Stillwater, Minnesota] a hundred years ago. In later years, some people logged just to keep their own families and neighbors warm. One such man was Jeb, and he liked to gamble a lot with his friends.

So one night Jeb was gambling, and he cleaned out all the rest of his partners. The next day Jeb was feeling pretty good, and so he decided to go into town to see what he could get with his money. In town, he stopped in front of a hardware store. He was looking in the window when the store owner came along and put a new-fangled–looking thing in the window.

"What's that?" asked Jeb.

"This is a brand new power saw. It cuts wood ten times as fast as you can with an ax. And it's a hundred times as easy," replied.

Jeb thought about it for a few minutes, and then he decided that if it could do even half of what the store owner said it could do, it would save him a hell of a lot of work and all his neighbors would be jealous of him.

"How much is it?" asked Jeb.

"Seventy-five dollars," replied the store owner. "And if you don't like it, you can just return it within a week."

So Jeb bought the power saw and took it home to see how it worked. About a week later, the store owner was working as usual when Jeb came back with the saw.

Jeb said, "This here new-fangled device don't work a bit. Why, I can cut wood twice as fast and twice as easy with an ax than with this thing."

"That's impossible," said the store owner. But being a fair man, he decided to give Jeb his money back. So he put the money on the counter, and bent over and yanked on the starter. The motor started roaring away.

"What in tarnation is that?" yelled Jeb. He was so scared, he picked up his money and ran out the door.[185]

The use of generic rural terms foreign to the dialect of Upper Midwesterners ("tarnation" and "new-fangled") and his selection of a biblically named, probably WASP, protagonist suggest that the teller was influenced as much by television's *Green Acres* and the *Beverly Hillbillies* as by regional life.

The DNR Says

There was these couple of ladies been shopping, and they were kind of tired, so they thought, "Well, we'll go over in the park and rest awhile before we go home." And in the park, there was a teeter-totter. They hadn't been on a teeter-totter in years, so they thought they'd ride on the teeter-totter.

So while they were riding on the teeter-totter, one end was a little heavier than the other, so one woman slid down the teeter-totter. Well, low and behold, she gets a sliver in her. So she goes to the doctor. "Doctor, take the sliver out."

So the doctor looked at her and he said, "Ladies, I can't take that sliver out."

"No? Why can't you?"

"Well, the DNR says, 'There's no lumbering in restricted areas.'"[186]

Wisconsin's DNR (Department of Natural Resources) and similar agencies in the Upper Midwest are controversial for their regulations regarding lumbering, hunting, fishing, and farming. For a pair of rural jokes told at the expense of regulatory agencies, see Texts 232 and 233.

The Miners

Except for Minnesota's Mesabi Range, the iron, copper, and lead mines that once employed thousands are largely closed today. Most of the region's mine workers—who labored underground, in open pits, on docks jutting into Lake Superior, and in "lakers" transporting red iron ore and taconite pellets to smelting plants—have died, retired, found other work, or moved away. Nonetheless, the memories of mining are strong. Rusting head frames, piled "overburden," and boarded shafts in communities like Hancock, Hurley, and Ely still mark the landscape.

Miners' jokes also persist, peopled by skilled Cornishmen, like the stock figures Bill and Jan, and by less-experienced Finns, Italians, Scandinavians, and Slavs. Raconteurs, most of whom have worked in mines, take special pleasure in wrapping their tongues around various dialects and parading occupational jargon. The themes of their tales match real life concerns: whatever their ethnicity, fictive miners chafe under overbearing foremen, grumble about piecework and long hours, struggle to communicate across linguistic barriers, long for advancement, and make light of danger.

The Would-Be Captain

One of the characteristics of a Cornishman is the fact that he doesn't admit he doesn't know everything that you're talking about and has no knowledge of it, or that he can't understand or figure out anything that you're talking about.

And there was a couple young fellows that were working in the mine that decided they wanted to be captains in the mine. In order to be a captain, you must have a little education, to be able to keep time and figure some small sums.

So they decided to go to night school. And after having attended for some time, they met on the street, and one said to the other, he said, "Jack, how are you coming along with the schooling?"

"Oh, tolerably well, thank you. How are you?"

"Well, pretty well. Only one thing: I can't understand the problems."

"Huh! They're easy as pie for me."

"Well, then, I'll give you one."

"What is it?"

"Well, here are eleven pounds of mackerel, eleven cents a pound. What'll it come to?"

"Wait a minute, I'll have it for 'e." And he takes a little pencil and paper to figure, but he couldn't do it. And he says, "Jack, give me that problem once more, will 'e?"

"Eleven pound mackerel, eleven cents a pound."

"I'll have 'em in a minute. [Pause.] Now give me that problem exactly right. I want to git 'em for 'e."

"Well," he said, "eleven pound mackerel, eleven cents a pound."

"Mackerel, eh, mackerel?!? Well, no wonder I couldn't get it right. 'Ere all the time I been figuring eleven pound 'erring."[187]

Down on the Fourteenth

They were down on the fourteenth one time. Captain come in to see how they were. Jan said, "Look 'ere, captain, we got some problem 'ere," he said. "We don't know 'ow to 'alf up our payday."

"Well," the captain said, "'ow much have ye got?"

"Look, cap, three five-dollar bills."

"Oh," cap said, "let me have them." So the cap took the three five-dollar bills. He gave Bill one, he gave Jan one, he put one in his pocket, and he walked out.

And after he was gone, Bill looked at Jan, and he said, "Something grand to have an education isn't it?"[188]

Miners' Mathematics

I have one that somebody told me. I always chuckle at it. It was told about one of the old shift bosses, Captain Nankervis. Well, anyway, in the early days when they started the mines, they brought a lot of Cornish miners over. A lot of "Cousin Jacks," they called them.

Anyway, they tell about this guy. He had three men in the shaft. They were in the shaft, and he come down and he hollered up at them. And he said, "Eh," he said, "how many up there?"

He says, "Three."

He says, "'alf of you come down."[189]

Although the Cornish dominated the ranks of mining foremen, or "captains," many were also illiterate and baffled by simple arithmetic as exemplified in these three tellings.

Jan's Accident

Bill and Jan were working in Centennial Mine. Fourteenth level. Always worked on the fourteenth. They loved it down there. Well, this day Bill went back to the shaft to get more drills. Jan was working on the machine, and the machine dumped over. Jan got hurt.

So Bill had to take him up to Calumet-Hecla hospital. So old Doc Curtin had Jan laid out on the table. And Bill was watching him. And Bill said, "Doc, what are you going to do now?"

"Oh," Doc said, "I'm going to give him a shot. In a few minutes, he won't know nothing."

"Oh," he said, "save your time, Doc, 'e don't know nothing now."[190]

The stock Cornishmen, Jan and Bill, work here for the Calumet-Hecla mining company that dominated the "Copper Country" of Michigan.

Patience and Perseverance

They were down on the fourteenth level. The captain came down this morning and said, "You fellows got to go down on the twenty-fifth."

Well, they got down on the twenty-fifth, and they weren't happy. They weren't used to it down there. About ten o'clock, the captain come in to see how the boys were getting along.

And Jan said, "Look 'ere, captain," he said, "we can't make any money 'ere. This rock is too 'ard."

So the captain got the boys together, and he gave them a little pep talk. And before he went out, he said, "You fellows got to have patience and perseverance." And he went out.

And after he was gone, Bill looked at Jan. He said, "Jan, what did 'e mean, 'patience and perseverance'?"

He said, "You fool, Bill, that's them two Italians up on the next level."[191]

The distress Jan and Bill have over being moved to a different level has to do with the piece work system; they would only be paid for the ore chiseled from hard rock.

Lagging Sprags

Maybe you heard this, about an iron ore miner? There was a Finn and a Swede working together in an iron ore mine, and they were putting up timber. You put your sets up. And they were cutting lagging sprags, and one side had to have a bevel on it, or both sides. If you're putting it on a round log, you'd chop a little space for it, and then they'd wedge it and you'd put a couple of spikes in.

And the old Swede was up on the stage waiting for it. And the Finlander calls up, "How much bevel you want on it?"

He says, "Cut it straight, have bevel enough."[192]

The Finn of this telling was getting carried away with his beveling, and the Swede's command to "cut it straight" was an inverse way of saying "don't cut it." See accompanying note.

The Lank

Did they ever talk about how they murder the English language here? Just like they used to say on the other end—I don't know if I told you this one?

Usually, in the underground—they had underground on the east end of the range; not so much on the west end, but they had some over there—and they usually used Finnish crews or Honky crews or Italians.

And one day, one of the partners didn't show up, so they put a—I can't tell dialect jokes very well—they put a Finn and a Honky together. So they had them working in the drift. And they blasted. And they were supposed to go back in there and crib it up and stuff.

So the Finn was in there, and the Honky was supposed to be handing him stuff. And he says, "Give me the 'lank." You know, "Give me the 'lank."

So the Honky's looking around. "The 'lank. The 'lank." Give him everything—lantern and a pick, you know.

Finally the Finn got mad, and he come out of the hole there and he says, "Here. The 'lank." And he took the piece of timber.

And the Honky says, "Well, whatsa matter you?" He says. "Fifteen years in this country, you still can't say planka."[193a]

I understand that when old Luigi first came over from Italy, he was put on the job in the mine with Heikki as his partner. Heikki was an experienced miner. He had been in this country maybe ten years or so.

And there was some communication problem between these two immigrants from different countries.

But at one point, Heikki was holding up that big old drilling machine, and he wanted to brace it. So he pointed at a board that was leaning up against the wall of the stope. And he said, "Luigi, give it for me that 'lank." Well, Luigi didn't know what he was talking about. But wanting to be helpful, he picked up a pickax and he handed it over.

And Heikki said, "No, no I don't want that pickax. Give it that 'lank." Luigi looked around and picked up a dynamite box and handed that over. "No, no, don't give it the box. Give it the 'lank."

Well, this went on for some time with Heikki struggling to hold that drilling machine, until through the process of elimination, Luigi finally handed him the plank. And Heikki took it and braced the machine. And he said, "Yah, that's what I wanted was that 'lank."

When Luigi finally found out what it was that Heikki had been asking for, he got rather irritated and excited, and he jumped up and down. And he said, "Whatsa matter you? You been this country ten, fifteen years and already you can'ta say planka?"[193b]

In the early days, most of the time, they had one Slovenian and one Finn working together. They had a language problem, so they couldn't fight. That's probably the main reason. They couldn't argue and fight because they couldn't talk too much to each other.

But the Finn, Finlander was up in the raise. The raise was a four-by four-foot hole that goes up into the pillar, and they dump the ore or hoist timbers through it or they had ladder roads in it. It's something like a laundry chute. He was up in the raise fixing it. And he says to his partner, he says, "Hey partner, send me up a 'lank."

And the Slovenian says, "Look at that bugger; he's been in this country twenty years, and he can't say planka in English good."[193c]

This joke is widespread throughout mining communities in the Upper Midwest. As in these versions, a Finn invariably requests the "'lank," but the partner may be an Italian, a Slovenian, or a "Honky" (sometimes called a "Hunky," that is, an immigrant from the old Austro–Hungarian empire and, usually, a Slav).

The Immigrant's Impressions

So they tell this story about the Slav, the young Italian, and the young Finn were all working down in this mine together.

So the Italian said, "You know, I no greenhorn. I come from Roma, the eternal city. I come to this country to be somebody. But I was somebody in Italy, too. And when I come down that gangplank in New York City, I've got patent leather shoes, gray striped pants, Borsalino hat, cutaway coat. When I walk down that gangplank, they look up and say, 'Who that?' 'I don't know. Must be Prince Umberto.'"

Well, this young Slav wasn't going to be left out. So he said, "Just a minute now on this. I come from Belgrade. Belgrade was a city before Rome was founded. I come to this country, too. I come down that same gangplank in New York. I got a nice gray Fedora hat. I wear the spats. And I got a nice suit of clothes. And a nice gold watch. And everybody look up when I come down and say, 'I don't know who that fellow is, but he's from over there somewhere in Austria-Hungary. Must be that young Prince Peter.'"

So the Finn is sitting there. And he said, "Chust one minute now. I come from way up nort at Arctic Circle. I come, my papa, he make me a nice coat from the reindeer. My mama, she make me a nice fur cap. Uncle, he make me a nice s'oepack." He says, "I come that New York, too. And I come down that same gang'lank. And I never forget that," he says, "I land in that New York on fourt' Yuly. And I walk down that gang'lank, and everybody look up and they take one look at that young Finn, and they say 'Yesus 'Rist.'"[194]

The teller's description of clothing is masterful. The "s'oepacks," or shoepacks, worn by the Finn were useful footwear for all ethnic groups in the Upper Midwest for outdoor winter work in the woods, in open pit mines, or on ore docks jutting into Lake Superior.

Underground Mining

There's the time the Bohunk, the Finlander, and the Norwegian were signing up for underground work. That's all that was left, underground mining. They ask the Bohunk, "You ever work underground?"

He says, "Why sure, I worked underground."

He says, "How far?"

"Well, six, seven feet. I dug ditches."

"Aw, that don't count." So they ask the Norwegian, "You ever work underground?"

"Oh, hell, yes," he says, "I work underground. I dug storm sewers. Oh ten, twelve feet underground."

"Aw, naw, you'll never make it, you know."

So Toivo's listening to this. He thinks, "Oh, I'm going to show that guy how many times I can work underground."

He says, "Toivo, come here. You every work underground?"

"Oh, son-of-a-pitch," he says, "I work underground long time."

"How many years?"

"Ohhh," he says, "fifteen, twenty years."

He says, "How far underground you work?"

He says, "Holy 'Rist." He says, "Nine, ten, twelve hundred feet. We don't care. However far down they want us to go, we go." Toivo's bullshitting.

So the guy says, "Good." He says: "You got the job." He says: "What kind of lights did you use when you worked underground? Did you use electric light or gas or what?"

"Kot tammit, sir," he says. "I don't know. I always worked on day shift."[195]

The struggle for employment (often contingent on passing a test of some kind) in this and the next joke is a common theme in the Upper Midwest, especially in the humor of Finnish-Americans, who have been involved historically in mining, logging, and "hardscrabble" farming on cutover acreage.

We Need Some Work

I know a joke about the Finlander and the Swede and the Chinaman. They were getting pretty hungry and they decided they'd get a job. They haven't worked for a while, and they'd been applying at every place possible. And finally they went to this mine.

So the foreman came and talked to them. He said, "No, we haven't got any work for you at all."

They begged him for a job. They said, "We have tried for two weeks to find a job. And we're starving. We need some work. Give us anything; we'll do anything."

So the foreman said, "Okay, I got a job for you. It isn't going to pay good. You go down to the deepest mine, which isn't a safe place at all, and you're going to go down there and work." And the foreman looked at the Finn, a big husky guy. And the Swede is a big husky guy. And the Chinaman is a tiny little squirt. He says, "What am I going to do with him?"

So they go down in the mineshaft, all the way down to the bottom. And he gives the Finn a pick. He says, "Here, you pick on that wall there. You put the ore in this thing. The Swede is going to wheel the bin back, and he's going to put it in the buckets on the pulley, and he's going to pull it to the top." And he looks at this scrawny Chinaman, he says, "You just take care of supplies, okay?" Fine.

So at the end of their shift—they worked a sixteen-hour shift—the foreman come back down there. And there's the Finn just picking like crazy, had gone forty feet farther into the mine. And the Swede had it all on top. And he asked these guys, "What happened to the Chinaman?"

"We don't know. We haven't seen him all day." The Swede says, "You know, the last I saw, he was going down over there, that mine shaft over there."

So the foreman, he walks back there. And he keeps going and going and going. And all of a sudden, in the dark, here jumps that Chinaman. "Su'plise!" [Surprise.][196]

Few, if any, Chinese have mined in the Upper Midwest, although they have run small businesses in cities throughout the region since the late nineteenth century. Their presence in this telling is required by the punch line, but the joke probably had its origin in another region and another occupational setting.

Six Twelves

Oh, this is an old ethnic joke. When they used to have—at one time, years and years ago—the foreman on the job, the line foreman, could hire and fire people.

So Toivo and Waino—and this is supposed to be a true story—Toivo and Waino and all them guys are working underground. And they worked like six twelves, that's six days a week, twelve hours a day. And on Saturday night, they'd close the mine. Saturday afternoon shift was the last one, and at midnight they'd close the mine until Monday at six. So them guys had a part of a day off.

Well, Toivo was going to leave early on Saturday night. And this is true. Or supposed to be true. This is passed on. And Toivo left at ten o'clock. And he went to his house, which is an Oliver house that U.S. Steel had built and all of this shit. And he went home, and he walked in the door quietly. He was going to surprise his wife. And there was this foreman banging his old lady.

He looked in. "Oh, my god." He ran back to the job. He told the guys on the job, he says, "Kot tammit, I come close. I almost got caught leaving early."

And that's supposed to be true. Now whether it is, I don't know or not, but that's one of them that tells how scared they were. These were line foremen, not superintendents or anything. These were just your foremen on the job that you were working on. That's getting back in the olden days, but that's the stories that we hear, and we catch onto, and we love.[197]

The Devil in the Mines

Here's a good one. There's this old Finlander. He had been working in the mines long enough. And he had a devil for a foreman and a devil for a partner.

And he told the captain, he kept telling the captain, "I want to change partners. That goddarn devil, I can't get along with him."

Then finally, after about a year or so griping and that, finally the captain went and changed his partner. Couple months later, the captain come by. He says, "How you like your new partner?"

He says, "You son-of-a-gun, first you give me the devil, then you give me his brudder."[198]

Telling the Foreman

Here's another one about an old Finn. He was in the mine long time. And he couldn't speak English at all. He just couldn't learn it, couldn't learn it.

And a young guy started. He was Finn, too. They were getting along good, and the boss come there one time, giving them a bad time, and the young fellow started telling the boss where to head in.

The old guy told the young guy in Finn, "*Sanopa vain poika, kun puheessa parjat.*" In other words, "Tell him good now that you got somebody that can understand the language."[199]

Although these three tellings are presented as jokes, they reveal the truth about working conditions early in this century and represent vented anger against overbearing supervisors.

Life in the Location

Bill and Jan walking home from night shift. Walking down through the location. Cold, clear morning. Snow on the ground.

Bill give Jan a poke. He said, "Jan, look at the smoke coming out of that there chimney."

Jan looked up. He said, "Pretty, isn't it."

Bill said, "That's the kind of woman to 'ave. The 'ouse is nice and warm. Good 'ot breakfast waiting for ye."

Jan said, "Something grand."

And as they walked down through the street, they looked to the right and the left. Smoke out of this one, smoke out of that one. When they got to Bill's house, they looked up. Smoke coming out of Bill's chimney. Bill went in the house. Jan continued down the road. Looking to the right, to the left. Smoke out of this one, that one.

When his own house came into view, there was no smoke. So he ran down the road, ran in the house, drew a pail of water, went up over the stairs hollering, "Fire, fire."

Mary Jane woke up. Said, "Where, where?"

He gave her the pail of water. Said, "In every bloody 'ouse but ours."[200]

This telling recalls the old mining "locations," clusters of company houses a stone's throw from the mines so workers could walk to and from their jobs.

A Bullgang Joke

We got some good ones, like I was explaining before, about the bullgang being dumb and stupid, being just big and dumb with a size fifty-two shirt and a size two hat. It isn't anymore. We got teachers working on the bullgang, and beauticians. I'm a barber and a teamster and the whole works. But I'm working in the pit, and I'll be damned if I know why. I don't know if you heard this joke, but I got a good joke for you.

They decided when they hired people—they hired a laborer, which was just common laborer, they hired a welder, who does welding, and they hired a bullganger, which is a dumb millwright supposedly, out in the field, doing pounding and stuff. So they all did their written tests, passed pretty good. Bullganger got the lowest score, naturally, because we're dumb. And they thought, geez, what are we going to do for a practical test? We have to be fair.

So they thought and they thought, and they said, "Jeez, we'll take each in a room individually and we'll throw three steel balls up in the air." About inch balls or so, just steel, bearings or whatever you want to call them.

So they brought the laborer in the room. The foreman threw three steel balls up in the air and left the laborer in the room. They watched him on the TV camera and listened to him. He looked at the three steel balls. He went over there and picked them up. He put them on a shelf, and he put a rag over them and covered them with dust so nobody would see them.

"Oh, yeah, that's okay for being a laborer. You did good."

They got the welder in there, threw the three steel balls up in the air, told the welder, "Do what comes naturally." They watched him.

He went over, got his welding machine, dragged it over there, welded the three steel balls together. Brought them out and said, "Here. I done a nice job of welding."

"Hey, yeah, you're okay. You're going to be a welder."

Brought the bullganger in there, threw the three steel balls up in the air, said, "Do what comes naturally."

Bullganger looked at them for about five minutes, scratched his head, scratched his ass, went and had coffee, came back a half an hour later, broke one, lost one, and stole the other one.

That's a bullgang joke. If you can't get a job nowhere else, come to the bullgang. If you can't get in the volunteer army, come to work on the bullgang.[201]

The teller gets a trickster's pleasure out of playing with the strong-but-dumb, happy-go-lucky stereotype of bullgangers. He at once denies the validity of the stereotyping while arguing its worth as a means of making work human instead of mechanical.

The Farmers

Whether dairying in the rolling hill country of southern Wisconsin, raising wheat on the western Minnesota prairie, or eking out a "hardscrabble" existence on logged-off Upper Peninsula acreage, Upper Midwesterners have been farmers. Cows, corn fields, barns, silos, and granaries proliferate in the rural landscape, while "farmer jokes" have been exchanged vigorously throughout this century at church suppers, auctions, feed mills, cafes, and taverns.

The most recent diminishment of family farms, resulting from economic changes and government policies, yields dark humor. Older narratives still in circulation are lightened through their evocation of an age when farmers dominated the region. These tellings traverse good land and bad, ruminate over meteorological extremes, and celebrate extraordinary crops. They consider bulls, cows, poultry, pigs, and horses that are smart and stubborn, potent and flatulent, docile and dangerous. They explore relationships between neighbors, between the farm family and their hirelings, and between farmers and assorted urbanites like salesmen, tourists, and government officials. Since farmers plow the soil while managing the sexual and scatological behavior of beasts, their jokes are full of "earthy" metaphors.

Hardscrabble

It was one that Henry Schneider always told about the hardscrabble country. About the guy that went out there with the wagon.

He threw his shovel down. It was all good, rich, black dirt. And he thought, "Holy Moses, this is like the Promised Land." And so he hurried back into town to close the deal.

And hell, he got back there and never could find the spot. Ever.[202]

Failed and successful efforts at claiming good homestead land are still part of the legend of European settlement in the Upper Midwest.

Farming the Coulees

There were three levels. See the guy that owned the cow up on the hill there, he'd milk her for a while, and then she'd roll down into the next man's pasture and he'd milk her, see. Finally, she got down to the valley, and then they'd have to start all over again.

And the corn, you shot it across the valley in a shotgun because you couldn't use a planter—it's too hilly.

It was so windy, the hen laid the same egg three times.[203]

According to the teller, he heard this tripartite tall tale during his youth in Monroe, Wisconsin, in the "coulee region," or "driftless hill area"— unglaciated terrain marked by high ridges and deep valleys.

Irishman's Oats

There was an old Irishman. He had a livery barn, and he used to raise oats for his horses. But he didn't give them very much oats by the looks of them.

Anyway, he was telling about the fine crop of oats. He said, "I got sixty acres of the finest oats you ever seen in your life on my back forty. Every kernel is as big as the end of me thumb."[204]

Rural Irishmen, in both Old World and New, were not widely regarded, especially in jokes, as expert farmers. They were, however, commonly associated with horses, which they raced, sold, traded, and rented.

Earl Lester's Team

My dad used to have a man whose name was Earl Lester working for him. And Earl Lester was a tobacco farmer, and he always used horses to plow the tobacco. He told me this story when I was a kid. I only heard it once, and I've repeated it many times. It just stuck in my mind as a kid.

Earl told me about a new breed of horses that he was perfecting. He said that they were just beautiful: they were golden, they were proud, they were prancers, they could pull a plow just something fantastic. And the thing that was so rare about these horses was it didn't cost anything to feed them, because he had perfected the breed to the point where he didn't have to feed them. And he said he got the things just perfected, and the damn things died on him.[205]

This telling is AT Type 1682, an ancient tale dating to the fables of Aesop: "The groom teaches his horse to live without food. It dies."

A Horse for Sale

This farmer had a farm, and he wanted to sell a horse that wasn't so good. And he had to advertise the horse for sale, and people came out to look at the horse.

And this one gentleman came and looked at the horse, and he said, "Well, it's kind of dark in the barn. Would you bring the horse out in the yard so that I can see him?"

"Certainly." So he brought the horse out.

And the prospective buyer looked at the horse from the front to the back and asked him, "Would you open his mouth? I'd like to see his teeth." So he looked at his mouth and, "Hmmm." Looked him over. So he said, "Well, now," he said, "I'd like to see him perform. I'd like to see him run. Would you show me how he can run?"

So the farmer said, "Yes, sir." And so he slapped him on the buttocks, and away the horse took off, and he ran straight into the side of the barn.

And the buyer said, "Why, man, that horse is blind."

And the farmer looked at him and said, "Oh, no, he just doesn't give a damn."[206]

This tale about a probably-blind horse parallels Text 114.

Distinguished Horses

There were two farmers who had pastures side-by-side, and each had a horse. The horses used to jump the fence between the pastures, and then the farmers could not tell whose horse was whose.

So they tried to make the fence higher, but this didn't work. So they tried to figure out a way to tell the horses apart.

One farmer tied a ribbon to his horse and this worked for a while, but when the ribbon fell off, they had the same problem. The other farmer decided to clip his horse's mane, and again it worked only for a while. Same problem with cutting the tail—it grew back.

So finally the farmers decided to measure them. And sure enough, the black horse was a hand-and-a-half taller than the white one.[207]

Baughman offers motif J2722, "Telling their horses apart." The joke has Polish, Norwegian, and other ethnic variants.

The Barn Door

A farmer bought a mule and was trying to get him in the barn. The door was too low, so he was sawing part of the door off on top. His wife said, "Well, it's a dirt floor, why don't you take a shovel and dig deeper?"

The farmer said, "Well, it ain't his legs that is too long. It's his ears."[208]

This telling shares the element of a beast supposedly too large for an entry way with AT type 1295B*, "Man on camel has doorway broken down so that he can ride in. It does not occur to him to dismount."

What The Preacher Said

One of the local farmers found his mule dead one day, so he started to bury it. A lady came along and asked what he was doing. He told her his mule had died, and he was going to bury it.

The lady said, "Well, you know the preacher said that the Bible calls those asses."

The farmer looked up at her and said, "Well, lady, I guess you could call this an ass hole then."[209]

Where to Breed the Goat

There was this little cantankerous old lady living in town. She thought things were getting too expensive, so she decided to move to the country and become self-supporting. She bought herself a nanny goat for milk, but she couldn't get it to give milk. One of her neighbors came over and told her that before she could get milk from a goat, she had to get it bred.

So the little old lady tied a rope around the goat's neck and took it to town to get it bred. When she was walking down Main Street, she saw an old farmer sitting on a rocker on a porch and yelled to him, "Hey, you lazy old man, where can I get my goat bred?"

The old man slowly got off his chair and strolled over to the goat. He lifted up the goat's tail and said, "Second hole down."[210]

Cows and Potatoes

What's that one about—we were talking about breeding cows. This one fellow, he was going over to his neighbor with a cow to get bred. And on the way over, he stopped and talked to this fellow that was digging potatoes.

And he talked to him a while. And he says, "How did your potatoes turn out?"

He says, "They didn't," he says, "I had to *dig* them out."

So he was really teed off. He says, "I'll get even with him." So, he went over and had the cow bred. And he came back, stopped there again.

The guy that was digging potatoes, he says, "Well, where did you get your cow bred?"

He raised up the tail and said, "Right under there, you dumb bastard."[211a]

This joke pertains to years back, when my father was telling me. I was a little girl, I wasn't supposed to hear it, but I did. And the reason that I remember it is that I wasn't supposed to hear it.

So it's about farmers that didn't get along. They were forever fighting, and they had disputes of all kinds.

So anyway this one farmer decided, "It's about time we made up." Okay, so he seen the other farmer planting potatoes. So he walked up to the fence, and he asked him, he says, "Well, neighbor, what kind of potatoes are you planting?"

And he told him. He says, "Well, raw potatoes."

Well, okay, if that's how you feel about it. So he [the first farmer] walked away from it.

So a few days later he [the second farmer] sees the other farmer walking with a cow down the lane. So he figures, I wasn't very nice about it. I'll go talk to him.

He walked up. He said, "Well, neighbor," he said, "where you taking your cow to get it bred?"

So he lifts up the tail and he says, "Right there."

So that was the love between the two farmers.[211b]

These tellings share a preoccupation with the "holes" of beasts, a forward old woman, and a wisecracking farmer. They also comment inversely on the importance of cordial relations between rural neighbors.

Raising the Bull

Someone back in the family had this great bull, and he was often used for breeding. This time the neighboring farmer had so many cows that, instead of bringing them over, it was decided they would just take the bull over there. The plan was to lead the bull up the ramp and into a truck, but he definitely had other ideas and simply refused to go.

Then someone had the great idea of using the hay sling and rope—putting the sling on the bull, raising him up in the barn, and then lowering him into the truck which would be positioned underneath. Sounded great. Three men managed to get the sling around the bull. The rope was tied on that went around a pulley on the main barn beam. Someone went around the barn and tied the rope to the waiting team of horses. Then some overly enthusiastic helper really "geed-up" the team. They lunged forward, and before you knew it they had hauled the bull right up to the roof. The bull bellowed, and the scared horses refused to budge. It appeared the bull might fall from the sling, so somehow all the men managed to lower him into the haymow where he proceeded to race around, tossing hay and creating a great dust cloud. By now he was so mad, no one dared go near him.

Whatever happened to the bull? Oh, they just left him there, and went back to bringing the cows to him.[212]

In the era before artificial insemination, stud bulls might be loaded onto cattle trucks via a permanent ramp built into a barnyard fence. Many such ramps can be seen throughout the Upper Midwest. Although the teller told this as a true story, its absurd bull-hoisting recalls AT Type 1210: "The cow is taken to the roof to graze." In a variant, Type 1210*, an ass is hoisted to a tower, but it dies as a consequence.

The Old Bull's Advice

A young bull and an old bull were standing on a hilltop looking over a pasture of cows. The young bull says, "Let's run down and screw a couple of cows."

The old bull turns to the young bull and says, "No. Let's walk down and get *all* the cows."[213]

Some Pills

Old farmer had a bull that wouldn't service the cows. So the farmer, he calls the vet and asks him what he can do for his bull here.

Vet says, "I don't know exactly what's wrong with him, but here's some pills. Try these and see if they might do the trick."

So the farmer tried it. First day, the farmer gave him one pill, and the bull services one cow. Farmer's pretty happy with this.

Second day comes, and the farmer gives him another pill. This time the bull's lying under a tree. Jumps up and breeds two cows.

Farmer thinks, "Boy, this is working good," and gives the bull another. This time the bull jumps over the fence and breeds all the neighbor's cows.

Neighbor comes out and says, "Hey, what happened to your bull there? Before, he wouldn't service a single cow, and now he's breeding everything in the county. What'd you give him?"

Farmer says, "Don't know, but it tastes like peppermint."[214]

In a variant, the aphrodisiac works too well; not only are the beasts exhausted, but when the pills are tossed in the well, the pump handle rises.

Taking a Wheelbarrow

These two guys was taking the cow to get her bred. And one guy, he was leading the cow. And the other guy, he was supposed to take a wheelbarrow.

"Well, what do you want a wheelbarrow for?"

"Well, we got to bring the calf home." That was quick work. "We got to bring the calf home."[215]

In the first three decades of this century, urban ethnics from Chicago factories and Pennsylvania mines homesteaded on logged-off acreage in northern Wisconsin, often with mixed results. Counter-culture and hobby farmers likewise emerged in the 1960s. Stories about their foolishness, like the one above, abound in the region.

Breeder's Service

This is a new one that I learned about two weeks ago. This is a short one. A farmer had a cow. A farmer had a cow, and she was in heat. And he himself was unable to take her to get her bred. So I think he told his neighbor, and with some help, they sent the cow—to get her bred—to another neighbor.

And then the helper came back, and the farmer asked him, "Did you get her bred?"

"No. We couldn't get her to lay on her back. We couldn't get her to lay on her back."[216]

The Unwitting Inseminator

Farmer Jessup told his wife that neighbor Pretz was coming over to breed one of their cows. He then went to the barn, took a big spike, and drove it over the stall where the cow was.

Then he called his wife to the barn. "I have to go to town. See that nail there? Well, that is the cow to be bred." And off he went.

A few hours later, Farmer Pretz showed up to fetch the cow. Farmer Jessup's wife took him to the barn and showed him the cow. He happened to glance up and see the spike. "What's that for?"

"To hang your pants on, I suppose."[217]

Breeding is the subject of many farmer jokes. Bulls are large, fierce, and unpredictable; cows are sometimes skittish. New calves and "freshened" (milk-producing) cows depend on successful breeding.

Carnation Milk

There was a Norwegian couple that was always writing on these contests, but they never won anything. So he quit writing, but she kept on, and she won.

She met her boyfriend and said, "You know, Ole, I've won."

He said, "What did you write on?"

"I wrote on Carnation Milk."

"Well, what did you write, Lena?"

"I wrote, 'Carnation Milk is the best of all, no tits to pull, no shit to haul.'"[218]

The jingle echoes the dairy farmer's complaint regarding the drudgery of twice-daily milkings and incessant barn cleaning.

Bovine Affection

There was a young farmer and he had a girlfriend. And he took her out to show her his farm. And as they walked down through the field, there was a cow and her little calf. And they were smelling noses.

And he said, "I'd like to do that."

She says, "Go ahead. It's your cow."[219]

Chicken Chasing

One time there was a boyfriend riding with a girlfriend. This was horse and buggy time, too. They was going along a farm. And a rooster was chasing a chicken. And he got up on her.

And then she says, "Did you ever?"

And he says, "No, but I tried to."[220]

There is a cycle of rural jokes involving this sort of courtship-by-proxy.

The Old Hen's Opinion

There was this farm yard, and it was a rooster and a bunch of hens around, and the rooster was going around bragging how good he was. Oh, he was wonderful, you know.

And the old hens were going around behind him: "TALK-talk-talk-talk-talk. TALK-talk-talk-talk-talk."[221]

In a Norwegian-American variant an appreciative rooster struts past the hen house crowing, "*Takk ... takk ... takk ... takk ... takk,*" or "thanks.

The Satisfied Sow

Farmer had a sow and he didn't have any boars. He'd just started farming, you know. So he asked the neighbor, "How do I get little pigs?"

"Well, you take it and get it serviced."

He says, "Oh, is that right?"

"Yeah, just bring it over. Our pig'll get it serviced. You'll have little pigs."

So he gets the pig out, gets it in the wheelbarrow 'cause he didn't want to lose him. Gets him over to the neighbor's in the wheelbarrow, puts him in the pen with that boar. Jeez, the old pig took care of her. Put her in the wagon and took her back home.

Next morning, he got up and looked. Hmmm. No little ones. So he piles her in the wheelbarrow and back over there again. Gets her serviced again. Takes her back home again.

Next morning, looks out. Hmmm. No little ones. Does the same thing the next day.

Gets up in the morning, looks out the window, and here's the pig sitting in the wheelbarrow.[222]

Compare to Text 215.

The Fattest Pig Context

There were these three farmers who all raised pigs. Each one wanted to win the fattest pig contest at the county fair that year. So they all put their pigs on special diets. The first farmer decided to feed his pig nothing but grain. The second farmer fed his nothing but table scraps. The third farmer decided just to stick a cork up the pig's hinder.

And so time went by until the day of the fair. First pig gets loaded onto the scale. "Five hundred sixty-nine pounds," the announcer screams out. Second pig gets up on the scale. "Seven hundred thrity-two pounds," the announcer yells. And the second farmer smirks at the first. Then here comes the third pig. "Nine hundred sixty-eight pounds." And the third farmer wins the grand prize.

Well, now the farmer has a problem. How is he going to get the cork out? He decides to train a monkey to get corks out of bottles, and after the monkey gets trained, he sets the pig out in the middle of a field with the monkey behind him. The farmer also stationed three men at different distances behind the pig to watch and report what they saw later.

After the cork was popped, the farmer asked the first guy, "What did you see?"

"All I saw was miles and miles of pig crap."

Farmer asks the second guy, "What did you see?"

"All I saw was miles and miles of pig crap."

Finally the farmer asks the third guy, who was the closest, "What did you see?"

The man replies, "All I saw was a monkey trying to stuff a cork back up a pig's hinder."[223]

While this scatological joke typifies adolescent humor, it also parodies the excitement of livestock competitions at county fairs, as well as the questionable shortcuts taken by some farmers to increase their animals' weights for show or sale.

Pa and the Hired Girl

That's this one family, they had a hired girl and they had a boy about so big. [Indicates four feet tall.] And one day, the father, he had the hired girl there in the kitchen. She was on the floor, and he was giving her. And the kid happened to look through the keyhole. And he seen it.

So he said, "Mama, is that so that women go to heaven with their feet first?"

And she says, "Oh, what are you talking about?"

"Well, Pa was with the hired girl in the kitchen there. She had her feet up, all the way up in the air like that. [Lifts both legs slightly.] And she says, 'Oh Lord, I'm coming.' And she probably would've, but Daddy was holding onto her."[224]

The Hired Man's Romance

This farmer had a hired man hired. And he also had a daughter. And the daughter came out in the field where he was plowing. She'd been pestering him for a little love. And so he agreed. He started his love, and he didn't know a damn thing about it. But she, she knew how it was supposed to work.

She says, "Now, put it in." He put it in and he kept it quietly there. She says, "Now, pull it out." And he pulled it out. She says, "Put it in." He did. "Pull it out."

Then he says, "Make up your mind, because I got some plowing to do."[225]

In the second telling involving promiscuous acts with the "hired help," variations include the village idiot, a plowboy, a high schooler on his first date, and a "husky Polack" playing the fool.

Out Plowing

What was that one about this guy, a salesman, was going down the road? And he saw this farmer out there plowing without no pants on?

Then he says, "I'm just curious." He says, "How come you're out here plowing without no pants on?"

He says, "Well, yesterday I was out plowing without my shirt and my neck got stiff. So this is my wife's idea."[226]

Salesmen frquently query farmers-at-the-plow in jokes and are just as frequently rewarded with some absurd answer. Meanwhile, gibes about male virility are a constant in jokes concerning husbands and wives.

Depression Bargain

Talking about hired men, that reminds me of an old joke about this one farmer. A salesman was going through the countryside. And he stopped to sell him something and discovered he had a hired man.

And he said to the farmer, he said, "My gosh, in times like these [the Depression] how can you afford a hired man?"

He says, "I'll tell you, it's simple." He said, "That hired man works for me for two years, then I deed him the farm. Then I work for him for two years, and he deeds it back to me."[227]

The Lightning Rod Salesman

There was a guy come to sell me some lighting rods. I kept saying no. And, well, he kept egging me on and bothering me.

And I said, "Well, if the insurance company will give me cheaper rates, I might put them on. But otherwise, I don't want them."

Oh, and he kept egging me on. He says, "I'll give you a good buy on them."

And I says, "I'll give you a good-bye without them." And I went to work.[228]

The Salesman Snubbed

There was a salesman, he was going from city to city by a bus. And there was a school teacher, she was riding the same bus. The day was breaking in the morning and there was a flock of cattle out in the pasture. And the salesman was kind of kidding the teacher.

"What's that?"

"Them are cows."

Then, went farther, and there were a bunch of cows and a bull with the cows. And the salesman says, "What's that?" He pointed out to the bull.

"That's the traveling salesman."[229]

These three jokes set the sometimes credulous, sometimes crafty salesman loose in the rural scene. Although the schoolteacher is more often the butt of rural jokes, in the third salesman joke, she tells the equally maligned salesman that "bull" connotes both virility and excrement.

The Urbanite's Comeuppance

Two city women were driving down the road when they seen a farmer out working in the field. They thought they would go over and play a joke on him.

The lady walked up to the farmer and said, "Sir, we can't seem to find any wind for our windshields. Do you have any?"

The farmer told them, "No, but I do have some tail for your tailpipe."[230]

In his comeback, the farmer parallels the structure of the urbanites' query while relying on the rural use of "tail" for the penis in particular and for genitals in general.

The Lawyer's Epitaph

A farmer was walking through a cemetery, and he came to a big tombstone, and engraved on the stone was the words, "Here lies a lawyer and an honest man."

And the farmer says, "That's funny. Bury two men in one grave?"[231]

Lawyers have been maligned in jokes for centuries, and it is hardly surprising that farmers, aswirl in the complexities of modern agriculture, take a swipe at them. The farmer's comment may also be regarded as spurred by the tombstone's size and braggadocio.

Too Close to the Barn

This one farmer was visited by an inspector and was told several times that he was to move his outhouse. It was too close to the barn according to regulations. After being warned over and over, the farmer finally moved the outhouse way into the woods. When the inspector visited again, he asked where the farmer had moved the outhouse to.

The farmer replied, pointing, "Oh, way back in the woods over there."

The inspector looked sheepish and said, "Oh I didn't mean you had to move it that far away."

"That's okay. Now we just 'go' in the barn."[232]

The Bull and the Bureaucrat

A farmer caught a guy messing around in his milkhouse. He said, "What are you doing here? Who are you?"

The guy said, "Here's my card, here's my card." He was a farm inspector. The same guy who had him move the outhouse way out there in the field. The inspector had a call of nature and asked, "Where's your facilities?"

"Well," the farmer said, "way out there where you wanted it moved."

The inspector gets out there a ways and a bull takes after him. He yells to the farmer, "Help, help, help."

The farmer yells back, "Show him your card, show him your card."[233a]

This was about a farmer. And the DNR man came around and he said he wanted to check the crick down there.

And the farmer says, "You better not go over there; there's a bull in the pasture."

And the DNR man says, "I got a red button on here. My red button says I can go anywhere I want to."

So the farmer says, "All right. Let him go, let him go down there to the crick."

So he goes down to check the bushes in the crick. About ready to come back and here comes the old bull out. The DNR man starts hollering, "Help, help."

And the farmer says, "Show him your button, show him your button."[233b]

These tellings are obviously rural protests against increasing regulation by government agencies.

The Wrath of God

This farmer is out working in his field. The farmer is riding his tractor when it turns over and dumps the farmer in a gully. The tractor rolls over and pins the farmer down and crushes both his legs so he's stuck in the gully.

Then it starts to rain, and the farmer's stuck there under his tractor getting all wet when he hears this rumbling sound.

The farmer looks up, and he sees this big cascade of water coming down the gully and it would drown him.

The farmer looks up and says, "God, why me?"

This big black cloud forms over the farmer and from it comes this big booming voice, "Because you piss me off."[234]

No doubt precipitated by the farm crisis in America, this telling resembles the Book of Job with its divine torment of a faithful servant. It has been peopled by African-Americans and Jews in other variants.

Agricultural Economics

What can a bird do that a farmer can't?
Make a deposit on a tractor.[235]

Rural Sociology

Did you hear about the farmer who was charged with child abuse?
He willed the farm to his son.[236]

These two jokes were told in succession. The second joke combines the social evil of
child abuse, which the public has recently come to admit is a national problem, with
the economic hardships that farmers nationwide sustained during the widely publicized
farm crisis of the late twentieth century.

The Townsfolk

Small-town talk frequently extends beyond fact, philosophy, and rumor into the realm of humor, be it exaggerated reality or outright fiction. The formation of towns, schools, and churches, the local police force and volunteer fire department, the tavern, store, and blacksmith shop or filling station, all contribute incidents, scenes, and especially characters (fools, tricksters, wits, eccentrics, boasters, tipplers) to this group of jokes.

Cycles of jocular narratives commonly center around some remarkable individual whose words and actions charge everyday life with laughter: wily Charlie Ferg of Richland County, fearless Olaus Norwick of Rice Lake, and yarn-spinning Nels Bennett of Gotham. Some of the stories told about them may be grounded in fact, while others are localized versions of well-traveled anecdotes.

In keeping with the Upper Midwest's pluralistic nature, the jokes and humorous anecdotes of small towns concern the doings and echo the dialect of Yankees, the Irish, the French, Norwegians, Swedes, Poles, Bohemians, and Germans.

Boscobel

Boscobel got its name from a farmer who used to have two cows, and one was Boss and one was Belle.

And every night he would go out and call his cows: "Come Boss, come Belle. Come Boss, come Belle."

And hence it got its name.[237]

In America's dairyland, "Boss" or "Bossy" is a generic cow name.

Good Enough Teacher

The settlers built a schoolhouse. And the first teacher they hired, that taught the first year, there was one homesteader just didn't think that he was good enough teacher. And the other members of the board thought he was all right. And they argued with the fellow that was dissatisfied that the teacher was all right, there was no...it wasn't necessary to look for a new teacher.

And the one that was dissatisfied said, "Well, you know, I want my boy to be lawyer."

And the other one spoke up and said, "Well, when your boy be lawyer, my bull will be giving milk."

That's all of that.[238]

School board wrangles, common today, extend to the pioneer era—although the rural metaphors of debate have all but vanished, to be replaced by the current newspeak "educationese."

You and the Lord

In the early days, there was a settler settled out in the hardscrabble country. Oh, it was rocky and tough and rough. And as the country opened up, there was a minister was going to build a church out in the open. And the settlers were scarce.

So to get some money, he had to visit them all. And he went away out in hardscrabble to visit this settler out there. And the fellow that settled in the hardscrabble had worked hard and cleared up quite a nice farm. And the minister was congratulating him on how well he done.

He said, "You and the Lord has done a wonderful job in here."

"Yes, but you ought to have seen it when God had it alone."[239a]

A minister came to see a Norwegian farmer, and he was trying to raise money for the church. So he said, "My you have a nice farm here—you and the Lord. You have some nice cows here—you and the Lord." Oh it went on like that.

And finally the Norwegian farmer couldn't stand it any longer, so he said, "But you should have seen what it was like when the Lord had it by himself."[239b]

Numerous rural versions across the United States have been recorded. The first teller heard this story around 1910.

The Church Bell

They had a church meeting to see about buying a bell. They argued about it, and the bells were awfully expensive.

One of the fellows says, "Well, we got steam heat in the balcony, we got steam heat in the choir room, we got steam heat in the basement. Why don't we get a steam whistle?"[240]

The bells of Upper Midwestern churches were very expensive. Timber, stone, and labor were abundant locally and provided by parishioners, but bells were made outside the region and required scarce cash. The records of pioneer churches are filled with accounts of "how we got our bell".

Liturgical Humidity

And then they had a church in the area here, and that's fairly recent. And in the wintertime, they had to heat it up. Real cold outside. And the air would get so dry in the there, and everybody would be coughing and hacking, which complicated things in the service. So finally, the church board decided they'd put in a humidifier to see if that'd help.

So they had a humidifier put in for a couple weeks. And at the end of the service, the people were marching out, and old Ole Johnson was walking out and shook hands with the minister. And the minister asked him if he noticed any improvements since they put in the humidifier.

"Yah," he says, "I sure do," he says, "I don't think the sermon is as dry as it used to be."[241]

Saying Grace

And then there was a [Swedish] Baptist minister. And he invited me to dinner at his house one day, but he said the grace so long that even the potatoes closed their eyes.

Well, that's just a few things that happened in the country.[242]

While southern WASP preachers are noted for their dramatic, highly emotional sermon style, their northern Scandinavian counterparts have been distinguished, at least in jokes, by their scholarly reserve.

The Adulterer's Confession

A man went to the priest to confess.
"What are your sins?"
"Well, I stole."
"Well, what did you steal?"
"I stole a ham."
"What did you do with it?"

This fellow was wondering about all the questions, but the priest was the priest, so he answered. "I hid it under the bridge, under that railroad bridge that goes out toward the ore docks."

"Well, you just leave that ham there, and say three Our Fathers for your penance."

So the guy did what the priest told him. But he got to wondering, why should that ham go to waste? He went back to find it, but it was gone. That priest took it.

Next time he had to go to confession:

"What are your sins?"

"Father, I'm guilty of adultery."

"Well, who did you sin with?"

But he remembered that ham. "I'm not going to tell you!" [Pause.] He figured that priest would go visit her too.[243]

Deaf Penitents

There was a Catholic priest, and he had a janitor. And the Catholic priest, he was visiting this janitor's wife. And this janitor, he broke in the basement of the priest, and he took some cabbage, some sauerkraut, out of the barrel, and a ham, and something else. And then this janitor went to this priest, and he was confessing, but he didn't confess that he stole the ham out of the barrel or the cabbage.

And the priest knew about it. And the janitor didn't confess on that. And the priest said, "Well, how about breaking into my basement and taking out the ham and the cabbage?"

And this guy says, "I can't hear you." But he says, "Father, you come where I am, and I'll go where you are." So they agreed. The priest got out from where he was, and he went where that janitor was, where he was confessing. And when they changed themselves, then this janitor asked—as a priest, see—"Now, who's been going and making love with my wife?""

The priest says, "I can't hear you."

So the janitor says again, "Who's been visiting my wife and making love?"

"I don't hear you." He says, "For sure, you can't hear over here. For sure, you can't hear over here."[244]

These stories are common in eastern European folklore. Although a different tale from Text 243, AT Type 1792, "The Stingy Parson and the Slaughtered Pig," involves a pork-craving priest. Tales centered around lust and the confessional were also common, as is the case in the second story recorded here. Text 244 was one of several priest/janitor/confessional tales in this teller's repertoire and was derived from old-country priest/sacristan or coachman/trickster cycles. It follows AT Type 1777A, "I Can't Hear You," motif X44.1.1.

Volunteer Firefighters

There was a big fire south of Plover here. They called up the Plover Fire Department, you know. And the Plover Fire Department come roaring out there, you know, and they looked. And here this woods was burning pretty bad.

And this guy says, "I give you ten thousand bucks if you put this fire out, 'cause I got a big woods there. I want to save that timber."

They looked at him. They said, "Aww, nooo, not us guys."

So he called up Peterson down there. He come roaring out there with his fire truck. Yeah, he looked at it, you know. He said, "Oh, Jesus, not me."

Ten-thousand-dollar reward. So they called up the Polonia Fire Department. They come out there: *ding-ding-ding-ding-ding-ding*, right into the fire there. *Ppssschewww* [imitates the sound of spraying hoses]. They come out of there all burnt up and smoky and their eyelashes burnt and their hair singed and everything.

So the farmer walks out to them with a check, and he says, "Boy," he says, "that was a pretty good job. Here's your ten-thousand-dollar check." He says, "What are you going to do with the money?"

Chief says, "First thing we're going to do is get the brakes fixed on the truck."[245]

Jokes about volunteer fire departments are common in American folklore. The teller places this joke in Plover, the site for his telling, but the joke really concerns Portage County's major ethnic groups, Norwegians and Poles.

Red Norwick on Patrol

Now this supposedly was true. You remember they always had a fourth of July parade. And Red [Norwick] was in charge, the morning of the parade, to be sure by ten o'clock, when the parade was started, the main street was cleared of traffic.

So they had signs, whatever, and Red would go up and down the street and tell all the people, "Look, you've got to have your vehicle here off the street by ten o'clock, cause the parade's coming by." And he comes along about where? You remember, the Pal Lunch was somewhere there along the main street. Right about there, it was. This apparently really happened. Anyway, this guy is there, and his car hasn't moved.

And so Red comes up to him, and he says, "Hey, mister," he says, "you got to get this car out of here. This is parade day, Fourth of July. You're way past time. There's no other cars up and down here."

"Well," the guy says, "I was just leaving. I don't know that it's such a big hurry. I can get out of here okay."

And Red looks down there, and he says, "Where you from?"

The guy says, "I'm from Dallas."

"Vell, vat in t' hell are you doin' vit a Texas license?"[246]

Red Tracks a Thief

You know that story, don't you? About how Red was on his beat patrolling Main Street? Well, he's going along, and all of a sudden this merchant runs out. And he looks up and down the street, and he sees Red.

And he says, "Oh, Red," he said, "Severson just was in here, and he stole a can of tobacco from me, and I think he took off south. And I lost sight of him, but he's ducked into one of the other places here."

So Red is going down the pike, stopping in. "Have you seen Ole Severson?"

And he finally—Severson—meantime, had run into Otto Shudlik's harness shop, and he says, "Otto, you got to hide me," he says. "Red's after me."

"Well," Otto says, "I don't have any... Well," he says, "I do. Jump in the corner over there, and I'll throw this pile of leather scraps over you." So Severson jumps in the corner, and Otto throws the stuff over him.

Couple minutes later, old Red comes puffing in the doorway. And he says, "I think maybe Severson is in here."

"Ah," Otto says, "he was in here, but he run right through and run right out the back door."

And old Red is taking out his handkerchief, and he's wiping his brow and puffing. And he looks around the corner, and he sees that pile of leather, and he says to Otto, "What's in there?"

"Oh," Otto says, "nothing but a pile of bells." So Red went over, and he give her a kick.

And he [Severson] says, "Yingle, yingle, yingle."[247]

Shooting Schlick's Watch

Old [Red] Norwick was talking to brother Jim. Jim was quite a kidder, you know.

And he said, "What do you use that revolver for?"

And Red says, "Well, sometimes in self defense and sometimes not."

"Well," he says, "can you hit anything with that?"

He says, "Oh yes."

And Schlick had one of them big watches hanging out in front, you know, about two foot square. "Could you hit that, Red?"

"Oh, yah. But," he said, "not every time."[248]

Hobo in a Freight Car

You know, you've heard about the time he went up to get the hobo out of the car? They said there was a hobo in one of the freight cars, and Red went out there.

And he said, "If you're in there, come out. If you ain't, why say so."[249]

Red in the Hobo Jungle

Another time, he shot, you know—talking about whether he [Red Norwick] could hit Schlick's clock or not. They had a hobo jungle up north of what later was the brewery, but was a factory.

Yeah, there was a grove of white pine trees.

There was apparently a gathering of hoboes, back in the Depression days. And whether they were drunk or causing a disturbance, I'm not sure, but somebody complained, and Red went up there and stepped out of the squad car. And he goes up and approaches them. And they've got a big kettle and they're making a lot of stew.

And he figured, well, he'd show them. And he whipped out his forty-five and he just shot a big hole right in the stew pot.

Turned on his heel and took off.[250]

These five stories told in sequence by two tellers are part of the Red Norwick cycle. Olaus "Red" Norwick was a police officer in Rice Lake from 1912 through the 1920s. He had red hair in his youth and a fiery red face ever after.

A Hobo's Grammar

This hobo stopped at the back door of a fashionable house, and he asked for a handout.

The lady of the house said, "Young man, do you see that pile of wood that needs sawing?"

He says, "Yah, lady, I seen it."

She said, "Young man, your English is terrible. You should have said, 'Yes, lady, I saw it.'"

"Well," he says, "I tell you, lady, you saw me see it, but you ain't seen me saw it."[251]

The ever-present appetite, aversion to work, and quick wit of the classic hobo combine in this telling.

Charlie Ferg at the Revival

Charlie [Ferguson] had been over to Yuba, had a few too many, and went over the hill to Woodstock, a little town that had revival meetings. At the revival meeting, he was standing at a tent pole, and he got a crying jag on. He started to cry. And he cried. And the minister thought he had got to Charlie, and he went running down there to Charlie.

"Charlie, Charlie," he says, "have you found the Lord?"

Charlie wiped the tears out of his eyes, and he said, "No, I didn't know he was lost."[252a]

He [Charlie Ferguson] was going down the road one evening, and they was having a camp meeting and he stopped.

They said, "Did you find Jesus?"

And he looked up, and he says, "Why, find Jesus? I didn't know he was lost!"[252b]

Ferg's literal interpretation of "found," with its implication that Jesus is perhaps some neighbor who is lost, resembles AT Type 1833E, "God Died For You," motif J1788.4, in which a traveling preacher asks a rustic if he or she knows "God died for you." The response is, "We don't get the paper way out here."

To Work for Jesus

Then there was the time Charlie wandered into a revival meeting. He walked up to the front row and sat down.

The minister looked down at him and said, "My friend, how would you like to work for Jesus?"

"Well," answered Charlie, "I wish I'd a-knowed. I just hired out to Ham Deetz."[253]

Another Charlie Ferg joke, this one has variants in which a Swede and a Scandinavian reply to a preacher's solicitation.

For Jesus' Sake

Years ago, they had the revival meetings out in the groves. Sometimes they'd have a tent; sometimes it was just seats set up. And this one was on Fancy Creek. And the meeting was in progress. They were having communion when Charlie and his friend came by in their horse and buggy and they stopped. And they were using the common cup and passing it around.

And the minister kept saying, "Take a little sup for Jesus' sake. Just a little sup for Jesus' sake."

So Charlie took a sup and he said, "My! I could take a whole quart of this for Jesus' sake."[254a]

And the time he [Charlie Ferguson] staggered into the Methodist Church while they were having communion. He made his unsteady way up to the railing and knelt down. The minister gave him a cup—what else could he do?

Well, Charlie tossed it off in a gulp and banged the cup down on the railing and said, "Fill 'er up again, Reverend. I love Jesus." [254b]

Burying John Barleycorn

When Richland Center voted to go dry, some folks had quite a celebration. Charlie was walking down the street hearing all them church bells ringing.

So he went and opened the door to the Presbyterian church and stuck his head in. Seeing the preacher up there, he says, "What are the bells for? Are you burying somebody?"

The preacher, wanting to play a joke, says, "Yeah. Haven't you heard. We're burying John Barleycorn today."

"I know that," says Charlie, "but I didn't know he was a Presbyterian."[255]

In the first telling, Ferg's thirst for wine and not the "blood of Christ" is not only blasphemous but an affront to his community's temperance. The second telling sustains the anti-temperance theme. "John Barleycorn" is a British personification of grain alcohol or "spirits."

Baptism in the River

Another time he [Charlie Ferguson] happened along when the Baptists were having a baptism in the river.

The minister was standing out there in the water facing the people on the bank, and he lifted up his arms heavenward and cried, "Lord, Lord, save this sinner."

And Charlie says, "This ain't the Lord, Reverend. It's me, Charlie Ferg."[256]

In a related story, a sinner plunged in the river claims to have seen Jesus and all the angels at the bottom of the river. His companion sees only a big mud turtle.

Charlie Fools the Preacher

The preacher wanted to buy a cow. He got to looking around. Someone told Charlie that the preacher wanted to buy a cow, and he says, "We told the preacher he ought to look out for you. You might beat him."

And he says, 'There ain't no one can beat me on a cow.'"

And Charlie says, "Send him up." So he saw the preacher and told him to come up on a certain night.

So that night came, about three nights afterward, and the preacher wanted to look at the cows, and he took him out and showed him all of his cows. The preacher says, "I want to milk that cow."

And Charlie says, "I'd want you to milk her. I wouldn't want you to buy a cow without milking her."

So he goes and milks the cow, and she give about a twelve-quart pail full of milk. Boy! He wanted to know what Charlie wanted for her and bought her right off and took her home.

A couple of days afterwards, the preacher saw Charlie. "Say," he says, "That cow won't give so much milk. What's wrong?"

Charlie says, "Oh, you milk her too often." He hadn't milked her for about three days before the preacher'd milked her.[257]

A Good Milker

He [Charlie Ferguson] lived down there right by the fair grounds, and he had several cows there, and he'd been selling them. This guy wanted to buy a cow, and he looked her over.

He asked, "How much did she give?"

Charlie says, "Well, I tell you, she runs over a twelve-quart pail every night and morning."

Well, golly, if she gave that much, he wanted her. But when he took her home, why she didn't give very much. He come back and jumped on Charlie about it. He says, "You said that cow'll run over a twelve-quart pail every night and morning."

He said, "I did. That's right. Why?"

"Why!" he says. "Well, she won't give that much for me."

He says, "I didn't say she give that much. I said she'd run over a twelve-quart pail. There's the pail right over there. Every night and morning, she goes through that gate, and she runs over that pail, every night and morning." [258]

Charlie's Cows

One time Charlie had a couple of cows to sell, and the buyer asked how old they were.

"Nine and eleven," says Charlie.

Well, the fellow thought the price was fair enough for cows of that age, so he bought them. Next day he came back spitting mad. "I thought you said those cows were nine and eleven. I showed them to the vet, and he said by the looks of their teeth, they're twenty if they're a day."

"That's just what I told you," said Charlie. "Nine and eleven. And that makes twenty." [259]

Trading Horses

Charlie traded horses with a man one night. The man asked him if the horse had any bad habits.

Said Charlie, "No, he hasn't. He don't look too good, but he's an awful good horse."

The next day the man brought the horse back and said, "This horse you traded me last night is blind."

Charlie said, "I told you that horse didn't look very good." [260]

Knot Maple

The preacher one time wanted some hard maple wood, some knot-maple. And someone told him, well, "Charlie Ferg's out there selling a little wood. You might get some from him." He was living out on Horse Creek then. So he went to see Charlie and asked if he could get some knot-maple.

So Charlie says, "Sure, I'll bring you in a load." So he brought him in a load of wood.

When the preacher got in there with it, it wouldn't hold a fire like he thought it ought to. So he asked Charlie about it. He said, "Charlie, that wood's not maple."

And Charlie says, "That's right. I thought that was what you wanted. Not maple." It was basswood.[261]

Disrupter of church doings, Ferg also proves a trickster in these five tellings of clever trades, most of which rely on Ferg's deception through adherence to an unexpected double meaning. His dupe is frequently the preacher, a worthy foe since the preachers of folklore are often cunning, proud, and greedy.

Charlie Goes Fishing

Charlie was fishing before the season opened. A fellow came walking up the stream.

He says, "How you doing?"

Charlie says, "Never had such fishing before. They're really biting today."

The other fellow says, "You know who I am?"

And Charlie says, "No. Who are you?"

He says, "I'm the game warden."

Charlie says, "Do you know who I am?"

Fellow says, "No."

And Charlie says, "I'm the biggest damn liar in Richland County."[262]

Sometimes told about hunting as well as fishing, this is perhaps the most widespread game warden/sportsman tale in American oral tradition. Baughman offers motif J1155.1.1*(b) and cites versions from Alabama, Arizona, Indiana, New York, Kentucky, and Texas.

Charlie Ain't Fishing

There's another one. I don't know if it was Charlie or not, but it could have been.

This fellow was walking up a stream with his fishing gear and everything, and along comes the warden. He says, "Let me see your fishing license."

Charlie says, "I ain't fishing."

The warden kept following him, and every little while he would say, "You better let me see your license."

But Charlie didn't pay any attention.

Finally, after they'd been walking about forty-five minutes or an hour, he gets to where he wants to be, pulls out his license, and shows it to the warden, and says, "Now, I'm fishing."[263]

See Text 113 and its note for a related telling in which a licensed fisherman leads a warden on.

Tavern Fisticuffs

And one time they were having a fight up in a tavern, and they were really going at it.

So Charlie stood up and says, "Count me in."

And just about that time, when he says that, this fellow clips him right on the chin hard, and while he's falling down to the floor, he says, "Count me out."[264]

In some versions, this incident is set in Yuba, a "Bohemy" town where the local Czech Catholics' drinking and dancing scandalized Protestant Anglos.

On an Old Sow's Back

And this one I'll tell you I heard about Charlie Ferguson. He lived up in Cherry Valley. And when we were young, they used to drive pigs to market, just drive them through the street, you know.

One day, they were driving them to market, and they came down through Bloom City. And just as he got into Bloom City, old Charlie ran and jumped on an old sow's back and he said:

Here's Charlie Ferg, the son of Aunt Sally,
Riding an old sow down Pleasant Valley.[265]

Although told as true, this telling may well be related to AT Type 1838, "The Hog in Church," in which a hog locked by mistake in a church runs through the parson's legs and carries him among the congregation.

Charlie Pursued

I heard a lot of stories about Charlie. One funny one is that he was running around the barn with the bull chasing him, and he was just making the corner of the barn each time.

And he came around the corner, and he hollered at the wife, "Hurry, hurry, Miranda," he says, "my insurance is on the clock shelf. This is my last time around."[266]

The rustic barnyard and the genteel parlor with its clock shelf are juxtaposed in this obvious fiction as the bumptious Ferg, whose real wife was named Lelah, calls out to some figure of the teller's imagination.

At the Country Store

Ole and I got our supplies that summer of 1888 at Tom Pratt's store at Superior Junction [now Trego]. That was the only store there at that time. Tom Pratt was a big man, over six feet tall, with powerful shoulders and arms, sandy hair, and blue eyes. He was a scientific fighter. He never picked a fight, but he never avoided one. He never allowed any rough stuff or dirty talk around his store. On occasion, he waded in and put an end to several drunken brawls. The Indians all had great respect for him.

Tom had a great sense of humor and a great fund of stories. I remember one he told about Simon Bartosic, an early settler at Superior Junction.

He said Simon had some squaw make him a pair of buckskin pants. He wore them for years. Buckskin stretches when wet. Tom said that every time Simon's pants got wet, Simon cut enough off the bottom to make himself a pair of mittens.[267]

Tall tales about stretched buckskin have been common on the American frontier. The mittens alluded to would have been "chopper mitts"—leather over-mittens with woolen liners.

Flour-Sack Underwear

A second story he told was about the woman camp cook. In the early pioneer days, the women, being short of material for clothes, sometimes made their underthings of flour sacks.

He said a teamster was taking a woman cook out to camp one winter. She tumbled out of the sleigh headfirst into the snow. Her dresses flew up, and the delighted teamster read on one side of her underpants, "Pillsbury's Best," and on the other side, "Pride of the West."[268]

Although flour-sack underwear and women camp cooks were common enough, the head-first dive, precisely positioned twin brand names, double entendre, and rhyme suggest this was a tale that got around.

The Iron River Travelers

Well, another thing them guys [from Iron River, Michigan] used to do when they took a trip in their car—they went down to Green Bay—they'd change the oil and the water in the radiator. And they'd change the air in their tires. They thought that was the thing to do—put fresh air in their tires.[269]

This telling was part of a cycle regarding rustic loggers and backwoodsmen from Iron River, Michigan; see also Texts 170 and 184.

Filling Station Sunday

Years ago we had, my dad had, a filling station and he sold farm machinery and things of that nature. Lot of times we used to work on Sundays. We was working there on a Sunday afternoon. And normally the place would be closed, but the front door was unlocked, it was just open.

Neighbor came running in. And my dad's name is Rollie. Neighbor fellow came in, and he says, "Rollie, Rollie, Rollie, come quick, come on quick!" He says, "The old man hung himself." So we dropped what we was doing, and we went quickly with him and run way over to their place.

Dad says, "Did you cut him down?"

"No," he says, "he wasn't dead yet."[270]

Directions to Some Place

Same filling station. This was years ago. I heard my dad tell this many a time, and I thought it was pretty good.

This guy couldn't talk very good. He stuttered, and he had an awful time coming out with something. He happened to be at the station one day, and a car drove up and they wanted to know directions to some-place. He started out: "Y-y-y-y... w-w-w-w... f-f-f-first... you can get there faster than I can tell you."[271]

The situation involving lost (usually urban) drivers asking directions of some ruralite is a jocular classic. In more commonly reported parallels, the local answers something like "you can't get there from here"; see Baughman motif J1648.

Barroom Gossip

One little story that I used to like to tell about: Frenchman buddy of mine, he was a very good lumberjack friend of mine, he used to come into my business establishment, my barroom.

And he said he had a hired man so darn slow that he couldn't even stop fast. [272]

Like the filling station and the blacksmith shop before it, the small town tavern was a place for facetious banter.

Drunks on the Street

We were discussing taverns in and around Richland Center—a dry town. And Milford mentioned that you see very few drunks on the street.

We had a fellow here in town—I'll omit the name to protect the innocent—that was always getting himself pretty well twisted out of shape. He was down to Madison one time, and he stopped in at a few bars on State Street. And he got pretty tipsy. And he walked out of the bar, and he started walking down State Street, and he was weaving from the buildings to the curb and back and forth.

A cop came along and tapped him on the shoulder. He says, "Say mister, you're carrying quite a load there, aren't you?"

He looked around. He says, "Yes, sir. Yes, sir, officer. I really should have made two trips."[273]

Madison is regarded as a "wild" and "radical" city throughout much of rural and small town Wisconsin, and State Street, a mall stretching from the University of Wisconsin campus to the State Capitol, is the city's deviant heart.

Lights on the Brewery

I'm going to tell about a couple of Irish friends I had, Leo and Charlie. They'd been indulging quite a bit in home brew. No—it was the brewery then. And they were coming home.

And he said, "We might as well go, because we can't drink it all that they make anyway." And they come along, and there were lights on the brewery.

And Charlie says, "No, but we got them working nights."[274a]

Jim Flynn, after he quit drinking—he drank for about thirty years, steady, like two, three quarts a day, brandy, he drank Christian Brothers.

And he says when he was about eighteen, his old man took him down to wherever the Christian Brothers factory is down in California. Stood him up on a hill and told him, "Jim, you'll never drink them dry."

He says, "He was right." He says, "I never drank them dry, but I got them sons-of-bitches going three shifts."[274b]

Christian Brothers

Another thing Flynn always used to say, he says: "I quit drinking a few years ago. And when I quit, they laid three monks off at the Christian Brothers factory."[275]

Upper Midwesterners have consistently led the nation in per capita brandy consumption, and they are among the leading beer drinkers. Although there are no major distilleries in the region, breweries abound. Fifty years ago, nearly every town with a population of more than five thousand had a brewery.

The Tavern Business

When I was running Konkolville there, one night there was a couple of women come in there, and they was drinking highballs and they was getting kind of rough and tough there.

And I told them, I said, "Now, look, ladies, I'm in business here. My name is Peter. And I don't want you to get Peter sore, because there's nobody going to do any business with a sore Peter."[276]

Popular joke books link this text to the adage about robbing Peter to pay Paul: "one of these days Peter's gonna get sore, and what the hell you gonna do with a sore Peter?" (For source, see the note accompanying this text.)

Drinking Highballs

And another night, there was some of them drinking highballs, and they was getting pretty well polluted.

And pretty soon one of them says, "You know, a couple more of these, and I'm going to begin to feel it."

The other one says, "Well, a couple more of these, and I don't give a damn who feels it."[277]

This joke was strung together with the one preceding.

Barn Dance Sleigh Rides

We used to go on sleigh rides out east of town to barn dances, in the wintertime. People would sit on bales of hay and wrap themselves up in blankets.

Anyway, they'd tell this story about a bald fellow, John. His head would get cold, so he'd put a wig on. And what with that sleigh bumping over drifts and going around corners, his wig fell off. He went burrowing around for it in the hay, and somehow his hand went between Eleanor's legs.

"That's it, John, that's it."

"That ain't it at all. Mine was new, this one's old: it's got a hole in it."[278]

John and Eleanor are the teller's standard Anglo–American couple; they appear alongside Ole and Lena in Text 92.

Uncle Henry's Picture

Well, this couple, you know, they had, they come from Canada here, and they never saw a mirror in their life. So his uncle died in Canada, and he went to the funeral.

And he was shopping through town after the funeral. And he picked up a picture of his Uncle Henry. At least he thought it was. Instead it was a mirror. And he brought it home.

And he was showing his wife the picture he brought of Uncle Henry. She looked. She said, "Uncle Henry, hell. That's a picture of some whore you had in Canada."[279]

This text is AT Type 1336A, "Man Does Not Recognize His Own Reflection in the Water (Mirror)," motif J1791.7. The tale is known in Chinese, English, Finnish, Greek, Hawaiian, Indian, Indonesian, and Korean versions.

During the Depression

During the Depression, there was a couple ladies met in the Penney's store down there, and they were talking about the Depression.

And one of them piped up and said, "My, my, isn't that terrible—this Depression coming on top of all these hard times."[280]

"Hard times," of course, was the vernacular term, while "depression," like "recession," was coined by economic theorists.

The Frozen Horse

One morning, I don't know how cold it was, but the mercury dropped completely out of the thermometer.

I couldn't start the car, so I decided to take the horse out of the barn and give the car a tow with the horse and pull it and see if it would start. But the foolish horse, when he stepped out of the barn, he took a leak. And that immediately froze into an icicle and froze him to the ground, so I had to run to the woodpile.

Grabbed a chopping block and chopped him loose and put him back in.[281]

For the first part of the tall tale, Baughman offers motif X1606.2.2*, "Temperature drops so rapidly that mercury knocks the bottom out of the thermometer." Tales of frozen urine are fairly common in the Upper Midwest: animals or humans "piss ice cubes," or a logger topping a pine slides to earth on his frozen urine. In a related motif, X1606.2.4*, "Wild fowl are frozen into lake by quick, hard freeze."

Nels Bennett's Dog

We used to just figure on Nels coming over about every other Sunday forenoon. And we enjoyed his stories, too, and he told some good ones. I remember one time, we had a young collie dog there.

Nels says, "Do you think that dog's going to be any good?"

I says, "Oh, I don't know—pretty mischievous pup."

"Well," he says, "I can take that pup and really train him." He said, "I had a dog one time. It just happened I opened the big barn door, and I still had a ladder up there. Why, that dog of mine, I could just say 'Climb that ladder', and the dog would go right up that ladder. I'd say 'Come down the ladder', and he'd turn around and come right down head first."[282]

Bennett's Little Team

And he used to tell about all the horses, pulling teams he had. "One time," he said, "we was logging down in the bottom." Says, "They had a couple big teams hooked on to them logs, big ellum logs, and they couldn't pull nothing. I took my little team down there and hooked it on. Why," he said, "it just pulled the heart right out of them ellum logs."[283]

Deer Wrestling

He said that shortly after he bought that place down by the river, he didn't have any fresh meat for a while. He said he went back up on the ridge there. He told Lizzie he'd bring her some meat pretty soon. Then he climbed up in a tree.

And he says, "Pretty soon a big buck deer come walking along under the tree." He said, "I just dropped down on his back and took hold of his horns and steered him right down to the ground and cut his throat."[284]

The Snake-Bit Dump Rake

Nels used to tell me when he come down that he had a dump rake tongue down there that a rattlesnake bit. It swelled up so that he couldn't get the neck yoke off. That snake reared up and bit that tongue so that when he got back to the house, he couldn't get the neck yoke off.[285]

These four tales were all from the same teller. They concern Nels Bennett, a Richland County farmer. (See notes to each text for motifs and types.)

Hunters and Fishers

Locals and travelers who "Escape To Wisconsin," experience Minnesota's "10,000 Lakes," and "Say Yah To Da U.P." know the truth of slogans on license plates and bumperstickers. The Upper Midwest is a region where woods, waters, wildlife, hunting, and fishing abound.

In these tales, those who leave civilization risk confrontations with rolling hoopsnakes, gargantuan mosquitoes (the alleged "state bird" of Michigan, Minnesota, and Wisconsin), snarling wildcats, and fierce bears. Locals get a perverse pleasure out of inflating or inventing their coexistence with dangerous beasts, while they enjoy exaggerating the terrors of nature for gullible tourists. When not prey themselves, Upper Midwesterners hunt squirrels, ducks, and deer, or cast lines in hope of landing some game fish: trout, walleye, or muskellunge.

Since game laws impose numerical and temporal restrictions, deer hunting season and the "opening days" for catching various species of fish are festive events, closely monitored by game wardens. But these "brush cops," few in number, are often outwitted by poachers in everyday life, and even more so in jokes.

The Hoop Snake

He [a fellow in Muscoda] says these black snakes in this area has got a pointed tail, real sharp. And he says this tail is deadly poison. What they'll do, he says, if they can ever hit you with that tail, you're dead.

So, he says, him and the old man was just walking along with the ax, and, he says, all at once the old man says, "Throw yourself down." So they both did instantly. And sure enough, along came one of these black snakes, and he had his tail in his mouth, coming down the hill like a big [hands make hoop shape]. And when they ducked, this black snake let go of his tail, and he just missed both of them, and he hit a big oak tree. Just hit it, and he drove his tail right in the oak tree. And there that snake was trying to get out of there, but there was no way he could do it.

So the boy then, he jumped up with his ax. He said, "I'm going to kill it right now."

The old man says, "No, no. Don't do that." He says, "Let him die right there. It's good for him. It's just what he deserves. Just let him suffer there and die." So they went on with their wood cutting.

And he says the next day—now this is really something—the next day they went back through there. And he said during the night, the snake had died. But he said every leaf and everything fell off that tree. Now that was really something.[286]

Tales of hoop snakes have been told for at least two centuries in backwoods America. The story follows Baughman motifs X1321.3.1, "Snake takes its tail in its mouth and rolls like a hoop toward its victim"; B765.1(aa), "Snake rolls at person or object, strikes it with fangs in full force of momentum"; and X1321.3.1.2*, "Snake strikes tree or vine, causes it to wither and die."

Big Mosquitoes

A friend of mine returned from Eagle River and was telling me a story about the mosquitoes. He said his friend Jack was sleeping out in the tent, and he left the zipper open.

And two mosquitoes slipped into the tent, and they said, one said to the other, "Shall we eat him here or take him outside?"

The other mosquito said, "No, we better eat him here. The big ones will take him away from us out there."[287]

Fierce mosquitoes have long been a part of folklore in the Upper Midwest, where T-shirts and postcards sometimes facetiously dub the insect as Michigan's, Minnesota's, or Wisconsin's "state bird."

Bad Mosquitoes

Everybody was telling how bad the mosquitoes were. Well, I tell them, you haven't seen nothing.

I said I was out working, and they came at me so bad, I covered myself all up and they were cutting my head all the time. So I put my hard hat on. I thought, I'll fix 'em.

So they stung right through the hard hat. They were getting at me anyways. But I had a little hammer in my pocket, and I take the hard hat off. And I clinched them stingers all over. Put the hat back on.

Okay, didn't take long, they come thicker than ever. I do the same thing. I did that about four or five times. Had 'em all clinched over. And I thought, well, I got you. And I strapped my helmet on, and I thought, well, I'm all set now.

And all of a sudden they decided to leave. They all start flying and here I was going, starting to raise up, going in the air.

So I quick and unlatched my helmet, and away they went with the hard hat.[288]

This tall tale combines two subtypes of AT Type 1960M, "The Great Insect": Type 1960M1 (motif X1286.1.4), "Large mosquitoes fly off with kettle," with the modern construction worker's hard hat replacing the old cast metal cook pot, and Type 1960M2 (motif X1286.1.5), "Large mosquitoes carry off men or animals." Such tales are widespread throughout the United States and have been reported in earlier Michigan and Wisconsin versions.

Mosquitoes on a Windfall

I was talking to that one big German, big Hank. And he was telling, we were hollering—about the mosquitoes up there by Ned Lake.

And he said, "Yah," he said, "I just come out of the swamp over there," he said. "I heard something flapping around there," he says, "and there was a big old buck mosquito standing flat-footed on a pine windfall screwing a shitepoke."[289]

There are other versions in the region that involve an insect-bird hybrid. "Shitepoke" is a regional term for a species of heron that feeds by poking its long beak in the muck or "shite" (shit) of swamps. Since mosquitoes are likewise long-beaked swamp dwellers and are facetiously dubbed "birds," such hybrids make humorous sense.

Cow Killers

Then he said, that same German, he was telling about, he said he was down on a farm in Wisconsin working in the summertime.

And he said he heard the cow bell ringing out there. He went outside there. And there was the cow laying dead.

Mosquito had sucked all the blood out of the cow, and he was standing on the fence post ringing the cow bell to try to get the calf to come out of the barn.[290]

Versions of this tale are cited from Illinois, New Jersey, and other parts of the American South, particularly Arkansas. Baughman provides motif X1286.2.1.1*, "Mosquitoes eat cow, ring bell to call calf."

Kitten on a Limb

Rodney always had a real good story.

One day he was telling me, "You know," he said, "there was these people going through the woods, and they saw a nice kitten out on a limb. And they looked at each other," he said, "and 'gee, it's a shame for a nice kitten like that to be alone out in the woods.' And they didn't realize it was a wildcat.

"And the fellow said, finally he said, 'Well, I'll go up there and get him. We'll take him home with us.' So he crawled way out on the limb. And down came the limb. And down came the cat. And down came the man. They were going around and around."

Rodney says: "Fellow went up. 'Shall I help you hold him?'

"'No. Help me let him go.'"[291]

This one matches Baughman motif X584.3*, "Boy catches animal, calls for help to turn the animal loose," with versions reported from only North Carolina and Florida.

Barehanded Bear Hunter

One time, a fellow from Illinois come up, and Paul [Fournier] was his hunting guide. So in the morning, Paul got out of the cabin and decided he'd go out and look over the land. He told the man to pay attention, and he'd try to drive some bears back.

So Paul found a bear out in the woods, and he got in its way and made it mad. It chased him, and he was running toward the cabin. But he fell down, and the bear ran right past him and through the cabin door.

Paul jumped up, slammed the door, and hollered inside, "Skin that one, and I'll be back with another."[292a]

These guys were hunting. They were in the hunting shack and this guy was bragging. He said, "I can go out and get a bear, and I don't even need a gun."

Once he made that remark, you know, the guys kind of challenged him to that. So the following morning, they said, "Well, go get that bear like you said last night."

So the guy couldn't very well back out. So he goes out in the woods, scareder than hell, you know, without a gun. Sure enough, he runs across a bear. The bear took off after him, and he started running for the cottage and hollering, "Open the door, open the door." Just as he got to the steps, he tripped. And with the momentum the bear had, he went right up over him and into the cottage, see.

And he got up, he closed the door, and said, "Skin him out. I'll see if I can get another one."[292b]

Boasts about hunting are a common pastime in the Upper Midwest, as are accounts of panic and its consequences. The term "buck fever" refers to deer hunters who freeze up, but the phenomenon likewise applies to bears.

One-Pipe S'otgun

Well, you see, I was going in for that walk in the woods the other day. And I had that one-pipe s'otgun with me. It wasn't the two-pipe s'otgun; it was that one-pipe s'otgun. You know? Yah, I guess you know. And I was walking down the two-track road in the woods. And I look behind me. And here's a heck of a big black bear. And he's coming right at me. But I wasn't scared. But I thought what the heck, and so I climbed up that tree. And so I looked down. And here's that bear, he's climbing up that tree too. I wasn't scared. But I said, oh what the heck, so I climbed up to the very tippy top of that tree there. And I looked down. And that bear, he's still coming.

Now I wasn't scared. But I thought what the heck, and so stick-ed that one-pipe s'otgun down at him. And I said, "Now, look here, Mr. Bear. You better go away, or I'm going to put t'is goddarn s'otgun right in your mout' and blow off the backs of your head." Now that bear, he just kept right on coming, and he opened up his mouth real wide.

I wasn't scared. But I thought what the heck, so I stick-ed that barrel of that one-pipe s'otgun right in his mouth. But before I can pull that trigger, the bear, he bites off that barrel, and he spit it out right in my face. Now, I wasn't scared, but I got so doggone mad, I shit my pants.[293]

Everything the Bear Does

This guy goes out hunting, and he was a rookie at it. He says, "Well, what'll I do if I see a bear?"

He says, "Well, that's nothing. You just do everything the bear does, and he'll leave you alone."

So he gets out in the woods and, sure enough, all of a sudden, out of the brush, comes a bear. The bear goes, *"Rrraaahhh."*

He goes, *"Rrraaahhh,"* right back at the bear.

Bear goes, *"Rrraaahhh, rrraaahhh."*

He goes, *"Rrraaahhh, rrraaahhh."*

Right then Mother Nature calls the bear, and he sat down to start doing it.

"Why, you dirty double-crosser, I did that the first time you went '*rrraaahhh.*'"[294]

These two tellings incorporate Hoffman motif, X716.9, "Defecation through fright," a common element of jokes involving hunters and bears.

Loaded for Bear

Old Gideon came. He come over. Joe King had seen a deer, so he loaded the musket. And one of the other boys seen a deer, so he loaded the musket. And then one of them seen a bear. So they forgot all about the deer.

So they got to talking. They was wondering how they was going to get rid of that. Afraid the old gun would blow up.

Well, they said, "Gideon's coming over. We'll have him unload it first." There was a squirrel down by the creek. And he said, "Uncle Giddy, can you hit that squirrel from here?"

"Oh, sure, sure."

"Give him the gun," he said.

He got the squirrel, but he went pretty near as far as the squirrel did.

Backwards.[295]

Part of the humor of this telling derives from "Uncle Giddy's" misconception that the musket is charged for small game, not "loaded for bear." More exaggerated consequences accompany Baughman motif X1121.4*, "Lie: Recoil of great gun."

Sixteen-Pointer

We were deer hunting and this guy came over. We were parked, remember? We were in the back forty of my brother's farm. And I had a pickup with a little camper on it. And I'd just been downtown and bought me two eight-packs of Point Beer, right. And they call these, "pointers," you know. So this guy comes by.

"You guys got anything?"

I says, "Yeah, I got a sixteen-pointer."

"Christ," he says. He comes flying. "I never seen a buck that big." He says, "Let me see it."

I opened up my camper, and I had two eight-packs there.[296]

Point Beer is brewed in Stevens Point, Wisconsin. Beer drinking is a common part of the annual deer hunt, especially when the hunt occurs on one's own land, where deer haunts are well-known and the deer can be killed with an ease that allows plenty of time for sociability. A buck's "points," of course, are the pointed extrusions of the antlers. A rack of antlers over eight to ten points is considered impressive.

Road Kill

This guy walks into Hardee's, and he says, "Give me a hot beef sandwich." So they brought it over, you know.

And I says, "That's not a hot beef sandwich, that's venison, that's road kill."

The guy says, "How can you tell?"

I says, "There's tire tracks."[297]

Deer are commonly struck by cars on highways in the heavily forested Upper Midwest. Butchering "road kill" is legal outside of the official deer season. The "tire tracks" on the sandwich are marks from a barbecue grill.

Feathered Pedestrians

Here about a week or so ago—the wild geese, they're coming down now. I never had any geese at my place. And last week, there's eight geese come walking down there. And they stopped and rested for a while, and then they took off again.

My idea is, the reason they're walking, is these are the poor class of geese, and they can't afford to pay to fly. So they're walking down south.[298]

During their annual migration, Canadian geese stop over by the thousands in the cornfields and marshlands of southeastern Wisconsin.

Pat and Mike Out Hunting

Pat and Mike were out hunting. This is really, really old. This is one of the first jokes I ever heard. They were out hunting, and Pat—there goes a duck over—and Pat pulls the gun up and *BANG*, down it comes.

Mike looks at Pat and says, "Pat, what the hell did you shoot him for?" He says, "The fall would've killed him."[299]

The stock Irish numskulls take to the marshlands. Baughman offers a pair of motifs: J2214(k), "Boy tells master he has wasted powder and shot; the fall would have killed the bird anyway," and J2259*(e), "Hunter feels bad about death of duck he has shot. His friend tells him: 'That's all right. The fall would have killed it anyway.'"

The Warden's Finger

Guy goes hunting on the Mississippi, shoots a duck, and the game warden is right on top of him. Sticks his fingers up the duck's ass and smells it.

"This duck's from Wisconsin, you got a Wisconsin license?"

Guy's a little surprised, but he says, "Well, yes, I have."

So that's okay. Guy goes back hunting and shoots another duck. And right there's the warden. Does the same thing.

"This duck's from Iowa. Got an Iowa license?"

"Yes, I do."

Then he shoots another duck, and there's the warden again. Does the same thing.

"This duck's from Minnesota. Got a Minnesota license?"

"Yes, I do."

Warden says, "Say, you're pretty well prepared. Where are you from?"

Hunter's pretty damned upset by this time. Says, "You're so smart, stick your finger up my ass and find out for yourself."[300]

This telling, set in popular Upper Mississippi hunting grounds near the Iowa, Minnesota, and Wisconsin borders, was augmented by the teller jabbing his fingers up an imaginary duck's rear and sniffing them.

A Wonderful Hunting Dog

Burns Kaupanger is a great hunter, you know. And he had a wonderful hunting dog. And he went to the lake one day and he shot a duck, and he sent the dog after it, and the dog walked on the water—right straight out—and got the duck. And he thought, well, this I can't believe.

He shot another one, and the dog walked out and got the duck. And he thought, well, I can't tell this to anybody. They'll think I'm drunk or out of my mind.

So he went to town, and he got Spike, Spike Swenson, to come up and see it. So Spike went with him, and Burns shot a duck, and the dog walked out on the water. He looked at Spike; Spike didn't look surprised or anything.

And he said, "Well, what do you think? Didn't you notice something funny about that dog?"

"Well," he said, "I noticed that the darn dog can't swim."[301]

Other versions from Arkansas and Kentucky, none earlier than 1940, have been cited.

Marking the Spot

Urho and Eino, they went fishing. And they were at the lake, you know, in the lake on the boat. They were fishing. Urho was getting good whites right here.

"Urho," Eino says, "We'll mark this place right here on the water, and when we come back here we know where to fish." [302a]

Leo used to go. We used to rent that boat out at Sunset Lake, and you were pulling in the big ones. And I said, "How're we going to make sure we come here tomorrow, get some more, we'll get our limit? Should we line it up with that tree or something?"

Leo says, "Oh, hell no, we'll just put a cross on the bottom of this boat."

And I said, "Well, how do you know we're going to get this boat tomorrow?" [302b]

This is AT Type 1278, motif J1922.1, "Marking the place on the boat," widely reported throughout Eurasia and the United States. Whereas old country numskulls mark the boat at a spot where something fell or was dropped overboard, American fools invariably wish to relocate a good fishing spot— often wondering if they'll get the same boat the next day. Baughman types this variant as 1278A and cites five versions from oral tradition.

The Right Bait

Leo and I were trout fishing up there [in Canada]. Lake Trout. And I had quite a couple. About three-pounders or so. And we were going along, and Leo didn't have a strike.

So I realized it, and I said, "Here," I said, "maybe you should change your bait." So he reeled it in, and I said, "Here it is. But you really don't need any bait for what you're doing." So I says, "You don't need no bait if you're catching nothing."

So then I gave him my bait, put it on his line, and it was still no good. And half an hour went by again, and he still didn't have no fish. And I said, "Well, if you're not going to use that bait, give it back to me." [303]

Although Upper Midwesterners are justly proud of their region's fishing, many make periodic northern treks to the Canadian wilderness, where the fishing is better yet.

Fish of Science

You know what you get when you cross a carp, a walleye, and a Polack?
You get a Cawalski [Kowalski].[304]

Other "hybrid" versions in the Upper Midwest involve experiments by the Department of Natural Resources. See note for details.

Clever Carp

We come out here every once in a while. A few years ago, Ed and I went fishing out on the lake, and I set my wallet on the boat. And we went out, and in a few minutes Ed stood up, and my wallet dropped out of the boat.

Oh, I thought that was gone forever, but all of a sudden a carp came up with it—balancing it up on his nose, you know, like a seal sometimes does. And he threw it to another carp, and they were throwing it back and forth.

That's the first time in my life I ever saw carp-to-carp walleting.[305]

Bottom-feeding carp are common in southern Wisconsin lakes where sports fishers generally regard them as inedible "trash fish" overtaking the habitat—perhaps the inspiration for this veritable carpet of carp. The silly concluding pun on wall-to-wall carpeting is typical of "shaggy dog stories."

Some of the Joke Tellers

Earl Nyholm constructing a traditional wigwam at the Festival of American Folklife,
Washington, D.C., July 1989.
Photo by Lynn Swanson, courtesy of the Michigan Traditional Arts Program, Michigan State University.

Felix Milanowski plays button accordion in his home, Ashland, Wisconsin, November 1980.
Photo by James P. Leary.

John Berquist, Eveleth, Minnesota.
Photo courtesy of John Berquist.

Oren Tikkanen, Calumet Michigan, March 1984.
Photo by Michael Loukinen.

Emery Olson in the carpentry shop at the University of Wisconsin–Stevens Point, May 1982.
Photo by James P. Leary.

Floyd Welker ties a fly for trout fishing in his basement workshop, Eau Claire, Wisconsin, July 1988.
Photo by James P. Leary.

Harry Chaudoir outside his rural home, Rosiere, Wisconsin, May 1988.
Photo by James P. Leary.

Ed Grabowski in the coffee room of the Learning Resource Center at the University of Wisconsin–Stevens Point, May 1982.
Photo by James P. Leary.

Edwin Pearson outside his home, Maple, Wisconsin, July 1987.
Photo by James P. Leary.

Jack Foster, Calumet, Michigan, March 1984.
Photo by Michael Loukinen.

Joseph Doyle at the Doyle home, east of Rice Lake, Wisconsin, July 1987.
Photo by James P. Leary.

Keith Lea in the coffee room of the Learning Resource Center at the University of Wisconsin–Stevens Point, May 1982.
Photo by James P. Leary.

Rose and Max Trzebiatowski in the kitchen of their farm home in the Fancher community of Portage County, Wisconsin, August 1980.
Photo by James P. Leary.

Roman David "Bombo" Alexa, Jr., and Roman David "Bimbo" Alexa converse amid skidding pulpwood near Iron River, Michigan, July 1989.
Photo by James P. Leary, courtesy of the Michigan Traditional Arts Program, Michigan State University.

Art Moilanen, piano accordian, and Matt Gallmann, button accordion, play a duet in Art's Barroom, Mass City, Michigan, March 1981.
Photo by James P. Leary.

Walter Johnson holds one of his two LP
recordings, *Oulun Poika Laulaa* [The Oulu
Boy Sings], outside his home in Oulu,
Wisconsin, February 1979.
Photo by James P. Leary.

Oljanna Venden Cunneen poses outside a
bank in her handmade Norwegian *bunad*,
Mount Horeb, Wisconsin, July 1986.
Photo by Janet C. Gilmore.

Anselm "Andy" Polso in the shop adjacent to
his home, Kimball, Wisconsin, February 1981.
Photo by James P. Leary.

Thure Shelin in his garden, Delta, Wisconsin,
July 1979.
Photo by James P. Leary.

Rodney Lahti and William Kangas exchange jokes on Kangas's back porch, Oulu, Wisconsin, May 1988.
Photo by James P. Leary.

L-R: Warren Leary, Ella Doyle, Joseph Doyle, and Bud Drew share coffee and talk around the Doyles' dining room table, July 1987.
Photo by James P. Leary.

John and Ellen Leino at their kitchen table, Washburn, Wisconsin, July 1987.
Photo by James P. Leary.

L-R: Leary, Olson, Mason, and Garski, Hilltop Tavern, May 1982.
Photo by Janet C. Gilmore.

Mason and Garski, Hilltop Tavern, May 1982.
Photo by Janet C. Gilmore.

L-R: Leary, Mason, and Garski, Hilltop Tavern, May 1982.
Photo by Janet C. Gilmore.

Jack Bingel and Frank Strukel in the local office of the Steelworkers Union, Virginia, Minnesota, August 1978.
Photo by James P. Leary.

Pete and Florence Trzebiatowski in their kitchen with some local moonshine, Stevens Point, Wisconsin, June 1989.
Photo by James P. Leary.

Toivi Reini and Lauri "Tuggers" Koski enjoy a moment of rest at the Festival of Michigan Folklife, East Lansing, Michigan, August 1988.
Photo by James P. Leary.

L-R: Leo Garski, Jon Mason, James P. Leary, and Emery Olson during a joke-telling session in the Hilltop Tavern, Stevens Point, Wisconsin, May 1982.
Photo by Janet C. Gilmore.

Collection Notes

Each joke performed by a teller in everyday life is part of a complex sociocultural event, a richly human activity of which the texts in this anthology are but dim reflections. Nonetheless, a little biographical information about the tellers, their qualities as raconteurs, and the circumstances of their performances can convey at least a glimpse of the light, color, and animation of "being there."

The notes which follow offer that glimpse whenever possible. In a very few cases, not even the names of tellers were available, and in more, only names were provided. Working with telephone books at the public library, I was able to contact a dozen tellers previously known by name only, but as many eluded my search. I welcome further information from readers.

I also welcome other versions of the texts presented here, or of other regional jokes not reported. Like the tellers themselves, jokes have independent "lives," changing and adapting as they pass from one teller to another or find their way into print through the popular press or the specialized writings of folklorists. As opposed to traditional yarns, narrative folksongs, or legends, however, scholars still know very little about the cultural, historical, and regional dimensions of folk humor in the United States and, especially, the Upper Midwest.

The Indians

1. Recorded from Earl Nyholm, August 27, 1987, by James P. Leary at the Festival of Michigan Folklife, East Lansing, Michigan. Born in 1937 at Crystal Falls, Michigan, of Ojibwa and Swedish parents, Nyholm is an enrolled member of the Keeweenaw Bay reservation at Baraga/L'Anse, Michigan. He grew up speaking Ojibwa and English and learned many traditional tales from relatives. Apart from a fund of sacred narratives, restricted to seasonal tellings, he also acquired secular "Indian jokes" and was in demand as a master of ceremonies at powwows in the Western Great Lakes region. In the early 1960s, Nyholm earned a B.F.A. from the Layton School of Design in Milwaukee. He has taught the Ojibwa language at Bemidji State University in Minnesota since 1972. Nyholm's fondness for puns, talent for detail, subtle yet clear preoccupation with moral issues, and measured yet animated delivery are typical of Ojibwa raconteurs. Traditional versions of the Wenabozho cycle have been widely reported, most recently and comprehensively in Victor Barnouw, *Wisconsin Chippewa Myths And Tales, And Their Relation To Chippewa Life* (Madison: University of Wisconsin Press, 1977), especially chapters 2 & 3.

2. Earl Nyholm, August 27, 1987. Folklorist Jim Griffith reported to me that he heard a Southwestern version in Tucson, Arizona, in 1989.

3. Earl Nyholm, August 27, 1987. Transcriptions from the Ojibwa throughout these stories are by Nyholm.

4. Earl Nyholm, August 27, 1987. Like the preceding telling, homophony between "she" and *"zhii"* is noted though the actual meanings are unrelated.

5. Earl Nyholm, August 27, 1987. See Harold Wentworth and Stuart Berg, *Dictionary of American Slang* (NYC: Thomas Crowell, 1960).

6. Earl Nyholm, August 27, 1987.

7. Earl Nyholm, August 27, 1987.

8. Earl Nyholm, August 27, 1987. The first bilingual misunderstanding resembles a Cornish miner's joke. Davy asks the hoist man to warm his pasty by putting it near the boiler and finds the fellow has eaten it. "I didn't mean fer 'ee to eat 'im up but 'eat 'im up!" See Caroline Bancroft, "Cousin Jack Stories From Central City," *Colorado Magazine* 21:2 (1944), pp. 53-54.

9. Recorded from a 50-year-old male teller who wishes to remain anonymous, September, 1987, by James P. Leary, at the Red Cliff Ojibwa Reservation, Bayfield County, Wisconsin. Thomas Vennum, Jr., made the following observation in "The Ojibwa Begging Dance," from *Music and Context: Essays for John M. Ward*, ed. Anne D. Shapiro (Cambridge, Mass.: Department of Music, Harvard University, 1985), p. 69.

> Ojibwa at a recent powwow in Sisseton declined the stew offered them by Sioux hosts because the rumor had spread among them that it was *animoshwabo* (dog soup). (There is an in-joke current among the Ojibwa that the sentence "See Spot run" in grade school primers refers to a dog of the Sioux about to be butchered.)

Other versions of the "hot dog" telling presented here have involved immigrant Norwegians. I recorded one from Jon Mason (Hilltop Tavern, Stevens Point, Wisconsin, May 6, 1982) in which newly arrived Ole attends a baseball game and is given a hot dog with the same results. See also, Red Stangland, *Polish and Other Ethnic Jokes* (Sioux Falls, South Dakota: Norse Press, 1980), p. 17.

10. Recorded from Tim Condon, 1973, by James Michael Krotzman, Stillwater, Minnesota. Condon was a sixteen-year-old high school student who had learned about Henry Otis from an elderly neighbor woman. His version appears in Krotzman, *Folktales Found In The St. Croix Valley* (University of Wisconsin–Eau Claire: M.A.T. thesis in English, 1973), p. 19. The goose/yes anecdote is attributed to Otis by Harry W. Palm in *Lumberjack Days in the St. Croix Valley* (Bayport, Minnesota: Bayport Printing House, 1969), pp. 3-4. See Baughman for sources of motifs X972(b), "Long fight"; X973, "Remarkable wrestler"; and X1733, "Lies about sinking." With regard to X1733, people *did* sink into the sawdust streets of mill towns, but probably not to the extent suggested in the tale.

11. Earl Nyholm, August 27, 1987. Vance Randolph offers an Ozark version of this widespread anecdote in *Hot Springs and Hell, And Other Folk Jests and Anecdotes from the Ozarks* (Hatboro, Pennsylvania: Folklore Associates, 1965), #32. French dialect versions from the Upper Midwest appear in Richard M. Dorson, "Dialect Stories of the Upper Peninsula: A New Form of American Folklore," *Journal of American Folklore* 61:240 (1948), p. 127; and Mary Agnes Starr, *Pea Soup and Johnny Cake* (Madison, Wisconsin: Red Mountain Publishing, 1981), p. 42. Starr's version came from Victor Michaud of Chippewa Falls, Wisconsin, and concerned Pete Legault (see Texts 161a and 162).

12. Earl Nyholm, August 27, 1987. Here is another example of Nyholm's extraordinary ability to synthesize European and native–American traditions. Nyholm offers a "clean" version of this joke at powwows: the boy rubs Crisco on his head in hopes of growing taller. I recorded a Finnish–American version in 1981 from Walter Johnson (the teller of Text 108) in which Eino notices Toivo's large member in the sauna and is told to rub his "little one" with lard. Other versions appear in paperback joke books: Mike Kowalski, *The Polish Joke Book* (NYC: Belmont Tower Books, 1974), p. 71; and Ralph L. Marquard, *212 Spicy Stories* (NYC: Hart Publishing, 1976), p. 146.

13. Earl Nyholm, August 27, 1987. This joke was very common in my home town, Rice Lake, Wisconsin, in the mid–1950s and appears in Anonymous, *Locker Room Humor* (Chicago: Burd Publishing, 1954), p. 45.

14. Earl Nyholm, August 27, 1987. Joe Cloud's occupation as a guide has been a common one for the Ojibwa for generations. A farmer/tourist version of this joke appears in Lewis and Faye Copeland, *10,000 Jokes, Toasts, and Stories* (NYC: Garden City Books, 1939), #1464.

15a, 15b. The first text was recorded from Earl Nyholm, August 27, 1987. The second text was recorded from Leo Garski, August 14, 1979, at the Northside Bar in Stevens Point, Wisconsin. Born in 1928 into a large Polish Catholic family on a farm in Portage County, Wisconsin, Garski stayed in the army after the Korean conflict before taking a maintenance job with the University of Wisconsin–Stevens Point in the late 1960s. An active hunter and fisherman, he is known in joke-telling circles for his glib one-liners and for his proclivity, as in this instance, to insert himself as a character in his own tellings. Garski's performance techniques are treated in my "Style in Jocular Communication," *Journal of Folklore Research* 21:1 (1984), pp. 29-46. Another midwestern version is reported by Walker D. Wyman, *Wisconsin Folklore* (Madison: University of Wisconsin–Extension, 1979), p. 36.

16. Earl Nyholm, August 27, 1987. This is another "shaggy dog" story in which the description of native peoples in the modern world is more important than the silly punch line. Odanah is on the Bad River Reservation on the south shore of Lake Superior, and the "Cities" mentioned are the "Twin Cities" of Minneapolis/St. Paul.

17. Recorded from Mary Fowler, February 7, 1981, by Mark Wagler and Emily Osborn, for the Wisconsin Humor Project, Madison, Wisconsin. Place names derived from the languages of native peoples abound in the Upper Midwest. In Wisconsin, for example, 19 of 72 counties carry Indian names, as do scores of towns, lakes, and rivers. See J. W. Ashton, "Some Folk Etymologies for Place Names," *Journal of American Folklore* 57:222 (1944), p. 140; and Robert Gard and L. G. Sorden, *The Romance of Wisconsin Place Names* (New York: October House, 1968), p. 115.

18a, 18b. The first text was set down from memory by John Mihelich, July 10, 1985, for the course, "Folklore of Wisconsin," at the University of Wisconsin, Madison. Mihelich was born in 1963 in Oconomowoc, where he grew up. He earned a degree in Industrial Relations at the UW–Madison in 1985. As in the preceding telling, Mihelich's explanatory legend is regarded as a joke and belies the facts. See Gard and Sorden, *The Romance of Wisconsin Place Names* concerning the mingling of truth and fiction.

 The second text was recorded from Jean Larke, August 20, 1980, by Mark Wagler and Emily Osborn for the Wisconsin Humor Project, Waukesha. Larke's version of "I can no mo' walk" intersects with another common immigrant legend in which a Norwegian family finally chooses their farm when the wife declares, "Stop, I will go no farther," or "Stop, this is as far as we go." See Alfred O. Erickson, "Scandinavia, Wisconsin," *Norwegian-American Studies and Records* 15 (1949), pp. 190-191; and the *Rice Lake Chronotype, Centennial Edition* 101:1 (September, 1974), section G, p. 14. A third version was recorded from an unnamed teller, September 22, 1936, by "Potter," a fieldworker for the Wisconsin Folklore division of the Federal Writers' Project. In it a "white man and an Indian" are hunting and trapping partners who pursue an elusive old coon. One day the Indian captures it and declares to his partner, "Old coon no more walk."

19. Recorded from Bernie Hughes, summer, 1980, by Tom Barden and Mark Wagler for the Wisconsin Humor Project, UW–Superior. In an article on "Wisconsin Humor" in the *Ocooch Mountain News* 6:6 (late summer, 1980), pp. 8-9, Tom Barden describes Hughes as "a professor of education administration at UW–Superior [who] was one of the best informants we found at that location." I recall hearing this story several times in the early 1980s, including once during a radio broadcast by commentator Paul Harvey, but I have not seen it in print.

20. Recorded from Pete Trzebiatowski, June 13, 1978, by James P. Leary at the Trzebiatowski home, Stevens Point, Wisconsin. Born on a Portage County farm in 1907, Trzebiatowski did factory and carpentry work and ran a number of taverns throughout central Wisconsin. He often told jokes and anecdotes set in his various places of business. See my "Polish Priests and Tavern Keepers in Portage County, Wisconsin," *Midwestern Journal of Language and Folklore* 8:1 (1982), pp. 34-42. Another regional version as told by Jon Mason, August 14, 1979, heightens sexual tension by reducing a "couple women" to one and making her a spinster Sunday-school teacher leading children on a field trip. Printed versions also feature schoolmarms and are set in the American southwest: Anonymous, *Extra-Sextra Special* (NYC: Scylla Publishing, 1954) not paginated; Gershon Legman, *Rationale of the Dirty Joke, An Analysis of Sexual Humor* (NYC: Grove Press, 1968), p. 216; and Larry Wilde, *The Complete Book of Ethnic Humor* (Los Angeles: Pinnacle Books, 1978), p. 24.

21. Pete Trzebiatowski, June 13, 1978. Legman provides a similar "how" joke from Virginia, ca. 1953, in which an Indian standing on a corner asks pretty girls, "When?" in *Rationale of the Dirty Joke*, p. 223. An onlooker reckons he always thought Indians said, "How." The "brave" replies, "I know how, what I want to know is when." Other versions of Trzebiatowski's telling have the young woman returning from college, not work: J. M. Elgart, *Further More Over Sexteen*, Volume 4 (NYC: Grayson Publishing, 1955), p. 58; Jackie Martling, *Just Another Dirty Joke Book* (Los Angeles: Pinnacle Books, 1982), p. 6; and Wilde, *The Complete Book of Ethnic Humor*, p. 21.

The French

22. Recorded from an unnamed teller, probably Louis Blanchard, ca. 1937, by an unnamed fieldworker, probably Gregg Montgomery, in the vicinity of Chippewa Falls, Wisconsin. Montgomery was a fieldworker for the Wisconsin Folklore division of the Federal Writers' Project in the late 1930s under the direction of Charles Brown of the State Historical Society of Wisconsin. Her correspondence with Brown indicates that she worked in the Chippewa Falls area, the source of an unpublished manuscript, "Pea Soupers," presenting the tales of French–Canadian loggers in the Chippewa Valley. That Louis Blanchard is the probable teller is suggested by the fact that Blanchard is referred to in "Pea Soupers" and that several of the tales in the manuscript were later recorded from Blanchard by other fieldworkers in essentially the same versions. Louis Blanchard (1872-1959) was born at Jim Falls, Wisconsin, and logged, like his father, in the Chippewa Valley before farming on cutover land at Cornell. A vivid talker with a fine store of reminiscences and tales, he was interviewed by journalist Fred L. Holmes for *Old World Wisconsin, Around Europe in the Badger State* (Madison: 1944), p. 31. His life history was published by Walker D. Wyman as *The Lumberjack Frontier* (Lincoln: University of Nebraska Press, 1969).

23. Probably Louis Blanchard, ca. 1937.

24. Recorded from an unknown teller, ca. 1937, by Gregg Montgomery, in the vicinity of Chippewa Falls, Wisconsin. Like Texts 22 and 23, this anecdote appears in a manuscript, "Pea Soupers," compiled for the Wisconsin Folklore division of the Federal Writer's Project in the late 1930s.

25. Recorded from Joseph Doyle, July 30, 1987, by James P. Leary at the Doyle farm home in the Town of Doyle, east of Rice Lake, Wisconsin. Born June 4, 1903, on the nearby Doyle homestead, the informant worked in the woods "until the bugs got too thick," then he went "down to Ioway to see how they picked corn," and later spent "a couple of months in Dakota, thrashing." His dad's brother, a doctor, wanted "Joe" to follow the profession, but World War I intervened. With three older brothers in the Army, Doyle was needed on the farm, where he remained. Doyle still speaks with a trace of brogue, and his repertoire includes scores of humorous anecdotes about Irish, Bohemian, English, Norwegian, German, and French neighbors.

26. Recorded from Oren Tikkanen, March 17, 1984, by Michael Loukinen at the Tikkanen home, Calumet, Michigan. Born in 1944 near Calumet, Tikkanen grew up hearing dialect jokes from his miner father and an uncle, Ricky Saari. He has honed his talents as a "dialectician" in recent years by interjecting joke telling into his work as a substance-abuse counselor and into his musical performances with a number of Finnish–American bands, including "Thimbleberry."

27. Oren Tikkanen, March 17, 1984. Polish and Scandinavian versions of the dialect joke appear in these collections: William Clements, *The Types of the Polack Joke* (Bloomington, Indiana: Folklore Forum Bibliographic and Special Series, No. 3, 1969), p. 22; Stangland, *Polish and Other Ethnic Jokes*, p. 13; Paul F. Anderson, *Scandinavian Yokes* (Minneapolis, Minnesota: Eggs Press, 1979), p. 8; Charlene Powers, *The New Uff Da, A Collection of 189 1/2 Norwegian Jokes* (Crosby, North Dakota: The Journal Publishing Company, 1977), p. 6, and *Leapin' Lena* (Crosby, North Dakota: The Journal Publishing Company, 1984), p. 11.

The Cornish

28. Recorded from an unknown teller in southwestern Wisconsin for the Wisconsin Folklore division of the Federal Writers' Project, late 1930s; published by Charles E. Brown in a pamphlet, *Cousin Jack Stories: Short Stories of the Cornish Lead Miners of Southwestern Wisconsin* (Madison: Wisconsin Folklore Society, 1940), p. 2. Charles E. Brown (1872–1946) was born in Milwaukee and served as curator of the Wisconsin State Historical Society's museum from 1908 until retirement in 1944. He directed the Federal Writers' Project in Wisconsin from 1935–1939, and he published numerous pamphlets of traditional Wisconsin narratives. Another version concerns an Irish workman's response to assurances by an estate owner that his "barking dog never bites." Mike reckons *he* knows this, but "does that dog know it?" See Copeland, *10,000 Jokes, Toasts, and Stories*, #7061.

29. Brown, *Cousin Jack Stories*, p. 5. Baughman offers motif X826*, "Drunk man answers his jug," with the text from Brown as his only example. An Irish version told by Canadian blacks appears as #14 in the "Pat and Mike Stories and Tall Tales" section of Arthur Huff Fauset's *Folklore From Nova Scotia* (American Folklore Society Memoir 24, 1931).

30. Brown, *Cousin Jack Stories*, p. 3. The rodents are rats in Randolph, *Hot Springs and Hell*, #202.

31. Brown, *Cousin Jack Stories*, p. 1. The enumeration of nouns with added or deleted h's in this text parallels one in which a Cockney family names their first eight children "'Orace, 'Erbert, 'Enry, 'Ugh, 'Ubert, 'Arold, 'Arriet, and 'Etty." The last is called "Halice." See Copeland, *10,000 Jokes, Toasts, and Stories*, #6782; Powers Moulton, *2500 Jokes For All Occasions* (Philadelphia: Circle Books, 1942), #1889; and Wilde, *The Complete Book of Ethnic Humor*, p. 73.

32. Recorded from Warren D. Leary, Jr., June 12, 1978, by James P. Leary at the Warren Leary home, Rice Lake, Wisconsin. Warren Leary, my father, was born September 15, 1922, in Chippewa Falls, Wisconsin, and moved fifty miles north to Rice Lake the next year when his father, Warren, Sr., bought an interest in the *Rice Lake Chronotype*, northern Wisconsin's largest weekly newspaper. After receiving a B.A. in English from Notre Dame, serving in the infantry during World War II, and acquiring an M.A. in journalism from Columbia University, Leary worked briefly for the *Milwaukee Journal* in 1948. He was editor, then publisher of the *Chronotype*, and retired in 1986. Part of a "morning coffee" network of local raconteurs, Leary has a long skein of jokes and anecdotes concerning local characters which are invariably marked by deft phrases and a journalist's penchant for realistic detail.

33. Brown, *Cousin Jack Stories*, p. 1. Old Abe, the eagle mentioned, was sold by Ojibwa Indians to a trader, Daniel McCann of Jim Falls, Wisconsin, in 1861. It served as a mascot for the Eighth Wisconsin Infantry and survived thirty-six Civil War battles and skirmishes. After the bird expired, it was stuffed and enshrined in the state capitol until destroyed by a fire in 1881. By that time, Old Abe was too much a part of Wisconsin's heritage to be forgotten, and a replica was found and placed in the rebuilt capitol. In a printed version, an English family typically visits the United States and sees an eagle. The children mistake the bird for an "'awk" or an "'en," but the father

declares it's "han heagle." See Copeland, *10,000 Jokes, Toasts, and Stories*, #6695; James Schermerhorn, *Schermerhorn's Stories* (NYC: George Sully and Company, 1929), p. 139.

34. Recorded from Jack Foster, March 17, 1984, by Michael Loukinen of Northern Michigan University, at Foster's home, Calumet, Michigan. Born in 1909, of Cornish parents, in Michigan's Keeweenaw County, Foster lived briefly in Butte, Montana, until his mother died and the family returned to Michigan, where Foster's grandmother ran a boarding house at Centennial Mine. Here is a brief description of the boarders provided by Foster:

> There we were with all these Cousin Jack miners. And that's all I ever heard. They did more mining home after shift than they did in the mine because that's all they discussed—and telling stories. That's where I got interested in these stories. I never forgot them.... I can see that big hard coal stove, shiny all around. And you could see through the isinglass, that flame, you know. You were freezing over here—we used to undress behind the stove because it was warm—and these miners would be all around. Some drank heavy, others were very religious.... There was a big long table, and Sunday afternoon I used to see them sitting around. They never had much education, a lot of them. And then, this is where the stories started, in that big room, big long table. One would pop one—"Do you remember this?"—talking about the old country.

Foster worked for the railroad, then joined the Calumet Police Department, and later was chief of security for the Calumet and Hecla Mining Company. He has entertained audiences for several decades with a repertoire of some seventy jokes and anecdotes about Cousin Jacks.

35. Foster, March 17, 1984. This telling is paired with the following one. A tramp declares himself a self-made man, "I started out without a rag on my back and now I'm all rags." See Moulton, *2500 Jokes For All Occasions*, #397; also Paul F. Anderson, *Scandimania: A Smorgasbord of Fun* (Minneapolis: Eggs Press, 1985), p. 30.

36. Foster, March 17, 1984. This telling followed the preceding one. This joke is attributed to southern "hillbillies" in Jack Runninger, *Favorite Jokes of Mountain Folks in Boogar Hollow* (Lindale, Georgia: Country Originals, 1971), p. 18.

37. Foster, March 17, 1984. Like the pasty, saffron bread and buns are Cornish culinary specialties. This telling is paired with the next example; the two are variants of the same basic joke. Henny Youngman, known for jokes about his wife, presents one in which the family dog eats a pie intended for the husband. The punch line is the same as Foster's. See *The Best of Henny Youngman*, vol. 1 (NYC: Grammercy Publishing, 1978), p. 75.

38. Foster, March 17, 1984. This joke is paired with the previous one.

39. Foster, March 17, 1984. Dorson collected this joke, attributed to a pair of Cousin Jacks, from Rod McDonald in nearby Dollar Bay, Michigan, during 1946. See Dorson, "Dialect Stories of the Upper Peninsula," #68.

40. Foster, March 17, 1984. An Irish version appears in Larry Wilde, *The Last Official Irish Joke Book* (NYC: Bantam Books, 1983), p. 66.

41. Foster, March 17, 1984.

42. Foster, March 17, 1984. See Ronald L. Baker, *Jokelore, Humorous Folktales From Indiana* (Bloomington: Indiana University Press, 1986), #134; Daryl Cumber Dance, *Shuckin' and Jivin', Folklore From Contemporary Black Americans* (Bloomington: Indiana University Press, 1978), #100; Edmund Fuller, *Thesaurus of Anecdotes* (NYC: Crown Publishers, 1942), #1534; Randolph, *Hot Springs and Hell*, #112; and Larry Wilde, *More of the Official Irish Jokebook* (Los Angeles: Pinnacle Books, 1979), p. 100, and *The Official Religious Jokebook* (Los Angeles: Pinnacle Books, 1976), p. 100.

The Germans

43. Recorded by Lois Buss of Shawano, Wisconsin, June, 1986, from her own repertoire for "Folklore of Wisconsin" at the University of Wisconsin–Madison. Born ca. 1952 near Pella, Wisconsin, in a heavily German–American area, Buss heard numerous "Plattdeutsch" or Low German stories from her great-uncles and uncles while growing up. She now teaches elementary school in Shawano. This is AT Type 1321, "Fools Frightened." The language and traditional plot of this tale are reminiscent of the Old World, while fishing regulations and clashes with game wardens suggest the American Upper Midwest.

44. Buss, Wisconsin, June, 1986. Paired with the previous text, this is AT Type 1321A, Motif J2615, "Fright at the Creaking of a Wheelbarrow (Mill)." Thompson cites numerous Flemish versions, which fit well with Buss's Low-German source. Four versions appear in Rev. Thomas R. Brendle and William S. Troxell, *Pennsylvania German Folk Tales, Legends, Once-Upon-A-Time Stories, Maxims, and Sayings* (Norristown, Pennsylvania: Pennsylvania German Society, 1944), pp. 184-185. Dance reports a recent African–American telling in *Shuckin' and Jivin'*, #142.

45. Recalled by Lois Buss from the performance of her deceased great-uncle August Laude, June, 1986. A second-generation German–American, Laude (ca. 1895–1975) worked in lumber camps and mills around the Shawano area of northeastern Wisconsin. He was also known as a drummer who teamed with his accordionist brother, Bill, to play old-time music at weddings and birthday parties.

46. Recorded from Charles Robinson, June, 1941, by Robert Draves, for the Archive of Folksong of the Library of Congress, at a gathering of lumber-camp singers in Waushara County, Wisconsin. Robinson, born in 1865, was long retired from logging when recorded for a survey of folk music in Wisconsin directed by Helene Stratman–Thomas of the University of Wisconsin. His residence in Marion, Waupaca County, and his singing of "Fond du Lac Jail"—a complaint about bad food and bed bugs awaiting carousing lumberjacks—suggest that he worked along the Wolf River. For a "fine example of Dutch dialect," see "How 'Sockery' Set a Hen," reprinted from the *Poultry Monthly* in Melville D. Landon, *Wit and Humor of the Age* (Chicago: ca. 1901), pp. 540-541.

47. Recorded from Edward E. "Fred" Metz, July 24, 1980, by Tom Barden and Mark Wagler at the Stoughton, Wisconsin, Senior Center for the Wisconsin Humor Project. See Baughman motif K64, "Contest: pulling on steak with teeth." The contestants are an Irishman and a Dutchman in the two cited versions, one from Virginia (1922) and the other from Indiana (1942).

48. Pete Trzebiatowski, June 13, 1978. For biographical information, see the notes to Text 20. This is a German version of a joke that previously has been reported from only Anglo–American and African–American sources. The sought spouse is "Wash[ington] Cox," "Wash Butts," "Bob Peters," and "Bob Cock," respectively recorded in Robert J. Adams, *Raconteur and Repertoire: A Study of a Southern Indiana Storyteller and His Material* (Bloomington: Indiana University M.A. thesis in Folklore, 1966), #28; in *Locker Room Humor* (author anonymous), p. 63; in Dance, *Shuckin' and Jivin'*, #167; and in Henry D. Spalding, *Encyclopedia of Black Folklore and Humor* (Middle Village, New York: Jonathan David, 1972), p. 354.

49. Recorded from Janet Cox, December 7, 1980, by Mark Wagler and Emily Osborn at West Salem, Wisconsin, for the Wisconsin Humor Project. Cox was raised in rural Hillsboro, Wisconsin. Her father was English, but her mother was German and the source for anecdotes regarding the "older German lady." The following story is likewise told "about this same old German lady."

50. Cox, December 7, 1980. Paired with the previous example, this anecdote parallels one often told about a government inspector who asks a farmer if he has problems with bugs in the corn. "We just fish them out and drink it anyway." Randolph cites a version from oral tradition and numerous examples from joke books in *Hot Springs and Hell*, #377.

51. Joseph Doyle, July 30, 1987. For biographical information, see the notes for Text 25.

52. Recorded from George Russell, June 17, 1975, by James P. Leary at the Russell home in Bruce, Wisconsin. Son of Irish immigrant parents, Russell (1886–1975) was born in the farming community of Dobie, Barron County, Wisconsin. He worked as a timber scaler for the Canadian National Railroad in lumber camps in the Rainy Lake area on the Minnesota border. After serving in World War I, he farmed for many years in the Rice Lake area. Still a fine raconteur in 1975, Russell told me, "Fifty years ago I could tell you a lot more stories. I've heard stories traveling on trains. And I heard lumberjack stories. And all sorts of them." See my "George Russell: The Repertoire and Personality of a North Country Storyteller" in *Folklore On Two Continents, Essays in Honor of Linda Degh*, ed. Nikolai Burlakoff and Carl Lindahl (Bloomington, Indiana: Trickster Press, 1980), pp. 354-362.

53. Recorded from Vern Loew (Lowe?), September 30, 1980, by Mark Wagler and Emily Osborn at Wind Lake, Wisconsin, for the Wisconsin Humor Project. Even today, with the many mergers within the Lutheran Church, mixed Norwegian and German congregations are rare. The Norwegians generally belong to the Evangelical Lutheran Church of America, while the Germans are members of the Missouri Synod or the Wisconsin Synod. For parallel versions of this anecdote, see Stewart H. Holbrook, *The American Lumberjack* (NYC: Collier Books, 1962), p. 202; Wilde, *The Official Irish Joke Book* (Los Angeles: Pinnacle Books, 1974), p. 72.

54. Recorded from Gilbert Reichert, December 15, 1980, by Mark Wagler and Emily Osborn at Greendale, Wisconsin, for the Wisconsin Humor Project. I recorded the Depression version (see in-text annotation) from Emery Olson of Iola, Wisconsin, August 14, 1979, at the Northside Bar in Stevens Point. Also see Legman, *Rationale of the Dirty Joke*, p. 89; Martling, *Just Another Dirty Joke Book*, p. 21.

55. Recorded from Mark Schneider, July 5, 1989, by James P. Leary at the University of Wisconsin, Madison, where Schneider was enrolled in "Folklore of Wisconsin." Schneider was born in Wausau, Wisconsin, in 1967 and raised in nearby Edgar. He heard this joke from his dad, Walter Schneider, Jr., a telephone lineman, who in turn learned it from his father, Walter, Sr. The elder Schneider was born in 1892 in Marshfield, Wisconsin, where his parents had moved from the Port Washington area just north of Milwaukee. Walter, Sr., farmed all his life, but he also ran a small garage and car dealership in Colby during the Depression and later worked in a box factory.

The Irish

56. George Russell, August 21, 1974. For biographical information, see the note for Text 52. Russell was a steadfast Irishman throughout his life and often complained about the English who "treated Ireland cruelly." Jimmy Lyons attributes the Pat-and-Mike story to Irish vaudevillian Frank Fogarty in *The Mirth of a Nation* (NYC: Vantage Press, 1953). Instead of an Englishman, a Jew counters an insulting Irishman in Copeland, *10,000 Jokes, Toasts, and Stories*, #6551; Ed Cray, "The Rabbi Trickster," *Journal of American Folklore* 78:306 (1964), p. 344; and Moulton, *2500 Jokes For All Occasions*, #1673.

57. Pete Trzebiatowski, June 13, 1978. For biographical information, see the note for Text 20. Trzebiatowski told five Pat-and-Mike jokes, all of which involved the experiences of immigration and itinerant work in America. They were uniformly "old ones" in his repertoire. To some extent, these foolish newcomers, who were common to all ethnic groups, reminded Trzebiatowski of his rural Irish neighbors. Compare Pat and Mike to Casey and O'Brian, who battle in Lyons, *Mirth of a Nation*, p. 7. A southern version concerning blacks is told on a Brother Dave Gardner LP, *Rejoice, Dear Hearts*, ca. 1960.

58. Recorded from Val Schmidt, August 20, 1980, by Mark Wagler and Emily Osborn at Waukesha, Wisconsin, for the Wisconsin Humor Project. Schmidt was born in 1905 in Norwalk, Wisconsin: "I've been around 75 years. You got to pick up a story somehow or other." This Irishman-as-a-hod-carrier joke is reported from oral tradition by Herbert Halpert in *Folktales and Legends from the New Jersey Pinelands*, 2 volumes (Bloomington: Indiana University Ph.D. dissertation in Folklore, 1947), p. 187, and by Richard M. Dorson in *Negro Tales from Pine Bluff, Arkansas, and Calvin, Michigan* (Bloomington: Indiana University Press, 1958), pp. 252-253.

59. Recorded from Don Barney, August 20, 1980, by Mark Wagler and Emily Osborn at Waukesha, Wisconsin, for the Wisconsin Humor Project. Irishman jokes have long been told by African–Americans, and Dance records a half-dozen in *Shuckin' and Jivin'*, including #294 which matches Barney's telling. Ozark farm boys in town are similarly amazed in Randolph, *Sticks in the Knapsack* pp. 69, 152, where four other versions from print and oral tradition are cited, the earliest from 1908.

60. Pete Trzebiatowski, June 13, 1978. See Baughman J2259*k, "Fool discards about half the nails he picks up while hanging pictures. He explains that those nails are for the opposite wall (or that they have their heads on wrong)." See also Baker, *Jokelore*, #195; Clements, *The Types of the Polack Joke*, Type E14.4, "Nails on the wrong end"; Stangland, *Norwegian Jokes* (Sioux Falls, South Dakota: Norse Press, 1979), p. 42, and *Polish and Other Ethnic Jokes*, p. 30; and Gerald Thomas, "Newfie Jokes," *Folklore of Canada*, ed. Edith Fowke (Toronto: McClelland and Stewart Limited, 1976), p. 146. For a Polish variant, see Text 134.

61. George Russell, July 8, 1975. This Irish greenhorn gem recalled for George his own work in the woods. Printed versions invariably involve Irishmen: Anonymous, *500 Best Irish Jokes and Limericks* (NYC: Bell Publishing, 1968), p. 20; Lyons, *Mirth of a Nation*, p. 13; Schermerhorn, *Schermerhorn's Stories*, p. 250; and Wilde, *The Last Official Irish Joke Book*, p. 10. For another version, see Text 156.

62. Russell, July 8, 1975. The central action in this tale resembles motif K840, "Deception into fatal substitution," common to trickster tales worldwide, except for the fact that the dupe does not die. Leonard Roberts reports essentially the same version as Russell's—involving Pat and Mike and the line "a job like that'll get a man killed"—in *South From Hell-fer-Sartin'* (Berea, Kentucky: Council of the Southern Mountains, 1964), #54.

63. Recorded from Casmir Sikorski, June 13, 1978, by James P. Leary in Sikorski's room at the River Pines Health Care Center, Stevens Point, Wisconsin. Born in 1907 in rural Portage County, Sikorski was crippled with polio as a youth, but he practiced the electrician's trade nonetheless. He was not an avid joke teller, but he had a fine store of local anecdotes. Some of the anecdotes were incorporated in letters recalling farm life and published in the Stevens Point *Daily Journal*. Other versions of this Pat-and-Mike story appear in Max Roach's Laurel and Hardy comedy, *Habeus Corpus* (1928), in which Oliver Hardy climbs a street sign at night to read the same message. See also Arthur Pope Lewis, *Now That Reminds Me* (n.p.: The Caxton Press, 1927), #406; Thomas L. Masson, *The Best Stories in the World* (NYC: Doubleday, Page & Company, 1913), pp. 195-196; and George Posner, *The World's Best Humor* (Philadelphia: Pennsylvania Publishing Company, 1925), p. 202.

64. George Russell, August 21, 1974. Randolph cites an Ozark version and numerous printed sources, Irish and otherwise, in *Hot Springs and Hell*, #69. See also Baker, *Jokelore*, #115; Tommy Bocafucci, *The Italian Joke Book* (NYC: Belmont Tower Books, 1975); Gershon Legman, *No Laughing Matter, Rationale of the Dirty Joke: Second Series* (Wharton, New Jersey: Breaking Point, Inc., 1975), p. 201, and *Rationale of the Dirty Joke*, p. 668; and Wilde, *Official Irish Joke Book*, p. 63.

65. Recorded from Edwin Pearson, July 29, 1987, by James P. Leary, at the Pearson home, Maple, Wisconsin. Born in 1911 in Wahoo, Nebraska, Pearson moved with his Swedish parents to a cutover farm near Maple in 1920. He likewise farmed and was active in town government. Possessed of a dry wit and given to subtle exaggeration, Pearson is particularly adept at tall tales, although he has heard and told lumber-camp, Swedish, Finnish, and Irish jokes all his life. See AT Type 1313A*, "In the Open Grave." This telling shares motifs with J2311, "Person made to believe that he is dead," and X828*, "Drunk person falls in open grave with humorous results." Specific parallels are found in Baker, *Jokelore*, #136; Randolph, *Hot Springs and Hell*, #353; and Wilde, *Last Official Irish Joke Book*, p. 52.

66. Recorded from Patricia Berigan Leary, June 12, 1978, by James P. Leary at the home of Patricia B. Leary, Rice Lake, Wisconsin. Patricia Berigan, my mother, was born in Omaha, Nebraska, April 3, 1926. She received a B.A. from Creighton University and an M.A. in journalism from Columbia University. Shortly after her marriage to Warren D. Leary, Jr., she moved to Rice Lake, where she raised seven children. This is the only joke I have ever heard her tell. Despite its setting at a traditional Irish wake, she learned it from her mother, Gladys Anderson Berigan, prior to her wedding, and she told it to me prior to mine. A more plausible Mason-Elk-Ku Klux Klan triad is offered by J.M. Elgart in *Furthermore Over Sexteen*, vol. 4 (NYC: Grayson Publishing, 1955), p. 58; the wake setting and the structure alternating praise with "He was that" appear in an Irish joke in *The Laughter Library*, ed. J.H. Johnson, Jerry Sheridan, and Ruth Lawrence (Indianapolis: Maxwell Droke, 1936), #363.

67. Recorded from John Leino, July 28, 1987, by James P. Leary, at the Leino home, Washburn, Wisconsin. Leino was born on January 1, 1918, at home in the rural "Finn Settlement" near Washburn. Leino's father, Edward, "used to tell jokes all the time in Finnish; he had all kinds of them." Like his father, Leino worked in the woods (although for only one season in 1936) and farmed. He also drove a truck for several Ashland and Bayfield County firms before retiring in 1980. This "old one" in Leino's repertoire can be found in *Locker Room Humor*, p. 121; Ralph L. Marquard, *212 Spicy Stories* (NYC: Hart Publishing, 1976), p. 65; Stangland, *Uff Da Stories* (Sioux Falls, South Dakota: Norse Press, 1979), p. 21; and Wilde, *Official Irish Joke Book*, p. 46.

68. Doyle, July 30, 1987. For biographical information, see the note for Text 25. For risqué versions, see Dance, *Shuckin' and Jivin'*, #21; Legman, *Rationale of the Dirty Joke*, pp. 388-389. Variations on the joke include Hoffman motif Q569.6, "Sinners in hell find that girls have no cunts."

The Scandinavians

69. Recorded from Leo Thorson, July 24, 1980, by Tom Barden and Mark Wagler at the Stoughton, Wisconsin, Senior Center for the Wisconsin Humor Project. Stoughton is a heavily Norwegian–American town whose annual Norwegian Independence Day festival, *Syttende Mai* (May 17th), draws thousands. The largely Norwegian–American crowd at the Senior Center guffawed loudly at this tale's suggestion of Norsky cussedness. Leo Thorson, born in Stoughton in 1914, is a fourth-generation Norwegian–American. After graduating in agriculture from the University of Wisconsin in 1939, Thorson worked in agricultural research for private, state, and federal organizations; he also worked his family's farm for twenty-three years. Bill McNeil reports that in the South, the Quaker threatens to sell his cow to a Baptist or a Methodist.

70. Recorded from Jim Croone, ca. 1973, by James Michael Krotzman and included in Krotzman's M.A. thesis, "Folktales Found In The St. Croix Valley," p. 23. Born in 1926 in the old lumber mill town of Stillwater, Minnesota, Croone heard and told many Scandinavian dialect stories while conversing with clientele as a discount store manager in North St. Paul, Minnesota. This joke involves a "colored unit" under fire during World War I. See Boyce House, *Tall Talk from Texas* (San Antonio: Naylor, 1944), p. 59. Bill McNeil reports Appalachian and Ozark versions where cries go to heaven when "things get a bit too rowdy" at a dance.

71. Recorded from Keith Lea, May 31, 1978, by James P. Leary during a coffee break in the employees' lounge of the Learning Resource Center at the University of Wisconsin–Stevens Point. Born in 1923 in Lanark Township, Portage County, Wisconsin, Lea absorbed the speech and stories of his English, Irish, and Polish neighbors while growing up. He has worked as a journalist and a librarian, most recently with the University of Wisconsin–Stevens Point. In keeping with his journalist's background, he performs at a measured pace, careful of each word and attentive to detail. For other versions of Chinese and Norwegian names being confused, see Anonymous, *The Minnesota Norwegian's Favorite Jokes* (Guthrie, Minnesota: Gifts O' The Wild, 1985), p. 5. Sam Ting is named for a German, Hans Schmidt, in H. Allen Smith, *Rude Jokes* (Greenwich, Connecticut: Fawcett Gold Medal Books, 1970), p. 107; this version is found in Wilde, *The Complete Book of Ethnic Humor*, p. 59.

72. Recorded from Henry "Moose" Johnson, August, 1978, by Larry Danielson at the Johnson home, Eveleth, Minnesota, for the Iron Range Folklife Project. Born in Eveleth in 1900, the son of immigrants from Trondheim, Norway, Johnson earned his nickname as a high-school football player

and boxer. He logged on the St. Louis River in 1921 and, like his father, worked in the iron ore mines, before serving for thirty-eight years as a police officer with the Oliver Mining Company. In Johnson's telling of this joke, there appears to be something left out. Montreal, Wisconsin, is an old logging and mining town adjacent to the Montreal River, which forms part of the border between Wisconsin and the Upper Peninsula of Michigan. Presumably the Irish had tricked the Swedes into thinking that crossing state borders was equivalent to entering a country.

For examples of variations, see Text 247 in this collection; Anderson, *Scandinavian Yokes*, p. 37; Dorson, "Dialect Stories of the Upper Peninsula," #34; Cully Gage, *Still Another Northwoods Reader* (Au Train, Michigan: Avery Color Studios, 1989), p. 85; Johnson, et al., *The Laughter Library*, #437; and Moulton, *2500 Jokes For All Occasions*, #1948. A bawdy version involves a Scandinavian philanderer caught with someone's wife. He hides behind a trellis with his testicles protruding. The wife proclaims them bells, the cuckold gives them a rap, and the wounded lover yelps, "Yingle, yangle." See Legman, *Rationale of the Dirty Joke*, pp. 748-749; Wilde, *The Complete Book of Ethnic Humor*, p. 228.

73. Recorded from Matt Persson, July 24, 1980, by Tom Barden and Mark Wagler at the Stoughton, Wisconsin, Senior Center for the Wisconsin Humor Project. For other newcomer jokes, see Edward J. Clode, *Jokes For All Occasions* (NYC: Grosset and Dunlap, 1921), p. 203; Schermerhorn, *Schermerhorn's Stories*, pp. 302-303.

74. Recorded from Thure Shelin, July 28, 1987, by James P. Leary, at Shelin's home, Delta, Wisconsin. Born in Chicago in 1907, Shelin heard Scandinavian dialect jokes from his immigrant Swedish parents. He spent his honeymoon in 1928 in the Delta area of Bayfield County, Wisconsin, and retired there in 1975 after laboring as a draftsman and design engineer on government projects throughout the United States. For a Scandinavian version of this joke, see Dorson, "Dialect Stories of the Upper Peninsula," #62.

75. Edwin Pearson, July 29, 1987. For biographical information, see the note for Text 65. Dorson recorded several versions of this story in "Dialect Stories of the Upper Peninsula," #147; see also Gage, *Still Another Northwoods Reader*, p. 86; and Stangland, *Uff Da Jokes*, p. 6.

76. Thorson, July 24, 1980. Thorson can't recall where or when he learned this joke, only that "I heard it and liked it." The term "newcomers" was used long before "immigrants" to describe Scandinavian arrivals in the Upper Midwest.

77. Recorded from Emery Olson, June 7, 1978, by James P. Leary at Chet and Ruth's Tavern, Plover, Wisconsin. Born in Iola, Wisconsin, a Norwegian section of Waupaca County, in 1923, Olson returned there in 1966 after working in "the carpentry trade" in Toledo, Ohio. He heard his first jokes out behind the proverbial barn, and his dad was a good teller. Regarding his own joke telling, Olson confesses:

> I like to have fun, and hear stories, and cut up. I'm a big ham, and I used to be years ago. When I was younger, people'd tell me, "You ought to go on TV." And I really feel like I could've been a comedian if I had the training, 'cause I love to get with people and make an ass of myself.

Olson's joke telling is examined more fully in my "Style in Jocular Communication," especially pp. 40-42. For other ethnic versions, see Anonymous, *Lamour LaMerrier* (Fort Worth, Texas: S.R.I. Publishing, 1965), p. 29; Anonymous, *Sexorama* (NYC: Derby Press, 1955), p. 20; Dance, *Shuckin' and Jivin'*, #234; J. Mortimer Hall, *Anecdota Americana, Second Series*, reprinted from the 1934 edition as *503 World's Worst Dirty Jokes* (NYC: Bell Publishing, 1982), p. 30; Legman, *Rationale of the Dirty Joke*, p. 548; and Wilde, *The Official Irish Joke Book*, p. 18.

78. Recorded from Felix Milanowski, November 12, 1980, by James P. Leary at the Milanowski home, Ashland, Wisconsin. Born in 1912 in a Polish neighborhood near Ashland's ore docks, Milanowski is a retired millworker and an avid sportsman. As a very animated joke teller, Felix would rock his body back and forth, use gestures when appropriate, mimic dialects, and laugh at punch lines until his face turned bright red. From his mill days, Felix recalled a German, Bill Schmaltz, now deceased, who used to tell stories on the job. He was so good that occasionally fellow workers would tell him to sit down and entertain them with stories while they worked. Felix also heard plenty of Ole-and-Lena jokes from the Swedish mother-in-law of a Bohemian friend, Don Belske.

79. Recorded from Oljanna Venden Cunneen, March 10, 1987, by James P. Leary and Reid Miller at a performance for the University of Wisconsin's Folklore Program, Madison. Raised in Black Earth, Wisconsin, Cunneen (1923–1988) spent most of her life in nearby Blue Mounds, where she was a guide at Little Norway, an ethnic museum built around a pioneer homestead. She was a masterful raconteur known especially for stringing together diverse Ole-and-Lena jokes into a coherent cycle that she performed for regional Norwegian–American audiences. Cunneen was also renowned for her costume making, needlework, rosemaling, and the construction of Norwegian troll dolls. She typically performed in costume and was quite comfortable holding an audience from a stage. Cunneen's telling about Ole and Lena is very close in style and content to Seattle co-

median Stan Boreson's version on *Stan Boreson Tells Diamond Jim's Favorite Yokes* (Huntington Station, NY: Golden Crest Records, LP CR-31028), side 1, band 13; recorded at Diamond Jim's restaurant, St. Paul, Minnesota. Other examples appear in Anonymous, *500 Best Irish Jokes and Limericks*, p. 35; Stangland, *Norwegian Jokes*, p. 5.

80. Cunneen, March 10, 1987.

81. George Russell, July 8, 1975. For biographical information, see the note for Text 52. Russell learned this joke prior to World War I while living in Minneapolis. A joke with the same plot as Russell's, but with an Irish maid, is in Wilde, *The Official Irish Joke Book*, p. 8. A similar punch line appears in another version: a Swedish witness tells a prosecutor that a thrown stone is "so long, but not so t'ick" as the lawyer's head (see Moulton, *2500 Jokes For All Occasions*, #1952).

82. Cunneen, March 10, 1987.

83. Cunneen, March 10, 1987. For other Norwegian versions, see Powers, *Leapin' Lena*, p. 22; Stangland, *Son of Norwegian Jokes* (Sioux Falls, South Dakota: Norse Press, 1980), p. 26. An Anglo–American example is recorded by Rayna Green in "Magnolias Grow in Dirt, The Bawdy Lore of Southern Women," *The Radical Teacher* 6 (1977), pp. 26-31.

84. Recorded from an unnamed female teller, July 24, 1980, at the Stoughton, Wisconsin, Senior Center for the Wisconsin Humor Project. This Stoughton version appears in Anonymous, *The Minnesota Norwegian's Favorite Jokes*, p. 5 and in Stangland's *Norwegian Jokes*, p. 37. This telling may be related to an older joke in which a minister was to be given a post in Minneapolis, "but he went up there to preach a trial sermon and took his text from St. Paul, so it's all off" (from Copeland, *10,000 Jokes, Toasts, and Stories*, #5192).

85. Russell, July 8, 1975. This joke and the next two were told by Russell in sequence. A slightly different version appears in Legman, *The Rationale of the Dirty Joke*, p. 705. Here, a Swedish maid is "yumped" by the man of the house; she later confesses to his wife that "he fooked me—good!"

86. Russell, July 8, 1975. An alternative version, offered right after Russell's telling by his neighbor, Erwin Schroeder, concluded with, "I hollered and I hollered, but the only one that come was Ole." Schroeder had heard this one in the 1920s when threshing in North Dakota.

87. Russell, July 8, 1975. This telling worked especially well in the Rice Lake area, where Russell commonly went for a drink and to talk at Wolf's Bar or the American Legion tavern, because the city has dozens of families named Olson, Johnson, Peterson, Anderson, Swanson, and Carlson. For a 1910 example, see Legman, *Rationale of the Dirty Joke*, p. 164; for a more recent version, see Red Stangland, *Ole and Lena Jokes* (Sioux Falls, South Dakota: Norse Press, 1986), p. 34.

88. John Leino, July 28, 1987. For biographical information, see the note for Text 67. Legman links the two jokes with the same final line in *Rationale of the Dirty Joke*, p. 164.

89. Cunneen, March 10, 1987.

90. Recorded by John Berquist, 1985, on *Ya Sure, You Bet You*, Half Moon Records. Born in 1946 in Eveleth, Minnesota, Berquist is a self-employed researcher and performer whose work and art have generally concerned traditional songs, tunes, and narratives gleaned from old timers in the Upper Midwest. In keeping with his Swedish ancestry, he is particularly adept with Scandinavian dialect songs and stories. Norwegian versions of this telling appear in Powers, *The New Uff Da*, p. 27; Stangland, *Norwegian Jokes*, p. 27. Clements offers a Polish example in *The Types of the Polack Joke*, p. 37.

91. Olson, June 7, 1978. Olson's telling and a version of the next example, told by Jon Mason, followed one another during an extended joke-telling session.

92. Milanowski, November 12, 1980. On June 7, 1978, I recorded a version from Jon Mason, told along with the previous text, in which Ole places his penis on a bar to see "who had the big ones." In a similar Norwegian joke, Lars is seen by his sweetheart when all the men urinate at a picnic (Legman, *Rationale of the Dirty Joke*, p. 326).

93. Cunneen, March 10, 1987. This particular example appears in Mike Kowalski, *The Polish Joke Book*, p. 32, and in Legman, *No Laughing Matter*, p. 842.

94. Cunneen, March 10, 1987.

95. Cunneen, March 10, 1987. While a "snooty Mrs. Carlson" is effectively bamboozled in this telling, a "Mrs. Thorson" is confounded in Stangland, *Son of Norwegian Jokes*, p. 27.

96. Pearson, July 29, 1987. This telling has several points of comparison with Text 76.

97. Persson, July 24, 1980. Richland Center, the home of Arlie Felton, is an Anglo–American bastion in western Wisconsin, with Norwegian and Bohemian neighbors nearby. For other ethnic versions of this joke, see Anonymous, *The Minnesota Norwegian's Favorite Jokes*, p. 15; Stangland, *Norwegian Jokes*, p. 41, and *Polish and Other Ethnic Jokes*, p. 25; and Marquard, *212 Spicy Stories*, p. 23.

98. Cunneen, March 10, 1987. A variant was provided by a Norwegian (Emery Olson, June 7, 1978): "They had a survey in Iola [Wisconsin], y'know. And sixty percent of the people in Iola had hemorrhoids. And the other forty percent were perfect assholes."

99. Leino, July 28, 1987. Other Norwegian versions appear in Powers, *The New Uff Da*, p. 7, and in Stangland, *Uff Da Jokes*, p. 3.

100. Cunneen, March 10, 1987. Stangland offers an Ole-and-Lena version of Cunneen's telling in *Ole and Lena Jokes*, p. 32.

101. Cunneen, March 10, 1987.

102. Recorded from Leon Teeter, June 1, 1978, by James P. Leary in the barroom of the Wisconsin River Country Club, Stevens Point, Wisconsin. Born ca. 1935, Portage County, Wisconsin, Teeter manages the Wisconsin River Country Club, a restaurant and golf course his parents developed on their farm. Joke telling has been a useful part of Teeter's work as a bartender, and he has a good store of Irish, Polish, and Norwegian jokes.

103. Pearson, July 29, 1987. This joke appears in Powers, *The New Uff Da*, p. 42, and in Stangland, *Norwegian Jokes*, p. 36.

104. Pearson, July 29, 1987. St. Peter refuses to make pasties, the Cornish miners' food, for one Cousin Jack in a version recorded by Dorson in *Bloodstoppers and Bearwalkers, Folk Traditions of the Upper Peninsula* (Cambridge: Harvard University Press, 1952), p. 118. Art Lee attributes the joke to Hjalmar Peterson (1886–1960), a.k.a. *Olle i Skratthul"* (Ole from Laughtersville), a Swedish–American musician and *bondkomiker* (peasant comedian) who toured the country from his Minneapolis base in the 1920s and 1930s; *The Lutefisk Ghetto: Life in a Norwegian–American Town* (Staples, Minnesota: Adventure Publications, 1978), p. 152. For recent Norwegian versions, see Powers, *The New Uff Da*, p. 53; also, *Stan Boreson Tells Diamond Jim's Favorite Yokes*, side 1, band 5.

105. Recorded from Mary Fowler, February 7, 1981, by Mark Wagler and Emily Osborn in Madison for the Wisconsin Humor Project. Although no biographical information was available for Fowler, her voice suggests a woman no older than thirty. I have received other versions from students in my Folklore of Wisconsin course at the UW–Madison.

The Finns

106. Oren Tikkanen, March 17, 1984. For biographical information, see the note for Text 26. For another version, see Randolph, *Sticks in the Knapsack* (NYC: Columbia University Press, 1958), pp. 7–8, 137.

107. John Leino, July 28, 1987. For biographical information, see the note for Text 67. Leino's variant is paralleled, with Polish and Mexican fools, in Wilde, *The Last Official Polish Joke Book* (Los Angeles: Pinnacle Books, 1977) and in Elgart, *Over Sexteen* (NYC: Grayson Publishing, 1951), p. 48. Legman cites Elgart and makes the Enchanted Pear Tree comparison in *Rationale of the Dirty Joke*, p. 128.

108. Recorded from Walter Johnson, May 23, 1988, by James P. Leary at the home of Bill Kangas, Oulu, Wisconsin. Finnish transcription and translation are by Arnie Alanen. Walter Johnson was born in 1914 on a farm in the heavily Finnish Town of Oulu where he still resides. Like many in the area, he has been a rural jack-of-all-trades: farming, logging, fishing, and working construction. Since the 1930s, he has also been known as one of the finest Finnish–American singers in the Upper Midwest, drumming for dances while his wife, Ailie, played the accordion. Johnson likewise has a reputation as a joke teller and prankster. He liked listening to the old timers while growing up: "When they were on the boats, they'd talk about women. When they were on the shore, they'd talk about boats." Their talk naturally included plenty of jokes in Finnish.

109. Recorded from Bill Kangas, May 23, 1988, by James P. Leary at the Kangas home, Oulu, Wisconsin. Kangas was born in Oulu in 1952 and has lived there all his life. He works as a banker in nearby Port Wing. He has been singing Finnish songs since he was five and nowadays drums and sings with the Oulu Hotshots. Kangas has a fine command of Finnish–American dialect.

110. Recorded from Frank Strukel, August 4, 1978, by James P. Leary, at the Hoyt Lakes, Minnesota Community Building. Born in 1945 in Eveleth, Minnesota, on the Mesabi Iron Range, the Slovenian–American Strukel is a "bullganger," or mobile maintenance crew member, in an open pit mine. He is known as a "good bullshitter" among other miners, an honor he shares with certain elders:

> I'd hear these stories from Hank Kanipes, my dad, the people at the Slovenian National Home in Eveleth. Just the old timers. You go in there, and you talk, buy them a drink, and say, "Hey, tell us a few stories." And they do. And they enjoy it and we enjoy it. I love it.

Mining and Finnish jokes are staples for Strukel; "kot tammit" is a standard phrase in the latter.

111. Keith Lea, May 31, 1978. For biographical information, see the note for Text 71. Lea lived for a time in the Upper Peninsula of Michigan, where he learned numerous Finnish jokes. Lea once told this one as a Polish joke, but he stopped when a Polish–American woman poured a glass of milk down his neck.

112a, 112b. First text, Oren Tikkanen, March 17, 1984; second text, John Leino, July 12, 1987.

113. Keith Lea, May 31, 1978. Copeland offers a version in which a young boy saves his companion at the game warden's expense in *10,000 Jokes, Toasts, and Stories*, #6146.

114. Oren Tikkanen, March 17, 1984. For another Upper Midwest version, see Text 260 in this collection.

115. Oren Tikkanen, March 17, 1984. I heard Michael Karni, the editor of *Finnish Americana*, tell a version in 1976; Dorson cites another in "Folk Traditions of the Upper Peninsula," *Michigan History* 31:1 (1947), p. 59.

116. An anonymous photocopied sheet, *Toivo's Tail*, sent to James P. Leary on March 27, 1980, by Kay Pavlik of Northern Michigan University, Marquette. Folk doctoring involving trumpets thrust up cows' behinds appears in such jokes as Text 144 in this collection. Tikkanen tells a Finnish–American dialect version that roughly matches *Toivo's Tail*. Dorson offers an Upper–Peninsula Finnish version in *Bloodstoppers and Bearwalkers*, p. 205; a version from the Ozarks appears in Randolph, *Sticks in the Knapsack*, pp. 131-132, 166. I have also heard the folk-revival singer Utah Phillips perform an extended version set on the Great Plains. The Finnish–American or Finglish dialect is treated with wit and erudition by Heino "Hap" Puotinen in two publications: "The Anatomy of Finglish," *Michigan Academician* 3:3 (1971), pp. 93-100, and *Finglish Fables and Other Humorous Finnish Dialect Tales* (White Pine, Michigan: Privately Printed, 1969).

117. Oren Tikkanen, March 17, 1984. I recorded a version from Bill Kangas, May 23, 1988, in which Toivo, who doesn't know much about cars, asks his mechanic buddy Eino to check out a new machine. One Polish and two Norwegian versions appear in Stangland, *Norwegian Jokes*, p. 43, *Ole and Lena Jokes*, p. 19, and *Polish and Other Ethnic Jokes*, p. 47.

118. Strukel, August 4, 1978. Strukel suits this telling to his own miner's occupation. For Norwegian and Polish versions, see Anderson, *Scandinavian Yokes*, p. 24; Clements, *Types of the Polack Joke*, p. 22. Also see AT Type 1349D*, "What Is the Joke? Nobleman asks peasant to hit his hand. Withdraws it so that peasant hits wall. Later peasant tries this on friend—but friend is to hit peasant's face." Baughman assigns motif J2131.1(a) to the same episode, although the players are a stranger and a numskull.

119a, 119b. First telling, Oren Tikkanen, March 17, 1984; second telling recorded from Ellen Leino, July 28, 1987, by James P. Leary at the Leino home in Washburn, Wisconsin. Ellen Kainu Leino was one year old in 1921 when her family moved from a mining community—Verona Location, Ramsay, Michigan—to the agrarian "Finn Settlement" near Washburn. Her Finnish dialect jokes are paralleled by numerous true stories, like this one about a neighbor.

> He went in the dime store. He wanted a comb. So he said he wanted a "gomb." So the clerk gave him a package of gum. He said he went around until he found the combs, then he picked one up.

Walter Johnson of Oulu told me a version on May 23, 1988. Leino's version and the next two examples were recorded in succession.

120. Ellen Leino, July 28, 1987. See Powers, *The New Uff Da*, p. 49; Stangland, *Norwegian Jokes*, p. 15.

121. Ellen Leino, July 28, 1987. This is the last of Leino's trio about Eino and Toivo's fruitless search for work. I recorded a Polish version, about Stash and Wladic, in Stevens Point, Wisconsin, June 1, 1978. For Italian and Norwegian versions, see Wilde, *The Last Official Italian Joke Book* (Los Angeles: Pinnacle Books, 1978); Stangland, *Ole and Lena Jokes*, p. 44. Their truck-driver settings are predated by a railroad variant in which a Swedish track walker sees two trains about to crash. The Swede's response to "What did you do?" is, "Well, I said to mineself, 'Dis bane one hell of a way to run a railroad.'" See Johnson et. al., *The Laughter Library*, #150.

122. Oren Tikkanen, March 17, 1984. For an Ozark text and references to an oral tradition extending back to 1935, see Randolph, *Pissing in the Snow and Other Ozark Folktales* (Urbana: University of Illinois Press, 1976), #98, and Clements, *The Types of the Polack Joke*, p. 45.

123. A photocopy given by Anselm "Andy" Polso of Kimball, Wisconsin, to James P. Leary, February 9, 1986. Polso (1913–1987) was born in Ironwood, Michigan, and worked as a motorman in iron ore mines and later as a groundskeeper for golf courses and ski hills. Active in the Gogebic Iron Range Finnish–American community, he was always ready with a few jokes. Polso picked up this text from Finnish–American friends at work. For similar humorous ethnic application forms, see Alan Dundes and Carl R. Pagter, *Work Hard and You Shall Be Rewarded, Urban Folklore From the Paperwork Empire* (Bloomington: Indiana University Press, 1978), #53-63, "Applications and Tests."

124. Edwin Pearson, July 29, 1987. For biographical information, see the notes to Text 65. The Maple community, straddling Douglas and Bayfield Counties in northern Wisconsin, is an area of heavy Finnish settlement. Not surprisingly, Pearson knew a gentle array of jokes and anecdotes regarding his Finnish neighbors.

125. Recorded from Lauri "Tuggers" Koski, August 27, 1988, by James P. Leary at the Festival of Michigan Folklife, East Lansing. Koski was born in 1926 in Deerton, Michigan, a mining town. His father was a miner, and he, too, worked briefly in the mines. He also worked for a truck farm and as a logger before going into construction and carpentry. Koski usually tells his jokes "when there's a few Finns around." He likes "to work them in when something comes up."

126. Lauri Koski, August 27, 1988. Koski is a sauna builder and an excellent *viita* maker. He heard this joke in the late 1930s or early 1940s. Of the Cornish man or Cousin Jack in the telling, Koski says, "Whenever a Finnlander took a Cousin Jack in the sauna, he'd go running out of there saying, 'That Finnlander's crazy.'" See Dorson for a version with a different punch line, "what blace is de towel?" in "Folk Traditions of the Upper Peninsula," p. 59. Also Aili K. Johnson presents a text and cites four other versions in "Lore of the Finnish–American Sauna," *Midwest Folklore* 1:1 (1951), p. 38.

127. Oren Tikkanen, March 17, 1984. For another Finnish/Irish joke on this theme, see Text 177. I overheard another Finnish version in October, 1980, at the Silver Star Tavern, Wentworth, Wisconsin, and I recorded a version involving two bums and a priest from Leo Garski, May 6, 1982, Stevens Point, Wisconsin. These published versions involve beatniks, Norwegians, and Poles: Anonymous, *Party Jokes For Swingers Only* (NYC: Bee- Line Books, 1967), p. 35; Powers, *Ya Sure, Ya Betcha!* (Crosby, North Dakota: The Journal Publishing Company, 1981), p. 58; and Wilde, *The Last Official Polish Joke Book*, p. 198.

128. Oren Tikkanen, March 17, 1984. A non-ethnic rural trickster appears in Runninger's *Favorite Jokes of Mountain Folks in Boogar Hollow*, p. 5. All three motifs, or exchanges, as well as others along the same lines, appear independently in oral tradition, but they are also frequently conjoined, most notably in the "Arkansas Traveler." For a detailed examination, see Catherine Marshall Vineyard's "The Arkansas Traveler," *Backwoods To Border*, ed. Mody C. Boatright and Donald Day (Austin and Dallas: 1943), pp. 11-60.

129. Oren Tikkanen, March 17, 1984. Marquette, home of Northern Michigan University, is the largest city in the Upper Peninsula, while Baraga is a sawmill village. Generally the trickster's response to "This is piss" is "Yes, but whose?" See Baker, *Jokelore*, #130; Legman, *No Laughing Matter*, p. 942; and Marquard, *212 Spicy Stories*, pp. 92-93. This joke may be related to an older tale, AT Type 1832B*, "What Kind of Dung?" cited from French-Canada, in which a priest asks a boy what he's looking at. The priest says it's horse's dung, but the boy wonders if it came from "a horse or a mare."

130. Ellen Leino, July 28, 1987. The response is "Ole Olson from Nor' Dakota" in Powers, *Leapin' Lena*, p. 50. This joke is probably related to an earlier one in which a Jewish patient says hello to another patient in a hospital waiting room. The second patient says, "I'm aching from arthritis," and the first responds, "I'm Rosenbaum from Chicago." Moulton, *2500 Jokes For All Occasions*, #1675.

131. Oren Tikkanen, March 17, 1984.

The Poles

132. Recorded from Max Trzebiatowski, August 14, 1979, by James P. Leary at the Trzebiatowski home, rural Portage County, Wisconsin. Trzebiatowski was the only boy in a large Polish immigrant family that settled in the Fancher area of eastern Portage County. "I was born on a farm [in 1903] and stayed on a farm." The first jokes he learned were in Polish and involved foolish peasants, tricksters, and priests; not surprisingly, he also had a large fund of rural jokes. I comment at length on his repertoire, style, and aesthetics in "The Favorite Jokes of Max Trzebiatowski," in *Humor and the Individual*, ed. Elliott Oring (Los Angeles: The California Folklore Society, 1984), pp. 1-17. Max told this particular tale in a slow, halting fashion since he first heard it and normally tells it in Polish. I believe he was going over the narrative in Polish, deciding what should be delivered only in English and what Polish should be retained. Notably, he recognized that part of the tale's wit lies in the rhyme which he delivered in Polish. As for the relationship between gender and economics, Malcolm Rosholt made this observation in *Our County, Our Story, Portage County, Wisconsin* (Stevens Point: Worzalla Publishing, 1959), p. 138:

> The near-equal status of wife to husband among the Poles was carried over into Portage County in the first and second generations. A cattle broker, for example, when buying a cow from a Polish farmer seldom closed the deal before the husband went into the house to "see what the woman says." Her word on the price of the cow was final.

A wife who gets cheated in cattle dealings is a fool indeed.

133. Recorded from Jon Mason, August 14, 1979, by James P. Leary at the Northside Bar in Stevens Point, Wisconsin. Born in Spooner, Wisconsin, in 1922, Mason moved with his parents to the mill town of Schofield, near Wausau, Wisconsin, "when the Depression hit." He worked as an electrician in Portage County where he was known among tradesmen and sportsmen as a joke teller without peer: the man who not only knew the most jokes (I recorded nearly 200 from him) but also the jokes most difficult to perform. His biography, repertoire, and mastery of form, dialogue, mimicry, and gesture are sketched in my "Style in Jocular Communication," *Journal of Folklore Research*, esp. pp. 35- 37. A city girl is married to a fur king and a mountain girl to a "furking hillbilly" in Anonymous, *Toujour Manure* (Fort Worth: S.R.I. Publishing, 1966), p. 8.

134. Recorded from William Kluge, June, 1985, by his daughter Becky for "Folklore of Wisconsin" at the University of Wisconsin–Madison. Kluge was born ca. 1938, a "full-blooded German," on a farm where he still lives in Wisconsin's Fox River Valley.

135. Recorded from Leonard Thalacker, July 25, 1980, by Tom Barden and Mark Wagler at Montello for the Wisconsin Humor Project. Born in 1909 in Marquette County, Wisconsin, of German parents, Thalacker is a Lutheran minister who retired in 1971. His wife, who graciously answered my letter since her husband was in ill health, related that Rev. Thalacker "has always had a good sense of humor and enjoyed jokes and funny stories, but rarely told jokes." I recorded a Polish version from Emery Olson, August 14, 1979, at the Northside Bar, Stevens Point, Wisconsin. Clements cites Polish examples in *The Types of the Polack Joke*, p. 24. See Stangland, *Ole and Lena Jokes, Book III*, p. 24.

136. Sikorski, June 13, 1978. For biographical information, see the note for Text 63. I heard this as an exclusively Polish joke in Louisville, Kentucky, 1980. Sikorski's "combination Norwegian and Polish" joke is fairly common in Portage County, where Poles in the central part of the county interact with Norwegians in eastern Portage County and adjacent Waupaca County.

137. Keith Lea, May 31, 1978. For biographical information, see the note for Text 71.

138. Leon Teeter, June 1, 1978. For biographical information, see the note for Text 102. Irishmen confound Texan braggarts in Myron Cohen, *More Laughing Out Loud* (NYC: The Citadel Press, 1960), p. 129; Wilde, *The Official Irish Joke Book*, p. 12. A Swede and a Norwegian square off in Anderson, *Scandinavian Yokes*, p. 21; Powers, *The New Uff Da*, p. 11.

139. Felix Milanowski, November 12, 1980. For biographical information, see the note for Text 78. This joke is set on the Ashland ore docks where Milanowski once worked; indeed, his old neighborhood was in the shadow of the docks. No longer in use, the ore docks are elevated railroad tracks that jut into the harbor on Lake Superior. Though Milanowski presented the joke as a true story, it also appears in Stangland, *Norwegian Jokes*, p. 30, and *Polish and Other Ethnic Jokes*, p. 29.

Other Ethnics

140. Recorded from an unnamed teller by Jane Olson, ca. 1936, in the Cambria area. Olson was a fieldworker for the Wisconsin Folklore division of the Federal Writers' Project in the late 1930s. According to her correspondence with director Charles Brown, she resided in Madison, Wisconsin, in 1936. Cambria is an area of heavy Welsh settlement where Jones is a very common Welsh name. Fred Holmes in *Old World Wisconsin* (pp. 202-203) noted thirty-three Joneses in Cambria in the late 1930s; many were associated with their farm's name as a means of distinction.

141. Recorded from an unnamed teller, September 22, 1936, in New Glarus, Wisconsin, by "Potter," a fieldworker for the Wisconsin Folklore division of the Federal Writers' Project.

142. Recorded from Michael Patzlsberger, July 11, 1985, in Randolph, Wisconsin, by Rhonda Feil for "Folklore of Wisconsin" at the University of Wisconsin–Madison. In Columbia County, Randolph inhabitants include Germans, the Welsh, and the Dutch, most of the latter belonging to the conservative Dutch Reformed faith. For variants, see Moulton, *2500 Jokes For All Occasions*, #1543; Dance, *Shuckin' and Jivin'*, #133. Patzlsberger's variant is matched in Runninger, *Favorite Jokes of Mountain Folks in Boogar Hollow*, p. 13.

143. Recorded from Doug Cochenet, June, 1986, at the Cochenet home by his daughter, Lisa, for "Folklore of Wisconsin" at the University of Wisconsin–Madison. Born in 1935, in southern Door County, Wisconsin, Cochenet has been a meat cutter, sailor, factory worker, gas station mechanic, hobby farmer, and rural jack-of-all-trades. He has a reputation as one of the best joke tellers in the Sturgeon Bay area. Like many Belgian–Americans in everyday life, the Belgians of this and the next two jokes are farmers. For Norwegian and Polish versions, see Powers, *The New Uff Da*, p. 12; Stangland, *Uff Da Jokes*, p. 13; and Wilde, *The Last Official Polish Joke Book*, pp. 156- 157.

144. Recorded from Harry Chaudoir, May 3, 1988, by James P. Leary at the Chaudoir home, Rosiere, Wisconsin. Chaudoir was born in the Brussels, Wisconsin, area where his parents farmed. He has done some farming and has worked for the regional electric company since 1946. He is very active in the local Belgian club and returned to the old country in 1972. Although not himself a stellar

joke teller, Chaudoir has heard plenty and tells a few—all in the Walloon dialect, which remains lively.

145. Doug Cochenet, June, 1986.

146. Keith Lea, May 31, 1978. For biographical information, see the note for Text 71. Lea learned this joke while working in Sault St. Marie, Michigan, and his telling refers to a prominent local landmark. Although Lea doesn't attempt an Italian–American dialect, he was influenced by Bill Siriano of the Sault, "a master storyteller," who was a representative of the Michigan Educational Association and a habitué of the Italian Hall.

147. Keith Lea, June 7, 1978. Eagan and Johanson hate "Eyetalians" in Wilde, *The Complete Book of Ethnic Humor*, p. 14. An uncharacteristic Swede organ grinder is confronted by a Norwegian in Anderson, *Scandinavian Yokes*, p. 32, and in Stangland, *Uff Da Jokes*, p. 13

Loggers Notes

148. Recorded from Carl Gunderson, August 9, 1973, by Katherine Leary Antenne and Minda Hugdahl, in Rice Lake, Wisconsin, for the Barron County Historical Society. Gunderson's Swedish immigrant father moved the family from Bayfield to Ladysmith in 1900 after he suffered financial losses logging during a winter with no frost. Gunderson (1898–1973) went into the woods at the age of fifteen as a dishwasher in the cookshack. One day, when the second cook threw burnt pie crusts on his clean dishes, Gunderson broke the fellow's arm with a rolling pin. He was thereafter promoted to cook and worked for many years in camps and on drives on the Flambeau River. Later, he farmed in the Blue Hills east of Rice Lake and gave sleigh rides in the winter through "Gundy's Canyon." The following is a deciphering of the story's "woods talk":

> A "bull," or "bull of the woods," is the camp foreman. A "ground mole," "ground hog," or "ground loader" is one who uses a "cant hook," a kind of log wrench, to direct logs up a pair of "skids" (poles) onto a sleigh or railroad car. A "cross-haul man," positioned on the side of the sleigh opposite the "ground mole," would tend a chain used to pull the logs up the skids. "Crow baits" are the cross-haul man's horse team. "Sky piece" sometimes refers to a hat or cap, but in this telling, it must mean the same as a "sky hooker," "sky bird," or "top loader"—the person who stood on top of the sleigh or railroad car and positioned logs into place. "Taileroos," the "single-line swamp hook," and a "slash block" are all kinds of equipment: log tongs, a chain with log-gripping hook, and a block and tackle, respectively. The "sky piece" is injured when his experienced "ground mole" absconds to the whore house and an inexperienced man, a "punk," botches commands. Confronted with a crotched log (a "school marm") that will roll up the skids unevenly because it is much larger at one end than the other ("blue-butted"), the "punk" fails to "sag," or "Saginaw," the log (to slow the butt end) and instead uses the opposite technique ("St. Croix"). The out-of-control log ends up "gunned," with its butt end on the ground and the other end pointing skyward like a cannon's barrel. The log strikes the "sky piece," and besides suffering a broken leg, the teller cracks two ribs ("slats"). In the hospital, he is also rid of "seam spurs," or lice. The "hot logging" undertaken involves moving timber immediately from stump to mill.

For an introduction to woods talk in the Upper Midwest, see L.G. Sorden, *Lumberjack Lingo* (Spring Green: Wisconsin House, 1969). Other versions of Gunderson's account appear in Robert Gard and L.G. Sorden, *Wisconsin Lore* (Sauk City, Wisconsin: Stanton and Lee, 1976), p. 59; Agnes M. Larson, "On the Trail of the Woodsman," *Minnesota History* 13:4 (1932), pp. 364-365; John Emmett Nelligan, *The Life of a Lumberman* (Madison: State Historical Society of Wisconsin, 1929), pp. 64-65; and Robert Wells, *Daylight in the Swamp: Lumberjacking in the Late 19th Century* (Garden City, New York: Doubleday, 1978), p. 228.

149. Recorded from an unnamed teller, possibly Charles Lee, ca. 1936, by an unnamed fieldworker, probably Gregg Montgomery or Jane Olson. Olson and Montgomery were fieldworkers for the Wisconsin Folklore division of the Federal Writers' Project in the late 1930s under the direction of Charles Brown of the State Historical Society of Wisconsin. This story, as well as Texts 151a and 165, appears in an unpublished manuscript, "Lumber and Lumberjack Lore.

150. Harry Chaudoir, May 3, 1988. For biographical information, see the note for Text 144. This joke is well known in the region. I recorded versions from Jon Mason on June 1 and June 7, 1978, in Stevens Point and Plover, Wisconsin. On May 27, 1978, Alvin Konkol, of Amherst Junction, Wisconsin, prefaced his telling with, "It's an old one. Columbus told that to the Indian. That's how come the Indian had it against the whites." Dorson presents a French dialect version and cites another in Finnish dialect; see "Dialect Stories of the Upper Peninsula," #21, and *Shuckin' and Jivin'*, #148. For the first of Jon Mason's versions, see Text 294.

151a, 151b. The first instance was recorded from an unnamed teller, possibly Charles Lee, ca. 1936. Texts 151a and 165 appear in an unpublished manuscript, "Lumber and Lumberjack Lore." The second telling was recorded from Oscar "Flack" Olsen, 1955, by Ward Winton, in Shell Lake, Wisconsin. Born in 1877 in Norway, Olsen emigrated to Shell Lake, Wisconsin, in 1884. He followed his father into a Shell Lake planing mill in 1893, then worked as a cook and, subsequently, a clerk in lumber camps from 1895–1900. After cowboying one year in South Dakota, Olsen traveled to Chicago where he worked as a baker, a piecework inspector for General Electric, and a motion picture operator before retiring in 1953. Biographical information on Ward Winton, a raconteur in his own right, accompanies Text 183. Olsen's version is reprinted from Winton's *Washburn County Historical Collections* (Washburn, Wisconsin: Washburn County Historical Society, 1976), p. 226.

152. Tom Sheehan, ca. 1967, by Ward Winton, Shell Lake, Wisconsin. Born in 1888 in Rock Creek, Kansas, Sheehan traveled with his parents by wagon to homestead in Washburn County, Wisconsin, in 1899. He entered the lumber camps in the winter of 1907–1908 and worked as a logger, farmer, and horse trader. Sheehan's anecdote is reprinted from Winton's *Washburn County Historical Collections*, (Washburn, Wisconsin: Washburn County Historical Society, 1976) p. 115.

153. Oscar "Flack" Olsen, 1955. His telling is reprinted from Winton's *Washburn County Historical Collections*, p. 226. For other versions see Copeland, *10,000 Jokes, Toasts, and Stories*, #7244; Mildred Meiers and Jack Knapp, *Thesaurus of Humor* (NYC: Crown Publishers, 1940), #3760; Moulton, *2500 Jokes For All Occasions*, #1944; William Patten, *Among the Humorists and After Dinner Speakers* (NYC: P.F. Collier & Son, 1909), p. 171; and Wilde, *The Complete Book of Ethnic Humor*, p. 224.

154. Recorded from Mike McCann, September 17, 1953, by Ward Winton, Shell Lake, Wisconsin. McCann was born in 1898 in Springbrook, Wisconsin. His father, Jim, was a noted fiddler and saloonkeeper. Young McCann logged hardwood in Wisconsin before following the timber to Washington, eventually serving with the fire department in Spokane. His jocular place-name legend is reprinted from Winton's *Washburn County Historical Collections*. "Chippanazie" is said to be "the Indian name for 'crooked bark'" in Ethel Elliott Chappelle's *The "Why of Names" in Washburn County, Wisconsin* (Birchwood, Wisconsin: 1965), p. 4. "Chip-in-a-zee" is defined as the "practice of chopping a notch on the side on which a tree was to fall," according to Sorden in *Lumberjack Lingo*, p. 24. Both spellings appear in Gard and Sorden's *The Romance of Wisconsin Place Names*, p. 23, although "Chippanazie" is said to mean "crooked water."

155. Recorded from Gust Pietala, July 3, 1987, by James P. Leary at the Festival of American Folklife, Washington, D.C. Born in Ishpeming, Michigan, in 1906, Pietala moved with his parents to Bruce Crossing in 1908. He still resides in "Bruce's." Pietala worked one winter in the lumber camps in the mid-1920s, tending chain for a skidding crew. Thereafter he worked successively in iron ore mines, on his own dairy farm, and at the White Pine copper mine. Since retirement in 1972, he has used red oak, white ash, yellow birch, and ironwood to fashion skis, sleds, tools, and furniture. In Pietala's blacksmith telling, the Chicagoan injures the horse through ignorance, driving nails straight into the hoof. The "Pennsylvania Dutch" trickster Eileschpijjel, derived from the German Till Eulenspiegel, does the same thing out of malice. See "Eileschpijjel Shoes A Horse" in Brendle and Troxell, *Pennsylvania German Folk Tales*, p. 170.

156. Gust Pietala, July 3, 1987. This telling is paired with the preceding example. In "The Origin of the One-Man Saw," Eileschpijjel pretends to mistake the use of a crosscut saw and splits it in two; see Brendle and Troxell, *Pennsylvania German Folk Tales*, p. 170. A well dressed greenhorn hands the saw to the smaller of two men in the telling of Wisconsin logger, Louis Blanchard; see Wyman, *The Lumberjack Frontier*, p. 21. For another Wisconsin version and additional references, see Text 61 and its accompanying note.

157. Recorded from Roman David "Bimbo" Alexa, July 18, 1989, by James P. Leary in the cab of Alexa's pickup enroute from Escanaba, Michigan, to his home in Iron River. Bimbo's paternal grandfather, Albert Alexa, emigrated from Bohemia in the 1890s to the Gilbert Lake area of Iron County, Michigan, where he raised sheep on a small homestead and worked winters in the woods as a teamster. Albert's son and Bimbo's dad, John Alexa, the source of this telling, was born in Iron County in 1897. John and his brothers-in-law, Ed and Charlie Casagrande, immigrants from the Italian Tyrol, worked in and ran lumber camps throughout the Upper Peninsula of Michigan. Bimbo was born at Gilbert Lake in 1934 and began working in lumber camps with his dad in the 1940s. He quit school in 1950 to winter in camps through 1955. He has been a truck driver, a riverboat hand, and a logging equipment sales representative, but he has run his own logging operation since 1966. Currently Alexa is president of the Michigan–Wisconsin Timber Producers Association. During Alexa's early years in the camps, "Ninety percent of the men were single: Finns, Swedes, Poles, Russians, mostly born in the old country." Friendly and articulate, Alexa relished days when "we'd swap stories in the evenings." "That was one of the pastimes," he added. Regarding the snowbound sawyer, Bimbo reckoned his dad "could have made that up." He went on to say, "You know, lot of these jacks made up their own stories."

158. Probably Louis Blanchard, ca. 1936. For more on Blanchard and "Old Man Beliell," see the note for Text 22. Charles Brown, who directed the Wisconsin Folklore project, was a major proponent of Bunyan hokum, publishing a half-dozen pamphlets on Paul and his coworkers. Brown's

Bunyan Backhouse Yarns (Madison: Wisconsin Folklore Society, 1945) has a version of Blanchard's tale. This is AT Type 1889L, "Lie: The Split Dog." The element of flopping from one set of legs to the other carries Baughman motif X1215.11(c). A far more elaborate version from Louis Blanchard, ending with a description of the progeny of "Tige" and a wolf, appears in Wyman, *The Lumberjack Frontier*, pp. 83-85.

159. Recorded from Thomas O. Church, April, 1987, in Middleton, Wisconsin, by Dawn Brunner for "Folklore of Wisconsin" at the University of Wisconsin–Madison. Born in 1934 in Homestead, Wisconsin, Church received a degree in engineering from the University of Wisconsin and is currently employed by the UW's Physical Plant. His father, Glen Church, and especially his grandfather, Morris Church, were lumberjacks in Florence County, Wisconsin, on the Michigan border.

160. Tom Sheehan, ca. 1967. Reprinted from Winton, *Washburn County Historical Collections*, p. 115.

161a, 161b. The first example was probably recorded from Louis Blanchard, ca. 1936. Pete Legault was once the subject of many humorous French dialect anecdotes in the Chippewa Falls area, including Text 162. The second version was recorded from Maude Pratt Odekirk, 1968, by Ward Winton, Shell Lake, Wisconsin. Raised in the Town of Stinnet, Washburn County, Odekirk (1884-1970) was the daughter of Margaret Robinson Pratt and Tom Pratt, a storekeeper/raconteur whose tales were recalled by Jens Ingebretson (Texts 267 and 268). She married Marion Odekirk in 1910 and worked as a schoolteacher, postmistress, and homemaker. Joe Trepania (Trepannier) was a legendary strongman and good-hearted innkeeper who, like Legault, had come from French Canada in the 1840s to log in the Chippewa Valley. Odekirk's telling is reprinted from Winton, *Washburn County Historical Collections*, p. 502. Another Wisconsin version attributed to Pete Legault also mentions that "when in charge of a log drive which was being held up in low water, he made the situation known to his employers by sending a picture of a peavey stuck up in a log"; see "The Memoirs of Bruno Vinette," as told to William M. Bartlett, *Wisconsin Magazine of History* 9 (1925-1926), pp. 442-447. The illiterate logger is not named by Louis Blanchard in Wyman, *The Lumberjack Frontier*, p. 18.

162. Probably Louis Blanchard, ca. 1936. Legault points at the "U.S." stamped on Army blankets in another version I heard in the mid-1970s from my aunt, Marge Vaudreuill, a native of Chippewa Falls.

163. Carl Gunderson, August 9, 1973. Stewart H. Holbrook compares such dwellings to primitive caves—"the logger at home peered through a haze of smoke to see nothing but more logs piled up, one upon the other"—in *The American Lumberjack*, p. 50.

164. George Russell, August 21, 1974. For biographical information, see the note for Text 52. Vermin were a common problem in lumber camps, and they made a permanent impression on Russell. Once when I spent the night at his home, he assured me that there were no bedbugs.

165. Recorded from an unnamed teller, ca. 1936, by an unnamed fieldworker, probably Gregg Montgomery or Jane Olson, for the Wisconsin Folklore division of the Federal Writers' Project.

166. Edwin Pearson, July 29, 1987. For biographical information, see the note for Text 65.

167. Recorded from Elmer Gunderson, ca. 1975, by Rose Verville Swanson, Mason, Wisconsin. Gunderson (ca. 1905-1977) lived in the Swedish settlement of Grandview in Bayfield County where he worked in the woods, then ran a tavern and a gas station. He was fond of singing Swedish songs and, according to Rose Swanson, was a "real clown" who "could imitate anybody." Swanson recorded these jokes and an array of Swedish and country-and-western songs and tunes during a party at the Indian Lake Tavern of her brother-in-law, Fritz Swanson. The highly self-conscious introduction for this telling and Text 174 was Swanson's response to telling his joke on tape at a raucous party; he modulates his voice and concentrates on elocution in the manner of a radio performer. The Chinese cook is badly treated by military officers in Legman's *No Laughing Matter*, p. 940. A Polish version, set in the Marines, appears in Ned Novak, *The New Polish Joke Book* (NYC: Nordon Publications, 1977), p. 113.

168. Recorded from Loren Wolf, November, 1986, in Eau Claire, Wisconsin, by Shelly Wolf for "Folklore of Wisconsin" at the University of Wisconsin–Madison. Loren Wolf's stories were all learned from his father, Arthur Wolf. Born in Shawano, Wisconsin, the son of a logging camp foreman, Arthur Wolf (1905–1984) likewise logged on the Wolf River. He later ran a resort in northern Wisconsin before retiring in Eau Claire. George Corrigan recalls the April foolery of a big Polish cook, Kilarski, who changed his name to Killarney to match his Irish workmates in *Calked Boots and Cant Hooks* (Park Falls, Wisconsin: MacGregor Litho, 1977), p. 18:

> While making the pancakes that April Fool's Day morning, Killarney decided to cut some cheese cloth in the shape of pancakes which could be placed between two thin pancakes after browning one side. No one could tell the difference by looking at the dish of pancakes. We all took two pancakes on our plates, applied the syrup or bacon grease, or both, then each took our knives and fork to take a bite, but we could not cut them.

Killarney fooled the boys again at lunch with a red-pepper–laced apple pie.

169. Thomas O. Church, April, 1987. I recorded a lumber camp version from Pete Trzebiatowski, June 13, 1978, in Stevens Point, Wisconsin. Legman likewise offers woods versions in *Rationale of the Dirty Joke*, p. 566, and in *No Laughing Matter*, p. 357.

170. Thomas O. Church, April, 1987. Although Florence, Wisconsin, is equally wooded and remote, Church, his father (Glen), and his grandfather (Morris) liked to poke fun at their cross-state neighbors.

171. Edwin Pearson, July 29, 1987. Among Pearson's hobbies were woodworking and poking around nearby lumber camps with a metal detector; he had a fine collection of woods tools. The Ole Johnson mentioned was born in Sweden and worked cutting the original white pine in Wisconsin lumber camps. Pearson recalls Johnson living "on the Clevedon Road near the Brule River" with a "beautiful team of horses and a dog for companions." Johnson was quite a wit, and Pearson tells several anecdotes attributed to him; see Text 241.

172. Recorded from Jens "Jim" Ingebretson, ca. 1954, by Ward Winton, Washburn County, Wisconsin. A second-generation Norwegian–American, Ingebretson (1877-1969) was born at Wisconsin Dells, where his father made shingles in the winter, then rafted them down the Wisconsin and Mississippi Rivers to St. Louis. In 1888 the family homesteaded on Long Lake, Washburn County. Jens entered the logging camps at the age of sixteen and worked his first log drive in the spring of 1894. After marrying in 1902, he continued to work in the woods, but passed up the drives to farm. Phoenix Grey was a veteran woods worker from Maine who logged for the O'Brien Brothers of Stillwater, Minnesota, on the St. Croix River and its tributaries. He was a bachelor and inspired numerous anecdotes, including the following example and Text 183. Reprinted from Winton, *Washburn County Historical Collections*, p. 342.

173. Jens "Jim" Ingebretson, ca. 1954. The Namekagon River in northwest Wisconsin flows into the St. Croix. Reprinted from Winton, *Washburn County Historical Collections*, p. 343.

174. Elmer Gunderson, ca. 1975. This telling would appear to refer to large timber rafts that were towed down the Mississippi to St. Louis mills until early in this century.

175. Recorded from Clinton "Hank" Kanipes, August 8, 1978, by James P. Leary at the MinnTac Iron Mine, Mountain Iron, Minnesota. Born ca. 1923 on the Mesabi Iron Range, Kanipes was a working boss on the "bullgang," or mobile maintenance crew, in an open pit mine. He was much admired by younger workers for his anecdotes and imitations celebrating the humorous doings of old-timers in the mines.

176. Recorded from Frank Bohn, 1975, by Ward Winton, Shell Lake, Wisconsin. Born 1893 in Shell Lake, Bohn was the son of a millwright and eventual head sawyer in Frederick Weyerhaeuser's local mill. Frank Bohn himself was a carpenter, building mover, and general contractor. This story came from Bohn's father, Lawrence. Reprinted from Winton, *Washburn County Historical Collections*, p. 237.

177. Recorded from John Slattery, August 8, 1978, by James P. Leary at Hibbing High School, Hibbing, Minnesota. Born ca. 1920, the youngest son of an Irish shovel runner and mine superintendent, Slattery heard many mining and lumber camp stories from old-timers as a child. He worked for the Hibbing, Minnesota, school system as a business manager. His telling of this jocular tale was in the context of an interview regarding the culture of miners on the Mesabi Range. This partially accounts for the background detail, but Slattery was inclined toward extended vivid narratives. The version involving lice-infested Pat was recorded from Jacob Pete for the Oral History Library at Ironworld in Chisholm, Minnesota.

For comments on the Finns' custom of building a sauna in the lumber camps, where they were noted for being "very clean," see Robert Pike in *Tall Trees, Tough Men* (NYC: W.W. Norton & Co., 1967), pp. 60, 98. The following is an excerpt from Pike's book:

> [T]he majority of the old-time woodsmen believed that taking a bath in the winter season would bring on galloping consumption.... [S]ome loggers kept putting on one pair of socks over another and one suit of long red underwear over another...and were quite surprised, come spring, when they had their first wash, to find several layers of socks and long-johns that they had forgotten about.

178. John Leino, July 28, 1987. For biographical information, see the note for Text 67. Leino's father and his neighbors would "come home in the spring with all the lice on their clothes." They had to strip on the porch and clean up before entering the house.

179. Roman David "Bimbo" Alexa, July 18, 1989. Finnish transcription, translation, and idiomatic interpretation by Arnie Alanen. Prostitutes blaspheming at the sight of a client's organ are common in jokes. In a version I recorded from Jon Mason, June 7, 1978, Stevens Point, Wisconsin, a well-hung clergyman visits a prostitute. Her confession of faith takes on a double meaning as he drops his pants: "Just because I'm a prostitute doesn't mean I don't believe in—JESUS CHRIST!"

180a, 180b. The first telling was recorded from Charles Gaulke, 1974, by Katherine Leary Antenne, Rice Lake, Wisconsin. Born in Wausau, Wisconsin, Gaulke (1877–1976) ran away from home at the age of fifteen to work in the woods. He was a road monkey, a teamster, a sawyer, and a toploader who also rode logs on drives in the upper Wisconsin and Chippewa River valleys. In the late 1890s, he farmed in Marathon County ("I had stones down there you could dance a square dance on"), then ran a tavern and rooming house near Stratford, before moving to Rice Lake around 1917, where he logged, farmed, developed traps for various animals and ran a woodyard. He continued to cut wood for customers, on a small scale, until 1970 at the age of 93. The second telling was recorded from George Russell, August 21, 1974, by James P. Leary at the Russell home in Bruce, Wisconsin. For biographical information, see the note for Text 52. Legman gives a rural-accented version of this telling from New York state, 1938, in *Rationale of the Dirty Joke*, p. 447.

181. George Russell, July 8, 1975.

182. George Russell, July 8, 1975. Hoffman provides motif X722.2.1, "He's in her ass." For other versions, see Legman, *Rationale of the Dirty Joke*, pp. 483–484; Norman Lockridge, *Waggish Tales of the Czechs* (NYC: Candide Press, 1947), p. 176; and Randolph, *Pissing in the Snow*, #78.

183. Recorded from Ward Winton, July, 1975, by James P. Leary. Lawyer, judge, and county historian, Winton (1896–1980) compiled the *Washburn County Historical Collections*, including reminiscences, many of them tape recorded, from people whose tellings appear in this collection: Bohn, Ingebretson, McCann, Odekirk, Olsen, and Sheehan. Winton told me about Funnix Grey, who is the subject of Texts 172 and 173, during the "Folklore of Wisconsin" course when he was 80 years old. For other versions, see *Fleetwood Pride, 1864–1960: The Autobiography of a Maine Woodsman*, ed. Edward D. Ives and David C. Smith (Orono, Maine: Northeast Folklore Society, 1967) pp. 40, 57; Patrick B. Mullen, *I Heard the Old Fishermen Say: Folklore of the Texas Gulf Coast* (Austin: University of Texas Press, 1978), pp. 126-127.

184. Thomas O. Church, April, 1987.

185. Tim Condon, 1973. For biographical information, see the note for Text 10. This is a recent tale backdated to a half century ago. Reprinted from Krotzman, *Folktales Found in the St. Croix Valley*, pp. 20-21. Kentuckians, Poles, and Norwegians misuse chain saws in Baker, *Jokelore*, #184; Clements, *The Types of the Polack Joke*, p. 21; Stangland, *Norwegian Jokes*, p. 32, and *Polish and Other Ethnic Jokes*, p. 38; and Wilde, *The Last Official Polish Joke Book*, p. 142.

186. Janet Cox, December 7, 1980. For biographical information, see the note for Text 49.

Miners

187. Recorded from John Persons, August 2, 1946, by Helene Stratman–Thomas in Madison, Wisconsin, for the Archive of American Folksong at the Library of Congress. Born in 1859, probably in a heavily Cornish mining community in Iowa County, Wisconsin, Persons contributed a number of Cornish Christmas carols to a state survey of folksong. A couple of old fishermen have the same argument over codfish and shad in Johnson et al, *Laughter Library*, #934.

188. Jack Foster, March 17, 1984. For biographical information, see the note for Text 34. The "fourteenth" corresponds to a level in an underground or "deep" mine, and Foster places Jan and Bill at the same depth in Texts 190 and 191. Related punch lines by an illiterate Irish maid ("there's nothing loike education afther all") and a Norwegian maid ("it must be vunderful to have an education") in response to the mistress's claim that she can write her name in dust on the piano appear in Moulton, *2500 Jokes For All Occasions*, #335, and in Anderson, *Scandinavian Yokes*, p. 4.

189. Recorded from Ed Silver, August 10, 1978, by James P. Leary during a workshop on miner's folklore at Vermillion Community College, Ely, Minnesota.
Born ca. 1915, Silver attended the College of Mines (now Michigan Tech) at Houghton, Michigan, and began working for U.S. Steel as an engineer in 1943. He supervised operations in open-pit iron mines in northern Minnesota, made his home in Ely, and retired in 1975. The setting of this story in an underground or deep mine is uncharacteristic of much of northern Minnesota, but it does correspond to Ely, where such operations continued until 1967.

190. Jack Foster, March 17, 1984. Mine accidents were terrible in Foster's recollections, and their frequency was one reason he chose another line of work. The "machine" in the story is a power drilling machine.

191. Jack Foster, March 17, 1984. While the miners of Foster's jokes are chiefly Cousin Jacks, other ethnics, including Croatians, Finns, and the Italians of this telling, also worked the Upper Peninsula's copper and iron mines. "Patience" and "Perseverance" are assumed to be "them two bloody Finlanders workin' across the shaft" in Dorson, "Dialect Stories of the Upper Peninsula," #36.

192. Lauri Koski, August 27, 1988. For biographical information, see the note for Text 125. Koski's heavy use of occupational jargon baffled me for a while, but I was able to make sense of this anecdote with help from Paul W. Thrush's *A Dictionary of Mining, Mineral, and Related Terms*

(Washington, D.C.: Department of the Interior, Bureau of Mines, 1968). "Putting up timber" in "sets" refers to erecting a main support frame of wood in a tunneled-out level about to be mined. "Sprags" are short wooden props or struts wedged to brace the main timbers, and "lagging" is the process of inserting the struts. To fit snugly within the support timbers, sprags had to be cut at tapered angles, or beveled, at one or both ends.

193a, 193b, 193c. The first telling was recorded from Albert Stimac, August 9, 1978, by James P. Leary at the Stimac home, Hoyt Lakes, Minnesota. Born ca. 1922 on the Mesabi Iron Range, Stimac was a machinist in the mines and served as the first president of the Iron Range Historical Society. The second telling was recorded from Oren Tikkanen, March 17, 1984. For biographical information, see the note for Text 26. The third telling was recorded from Lee Brownell, August 10, 1978, by James P. Leary during a workshop on miner's folklore at Vermillion Community College, Ely, Minnesota. Born in 1908, Brownell began work as an underground iron ore miner on Minnesota's Vermillion Range in 1927. After retiring from the Pioneer Mine, he contributed a column of occupational reminiscences to the *Ely Miner*. The work setting varies in each of the three tellings.

In Text 193a, work occurs on the "other end," the western end of the Mesabi Range, where the pair labor in a "drift," one of the horizontal passages that collectively form a mine's levels. Their task is to clear out an area newly opened by dynamite blast, then construct a "crib" (a layered structure of horizontal logs akin to the walls of a log cabin) for support. A drilling machine figures in the second telling, where Luigi and Heikki work in a stope. Although in this telling "stope" may refer to a large "room" in an underground mine, the term is used more frequently in reference to a series of step-like vertical excavations used in following a vein of ore. In the third telling, the "raise" is a small, connecting passageway between mine levels that might be hacked out of a "pillar," a column of rock generally left unmined to provide roof support. A variant appears in Dorson's "Dialect Stories of the Upper Peninsula," #83. Some Swedish loggers are traveling home by wagon, and one asks for the "yig." Another Swede tells him, "Yesus Chris', Ola, you bin here two year, and you can't say yug yet." The German Schultz and the Scandinavian Olsen bicker about "shin" and "yin" (gin) in Moulton, *2500 Jokes For All Occasions*, #1957.

194. John Slattery, August 8, 1978. For biographical information, see the note for Text 177. Hoffman offers motif X615, "Resemblance to Christ." A German and a Frenchman brag they are mistaken for rulers of their countries. A Jew reckons a watchman in the market place said, "Jesus Christ, you here again," in Lockridge, *Waggish Tales of the Czechs*, p. 260. Christ becomes "Holy Moses" in Johnson et al, *Laughter Library*, #706, and in Moulton, *2500 Jokes For All Occasions*, #1707.

195. Frank Strukel, August 4, 1978. For biographical information, see the note for Text 110. See Texts 119-123 for Finns in search of work; for another miner's employment test, see Text 201.

196. Bill Kangas, May 23, 1988. For biographical information, see the note for Text 109.

197. Frank Strukel, August 4, 1978. As an active member of the Steelworker's Union, Strukel was very interested in the history of organized labor in his community. Dorson offers a Cornish mining version in "Dialect Stories of the Upper Peninsula," #38, as does Caroline Bancroft in "Folklore of the Central City District, Colorado," *California Folklore Quarterly* 4 (1945), p. 332. Office and construction workers appear in Legman, *Rationale of the Dirty Joke*, p. 736; Powers, *The New Uff Da*, p. 51; and Stangland, *Grandson of Norwegian Jokes*, p. 10.

198. Lauri Koski, August 27, 1988. Koski told this and the next anecdote in succession; they share the theme of complaints about bosses with the prior telling. The dust and grime of the mines might lend any miner a devilish aspect. The "devil's brother" element resembles the punch line of a joke in which some trickster dresses as the devil to intimidate a rascal, but the rascal (Pat, or Ole, or Ethan Allen) responds with, "Shake hands, I married your sister." See Benjamin Botkin, *A Treasury of American Anecdotes* (NYC: Bonanza Books, 1957), p. 139, and Stangland, *More Ole and Lena Jokes*, p. 16.

199. Lauri Koski, August 27, 1988. Finnish transcription by Arnie Alanen. Koski told this on the heels of the prior example, with his pal, Toivo Reini, chuckling in appreciation of the few words in Finnish.

200. Jack Foster, March 17, 1984. Dorson recorded another Cousin Jack version set in the Central location of Foster's Keeweenaw County in "Dialect Stories of the Upper Peninsula," #37. Cully Gage puts the Cousin Jack and his Jenny in Tioga, west of Ishpeming, Michigan, in *Still Another Northwoods Reader*, pp. 86-87. A farmer's lazy wife neglects the fire in two versions reported by Katherine Briggs, *A Dictionary of British Folktales*, Part A, Volume 2 (Bloomington: Indiana University Press, 1970), p. 152.

201. Frank Strukel, August 4, 1978.

Farmers

202. Warren D. Leary, Jr., July 30, 1987. For biographical information, see the note for Text 32. Henry Schneider (b. 1880), to whom this jocular legend is attributed, was a storekeeper,

entrepreneur, and violinist in Rice Lake in the first half of this century. The "hardscrabble country" described is also known as the Blue Hills, and its rocky, swampy, rolling, stump-laden landscape is dotted with marginal and abandoned farms. This area also figures in Text 239a.

203. Val Schmidt, August 20, 1980. For biographical information, see the note for Text 58. For the tale's first part, Baughman offers motif X1523.3*, "Animals in Steep Country." Milk pails, not cows, roll from farm to farm in Ben Logan's recollections from roughly the same vicinity; see *The Land Remembers: The Story of a Farm and Its People* (NYC: Viking Press, 1975), p. 5. Baughman motif X1523.2.1*(a) is "Farmers plant corn by firing seeds at hillsides with gun." "Wind affects chickens" is motif X1611.1.7*(c). A Nebraska hen lays the same egg five times in Roger Welsch, *Shingling the Fog and Other Plains Lies* (Lincoln: University of Nebraska Press, 1972), p. 18.

204. Joseph Doyle, July 30, 1987. For biographical information, see the note for Text 25. Doyle invested the liveryman's boast with a fine brogue, stressing the contradictory acreage and thrusting out his right thumb.

205. Recorded from Rodney Oppreicht, February 8, 1981, by Mark Wagler and Emily Osborn at Alma for the Wisconsin Humor Project. Although he is "German–Swiss–English–Irish," Oppreicht was raised in an Irish–Norwegian neighborhood around Gays Mills in Crawford County, Wisconsin, where his father, Amel, farmed. Since 1963, Rodney has taught language arts at Winona Senior High School in Winona, Minnesota. His father is mentioned as the neighborhood Santa Claus and part of a rural work ring in Logan, *The Land Remembers*, pp. 209 & 250.

206. Recorded from Delores Sundeen, December 15, 1980, by Mark Wagler and Emily Osborn at Greendale for the Wisconsin Humor Project. Born in Schofield, Wisconsin, in 1916, of German extraction, Sundeen was an elementary school teacher for twenty-eight years. This is her favorite story, learned from a brother-in-law, Carl Anderson, in the late 1940s. He probably learned it while growing up on an Illinois farm. Randolph reports an Ozark version and eight joke-book references in *Hot Springs and Hell*, #332.

207. Recorded from Norman Schroeder, June, 1986, by his daughter Vicki for "Folklore of Wisconsin" at the University of Wisconsin–Madison. Schroeder is a third-generation German–American farmer. This tale remains current in such field collections and joke books as Baker, *Jokelore*, # 244; Clements, *Types of the Polack Joke*, p. 28; and Stangland, *Norwegian Jokes*, p. 41, and *Polish and Other Ethnic Jokes*, p. 27.

208. Recorded from Marcus Ewert, June 28, 1986, by Lois Buss at the Ewert home in Shawano, Wisconsin, for "Folklore of Wisconsin" at the University of Wisconsin–Madison. Born in 1928 in rural Shawano County, Ewert comes from a solidly German–American extended family of joke tellers and musicians and has done farm work for much of his life. Ewert's hole-digging, long-eared variant appears in Anderson, *Scandimania*, p. 4; Stangland, *Polish and Other Ethnic Jokes*, p. 23; and Wilde, *The Last Official Polish Joke Book*, p. 158.

209. Doug Cochenet, June 23, 1986. For biographical information, see the note for Text 143. Cochenet told this joke and the next in succession.

210. Doug Cochenet, June 23, 1986. This joke matches the second part of Text 211. The mistaken association of indolence with the farmer's sitting place draws upon a regional term for lazy farmers: "porch climbers." Meanwhile, the imperious urbanite's comeuppance by a punning farmer recalls the "Arkansas Traveler" cycle; see the note for Text 128. A girl directs a boy to her vagina, "the second hole you come to," in Legman, *Rationale of the Dirty Joke*, p. 92.

211a, 211b. The first telling was recorded from John Leino, July 28, 1987. For biographical information, see the note for Text 67. The second telling was recorded from Alice Centala Kania, March 29, 1989, by James P. Leary at the Kania home, Metz, Michigan. Alice was born on a farm in Presque Isle County, Michigan, in 1926. As a young woman in the 1940s, she worked briefly in Detroit before returning to the family farm after her mother's death. She and her husband, Ed Kania, have raised six children. Her particular version, originally heard in Polish, was learned in the 1930s from her father, Clement Centala, a second-generation Polish–American farmer and fiddler for house parties:

> I remember as a kid, we used to walk to the neighbors a lot…and neighbors would come over. And they used to play cards a lot. You'd walk there, and while you're playing cards, pretty soon someone's got to tell a joke…. And I remember my dad telling that one. Just a bunch of kids running around. "Oh, that sounds funny, everybody's laughing." So I listened to it. Well, then it always stuck because they seen that we were listening. "You kids get out of here." … And I think that's why some of these things stick in your head. You remember it because you weren't supposed to.

The joke's first part, involving literal answers to broader questions regarding potatoes, recalls an exchange George Russell told me about on July 8, 1975:

> And the discussion come up, when we were cutting [wood], about planting potatoes. What time? With the moon? And everyone had their own idea about planting

potatoes. And Mr. Drost, the sawyer, said, "Well, I'd get up in the morning and plant them."

I have also heard, "I'd plant them in the ground." The second part of both the Leino and Kania tellings is doubtless related to Text 210.

212. Recorded from Fred Wollenburg, June 24, 1985, by Margaret Stine at the Wollenburg home, rural Pardeeville, for "Folklore of Wisconsin" at the University of Wisconsin–Madison. Born ca. 1950, Wollenburg is, in Stine's words, "a teacher for the emotionally disturbed, confirmed tinkerer, and punster."

213. Recorded from George Krammer, October, 1986, by Harley Lemkuil for "Folklore of Wisconsin" at the University of Wisconsin–Madison. Born ca. 1930 in Joe Daviess County, Illinois, just south of the Wisconsin border near East Dubuque, Krammer continues to farm on the place where he grew up. Noted for his store of jokes, rhymes, and proverbial expressions, he is also a rural jack-of-all-trades: blacksmith, electrician, mechanic. Legman cites several versions in *Rationale of the Dirty Joke*, p. 208.

214. Recorded from Jerry Brokish, June 24, 1985, by Peggy Hoge for "Folklore of Wisconsin" at the University of Wisconsin–Madison. Born 1950 in Dodgeville, Wisconsin, Brokish grew up on a dairy farm and works as a farm hand in Arlington, Wisconsin. He learned this joke from an older brother when he was young. Hoge captured this performance when Brokish took a break from cleaning the barn: "Jerry tells me with an unshaven face. He's leaning on a shovel handle and his clothes are covered with manure." I recorded a version involving a boar hog from Jon Mason, June 1, 1978, Stevens Point, Wisconsin. For variants, see Legman, *Rationale of the Dirty Joke*, p. 315, and *Jim Owens Hillbilly Humor* (NYC: Pocket Books, 1970), p. 108.

215. Max Trzebiatowski, August 13, 1980. For biographical information, see the note for Text 132. Trzebiatowski told this and the following joke in quick succession; indeed, he knew several more involving the ignorance of simpleton or fledgling (usually Chicagoan) farmers.

216. Max Trzebiatowski, August 13, 1980. This telling followed the preceding example. A school-marm who has a heifer is the fool in Legman, *Rationale of the Dirty Joke*, p. 137. In a variant, a cow won't sit down to be milked; see Briggs, *A Dictionary of British Folktales*, Part A, Volume 2, p. 184.

217. Recorded from an unidentified teller, possibly Fred Wollenburg, June 24, 1985. For biographical information on Wollenburg, see the note for Text 212. The Yankee and German names of Jessup and Pretz match the ethnicities of many farmers in southern and eastern Wisconsin. An artificial inseminator is told the same thing by a farmer's city-born spouse in Legman, *No Laughing Matter*, p. 715.

218. George Russell, July 8, 1975. For biographical information, see the note for Text 52. I recorded a Finnish version in February, 1981, from Charles Mattson of Covington, Michigan. Rural non-ethnic rhymers appear in Anonymous, *Sexorama* (NYC: Derby Press, 1955), p. 58, and Legman, *No Laughing Matter*, p. 369.

219. George Russell, June 24, 1975. Printed versions include Anderson, *Scandimania*, p. 3; Copeland, *10,000 Jokes, Toasts, and Stories*, #1531; Moulton, *2500 Jokes For All Occasions*, #1136; and Powers, *Ya, Sure, Ya Betcha*, p. 14. A bull and a cow are "mating" in Legman, *Rationale of the Dirty Joke*, p. 225.

220. Max Trzebiatowski, August 14, 1979. For another Trzebiatowski telling involving flirtation through references to breeding animals, see Text 229.

221. Janet Cox, December 7, 1980. For biographical information, see the note for Text 49. Cox's "talk" onomotopoeically recreated the hens' cluck. For the Norwegian-American variant, see Stangland, *Uff Da Jokes*, p. 13.

222. Jon Mason, June 1, 1978. For biographical information, see the note for Text 133. In the middle of the joke, Mason inadvertently referred to the sow as "him." His friend Ed Grabowski, raised on a cutover farm, remarked after the telling that "a lot of those [farmer jokes] are originally from the farmers themselves." Versions appear in Anonymous, *Party Jokes For Swingers Only*, p. 175; Botkin, *A Treasury of American Anecdotes*, p. 247; J. M. Elgart, *Fifth Over Sexteen* (NYC: Grayson Publishing, 1956) p. 18; and Legman, *No Laughing Matter*, p. 252, and *Rationale of the Dirty Joke*, p. 197.

223. Recorded by Margaret "Peggy" Hoge, June 24, 1985, from her own repertoire for "Folklore of Wisconsin" at the University of Wisconsin–Madison. Born 1965 in Franklin, Wisconsin, Hoge was completing a degree in wildlife ecology and planning to pursue veterinary medicine when she took my course. She recalls hearing this joke in grade school. Sellers' proclivities to artificially fatten their beasts and buyers' attempts to induce weight loss through defecation are treated in my "Stories and Strategies of the Omaha Stockyard," in *Workers Folklore and the Folklore of Working*, ed. Philip Nusbaum and Catherine Swanson (Bloomington, Indiana: Folklore Forum, 1978), pp. 29-41.

224. Pete Trzebiatowski, August 13, 1979. For biographical information, see the note for Text 20. Trzebiatowski had a string of farmer/hireling jokes, several of which (including Text 225) were in the repertoire of his first cousin, Max Trzebiatowski. On June 13, 1978, he combined this story with one in which the farmer's son hears his father say to the hired girl, "Turn out the light and I'll eat that thing." The boy asks his mother, "Does Daddy eat light bulbs?" Legman cites Idaho instances of the "coming" and "eat glass" variants in *Rationale of the Dirty Joke*, pp. 58-59. The adulterers are a wealthy man and a maid in Anonymous, *A Lei A Day* (Fort Worth: SRI Publishing, 1966), p. 19; J. Mortimer Hall *Anecdota Americana* (NYC: Humphrey Adams, 1927), # 216; and Wilde, *The Official Religious Joke Book*, p. 84.

225. Max Trzebiatowski, August 14, 1979. As the only brother of seven older sisters, two of whom married hired men, Trzebiatowski had to chuckle at this "old one" learned as early as the 1920s. His own sisters, however, "were well watched." According to Trzebiatowski, "They couldn't get out of eyesight with the hired men, or have any fun." For variants, see Anonymous, *Sexorama*, p. 62; Legman, *Rationale of the Dirty Joke*, p. 119; Martling, *Just Another Dirty Joke Book*, p. 110; and Wilde, *The Last Official Polish Joke Book*, p. 163.

226. John Leino, July 28, 1987.

227. Keith Lea, May 6, 1982. For biographical information, see the note for Text 71. Lea was prompted to tell this by a discussion of the Depression. He followed its telling with an account of a farmer who let his pigs run on the Stevens Point market square rather than sell them for less than the cost of feed. Other versions appear in Fuller, *Thesaurus of Anecdotes*, #2312; Johnson et al, *The Laughter Library*, #640; and Meiers and Knapp, *Thesaurus of Humor*, #3745.

228. Pete Trzebiatowski, August 13, 1979. Although told as a true story, this may be a traveled anecdote for several reasons: this telling has a jocular punch line, was told along with a string of "farmer jokes," and refers to a late-19th/early-20th–century era that predates the teller's brief tenure as a farmer. Rural con artists occasionally perpetrate lightning-rod scams today.

229. Max Trzebiatowski, August 14, 1979. Another Trzebiatowski telling, Text 220, involves flirtation through reference to breeding animals.

230. George Krammer, October, 1986. See Allen Walker Read, *Classic American Graffiti: A Glossarial Study of the Low Element in the English Vocabulary* (Waukesha, Wisconsin: Maledicta Press, 1977), p. 80.

231. Edwin Pearson, July 29, 1987. For biographical information, see the note for Text 65. An array of ethnic individuals and townsfolk also malign lawyers in Anonymous, *The Minnesota Norwegian's Favorite Jokes*, p. 2; Copeland, *10,000 Jokes, Toasts, and Stories*, #4833; Masson, *The Best Stories in the World*, p. 112; and Schermerhorn, *Schermerhorn's Stories*, p. 143.

232. Lois Buss, June 23, 1986. For biographical information, see the note for Text 43.

233a, 233b. The first example was recorded from Marcus Ewert, June 28, 1986. The second was recorded from Janet Cox, December 7, 1980. Ewert's niece Lois Buss told the previous joke with its similar theme; meanwhile, Cox paired this anti-DNR joke with Text 186. In Wisconsin, the dairy state, milk is graded, and milking systems must meet strict specifications for cleanliness. Such specifications have naturally had a powerful impact on the technology and economics of farming, as well as on the layout and design of farm buildings. Agricultural runoff into creeks has been strictly monitored, as have shallow streams where cattle might wallow on hot days. If its presence in print is any indication, the joke is also enjoyed by rural Minnesotans; see Anderson, *Scandinavian Yokes*, p. 34, and Anonymous, *The Minnesota Norwegian's Favorite Jokes*, p.4.

234. Recorded from Lyle Steckel, March, 1987, by his son Jack at the Steckel home in Oregon, Wisconsin, for "Folklore of Wisconsin" at the University of Wisconsin–Madison. For variants, see Baker, *Jokelore*, #298; Dance, *Shuckin' and Jivin'*, #134; and Legman, *No Laughing Matter*, p. 778.

235. Warren D. Leary, Jr., April 3, 1985. As a journalist who grew up and worked in agricultural Barron County, Leary naturally covered the farm scene; indeed, his morning coffee group, where all the latest jokes are exchanged, included several veteran farmers.

236. Warren D. Leary, Jr., April 3, 1985

Townfolks

237. Recorded from Ida Mae Marshall, October 28, 1980, by Mark Wagler and Emily Osborn in Jefferson for the Wisconsin Humor Project. Marshall was born in 1930 and raised on a farm near Gillingham, Wisconsin, "in an area referred to as Upper Fancy Creek." Since 1952, she has been a high school librarian and math teacher in Jefferson, Wisconsin. According to Marshall, her Czech mother, Emma Janacek Marshall, "was a storyteller and this is just one of many that she related to me and my six brothers and sisters as we were growing up." Marshall's farm home was not far from the Wisconsin river town of Boscobel. Sources for "Boscobel" are a Castillian vulgarism for "beautiful wood" and a wood that sheltered Charles Stuart after defeat in the battle of Worcester.

In support of the latter explanation, there are more Scots than Spaniards in southwestern Wisconsin. See Gard and Sorden, *The Romance of Wisconsin Place Names*, p.14.

238. George Russell, July 8, 1975. For biographical information, see the note for Text 52. George Russell's father, Patrick, was born in Ireland, then immigrated to Perth, Ontario, before coming to the Town of Oak Grove in Barron County, Wisconsin, to log and homestead. Patrick Russell was a town supervisor from 1885–1887, and George heard this anecdote from him.

239a, 239b. The first telling was recorded from George Russell, July 8, 1975. Russell was prompted by a four-wheel-drive trek we had made with his former hired man, Jerry Booth, to an abandoned farm. The "hardscrabble country" figures in Text 202. The second example was recorded from Lydia Goerz, October 28, 1980, by Mark Wagler and Emily Osborn in Jefferson for the Wisconsin Humor Project. Randolph cites its circulation in Missouri around 1900 and offers a dozen references from rural areas across the United States in *Hot Springs and Hell*, #236.

240. Recorded from Minnie Moser, February 9, 1979, by Mark Wagler and Emily Osborn, Gotham, Wisconsin. Versions of this anecdote appear in Schermerhorn, *Schermerhorn's Stories*, p. 68, and in Stangland, *Uff Da Jokes*, p. 39.

241. Edwin Pearson, July 29, 1987. For biographical information, see the note for Text 65. The old Swedish logger Ole Johnson appears in Text and note 171. Pearson told this anecdote and the following tall tale in succession. He also recalled a Swedish minister whose congregation couldn't quite support him. The preacher had a hayfield and cattle. One day it looked like rain, so he filled up half the church with hay. Pearson remarked, "A lot of preachers want to lead the flock; he wanted to feed his evidently."

242. Edwin Pearson, July 29, 1987. Since Pearson was a Lutheran and preachers seldom invite the congregation to dinner, this telling is facetious beyond its anthropomorphized spuds. The teller enjoyed "making up some of these exaggerations"; see also Text 281.

243. Felix Milanowski, November 12, 1980. For biographical information, see the note for Text 78. This is an old one Felix learned in his house-party days from Polish–American tellers.

244. Max Trzebiatowski, August 14, 1979. For biographical information, see the note for Text 132. Trzebiatowski first heard this in Polish from tellers of his father's generation. Although widely collected in eastern Europe, this tale has rarely been reported in the United States. For versions translated into English, see Olga Nagy, "Personality and Community in Klara Gyori's Repertoire," *Studies in Eastern European Folk Narrative*, ed. Linda Degh (Bloomington, Indiana: Folklore Institute, 1978), p. 519, and Kurt Ranke, *European Jests and Anecdotes* (Copenhagen: Rosenkilde and Bagger, 1972), #205.

245. Jon Mason, June 7, 1978. For biographical information, see the note for Text 133. I discuss the inter-ethnic dynamics of this joke in "The Polack Joke in a Polish-American Community," *Midwestern Journal of Language and Folklore* 6:1/2 (1980), pp. 26-33.

246. Warren D. Leary, Jr., July 30, 1987. For biographical information, see the note for Text 32. Olaus "Red" Norwick made a powerful impression on my dad, who lived just down the block from the Police Station; his father, Warren Sr., once put Red up to chastising his namesake for boyish mischief. These tellings were offered in sequence by Leary and Joseph Doyle. Dallas, Wisconsin, is a heavily Norwegian farming community some twenty miles south of Rice Lake. The illiterate Finnish sheriff of Ishpeming asks a speeder from Detroit just what he's doing with "da Misigan lizense" in Dorson, "Dialect Stories of the Upper Peninsula," #35.

247. Warren D. Leary, Jr., July 30, 1987. On other occasions, I have heard my dad designate Sockness Shoe Store—founded by immigrant Norwegians and once Rice Lake's longest-running business—as the theft site. The miscreant was sometimes Axel "Clam" Peterson, an alcoholic logger who spent time in the Rice Lake jail in the 1920s and was found dead on a river bank in 1953. This second of five anecdotes in the Red Norwick cycle is usually told as a Scandinavian joke; for another version and references, see Text and note 72.

248. Joseph Doyle, July 30, 1987. For biographical information, see the note for Text 25. This third of five anecdotes in the Red Norwick cycle is set on Rice Lake's Main Street, where a sign in the form of a watch hung outside Reinhold Schlick's jewelry store from 1907 through the 1920s.

249. Joseph Doyle, July 30, 1987. The fourth of five anecdotes in the Red Norwick cycle. Hoboes were common in towns with any rail traffic during the Great Depression.

250. Warren D. Leary, Jr., July 30, 1987. This is the fifth of five anecdotes in the Red Norwick cycle. The "jungle" described was adjacent to the Soo Line tracks and at the edge of town, where a train might still be traveling slowly enough to hop.

251. Recorded from William Skinner, July 24, 1980, by Tom Barden and Mark Wagler at the Stoughton Senior Center for the Wisconsin Humor Project. Skinner was born in Edgerton, Wisconsin, in 1906. The family moved to Madison and later to Stoughton, where Skinner resides today. Until retirement in 1971, he worked in his father's coal yard, as a shipping clerk and assistant foreman for Armour Condensery, as a gas station manager, and as a lab clerk for U.S. Rubber.

He doesn't recall when or where he heard this joke. A version appears in Moulton, *2500 Jokes For All Occasions*, #387.

252a, 252b. The first example was recorded from Floyd Welker, July 22, 1988, by James P. Leary at the Welker home in Eau Claire, Wisconsin. Welker was born in 1910 in Viroqua, Vernon County, Wisconsin. In 1931, Welker began farming in adjacent Richland County, the site of this telling. He met his wife there and married in 1935. In 1947, the Welkers moved to Eau Claire, where Floyd worked as a laborer for Eau Claire Elevator and as a maintenance man for the University of Wisconsin–Eau Claire until retirement in 1975. The second was recorded from Jesse Deets, December, 1974, by Mark Wagler at the Deets home in Bloom City, Wisconsin. Born in 1896 on a Richland County farm near Bloom City, Deets served in the Army during World War I, then farmed for a few years before running a general store from the early 1920s until 1970. According to Deets, the store was a hangout for storytellers:

> We always had a lot of loafers, and it made a lot of difference what kind of business you're getting. I had people off the ridge up here come in and say, "Well, I knew if I come down here, you'd be open." Some nights, they'd be some people come in there, and they'd keep me up till twelve o'clock just talking and telling stories.

Deets' words and stories are drawn from Mark Wagler, "Jesse Deets," *Ocooch Mountain News* (1975).

"Charlie Ferg" (Charles Ferguson), the subject of tellings 252-266, was born August 5, 1865, in Ohio, the son of John Thompson Ferguson and Sarah Robbin. He moved to Richland County, Wisconsin, with his family as a young boy. In 1904 Ferguson married Lelah Jones and the couple had four children: Thelma, Lucille, Charles Gordon, and Marion. He died September 22, 1944. He had the reputation of being a great wit, a shrewd trader, and a bit of a rascal. Many of the stories attributed to him are widespread as jokes or local character anecdotes, but a few of them probably happened much as they are told.

253. Recorded from Harold Stewart, April, 1975, by his wife, Janice Stewart, Chippewa Falls, Wisconsin. Harold Stewart (born ca. 1920) grew up on a dairy farm in Richland County. After graduation from LaCrosse College in 1942 and a stretch in the Navy, Stewart was a teacher and a school administrator in Shawano, Brown Deer, Oshkosh, and other Wisconsin towns until his retirement in 1981. He earned an M.A. from LaCrosse and a Ph.D. from the University of Wisconsin, Madison. Stewart heard anecdotes about Ferg from his father, whom he describes as "quite a storyteller himself." When Mark Wagler's article on Jesse Deets, cited in the previous note, appeared in the *Ocooch Mountain News*, a regional monthly from southwestern Wisconsin, Janice Stewart responded by sending in stories her husband told, as well as from others such as her father, LaVerne Smith, and his friend George McCumber. Reprinted from the *Ocooch Mountain News* (1975).

For a Swedish variant, see Copeland, *10,000 Jokes, Toasts, and Stories*, #7449, and Patten, *Among the Humorists*, p. 72. Also, a Scandinavian is working for Louie Sands, a Swedish logging contractor in the Upper Peninsula of Michigan, in Wells, *Daylight in the Swamps*, p. 169.

254a, 254b. The first example was recorded from Loraine Kent, March 15, 1981, by Mark Wagler and Emily Osborn in Richland Center for the Wisconsin Humor Project. The second was recorded from Harold Stewart, April, 1975, by his wife Janice Stewart in Chippewa Falls, Wisconsin. Reprinted from the *Ocooch Mountain News* (1975). In the Upper Midwest, where Catholics and Lutherans dominate religious life, revival meetings have not figured largely in community life and lore. Methodists, Presbyterians, and Baptists, however, are common in southwestern Wisconsin, especially near the Mississippi, and in 19th century lead-mining towns where the Cornish, the Welsh, upland Southerners, and Yankees formed the majority. Their influence has been especially strong in Ferg's Richland County. Its county seat, Richland Center, remained legally "dry," unheard of in the beer state, from Prohibition until the mid-1980s.

255. Jesse Deets, December, 1974. Reprinted from the *Ocooch Mountain News*, (1975).

256. Harold Stewart, April, 1975. Reprinted from the *Ocooch Mountain News*, (1975). Randolph reports three versions from the American South in *Hot Springs and Hell*, #39.

257. Jesse Deets, December, 1974. Reprinted from the *Ocooch Mountain News* (1975).

258. Jesse Deets, December, 1974. Reprinted from the *Ocooch Mountain News* (1975). This is the second of five Ferg-as-trickster tales.

259. Recalled from the telling of LaVerne Smith, April, 1975, by his daughter, Janice Stewart. LaVerne Smith (ca. 1898–1977) grew up on a farm between LaCrosse and West Salem, Wisconsin. Always fascinated by the mechanical side of farming, Smith sold milking machines and later was a manufacturer of engine components in Richland Center, where he knew Charlie Ferg and heard stories about him. His daughter recalls that "he was pretty good at telling jokes, but mainly he liked to tell about things that had happened when he was young, back on the farm." Reprinted from the *Ocooch Mountain News*, (1975). This is the third of five Ferg-as-trickster tales.

260. George McCumber, April, 1975. For further information, see the note for Text 253. Reprinted from the *Ocooch Mountain News* (1975). This fourth of five Ferg-as-trickster tales is widely told; see Text 114 and its accompanying note.

261. Jesse Deets, December, 1974. Reprinted from the *Ocooch Mountain News* (1975). Knot-maple is wind-twisted and especially dense maple that can "hold a fire." A little boy asks his dad what the holes in a board are. When told they're "knotholes," he replies: "If they're not holes, what are they"; see Moulton, *25000 Jokes For All Occasions*, #600.

262. LaVerne Smith, April, 1975. Reprinted from the *Ocooch Mountain News* (1975). This joke has been published since in folklore collections too numerous to mention, and it has long been a mainstay in such published joke books as Copeland, *10,000 Jokes, Toasts, and Stories*, #6158; Fuller, *Thesaurus of Anecdotes*, #1848; Johnson et al, *Laughter Library*, #872; Moulton, *2500 Jokes For All Occasions*, #1289; and Schermerhorn, *Schermerhorn's Stories*, pp. 46-47.

263. LaVerne Smith, April 1975. Since Smith is the source of the previous example and since this telling assumes that the trickster is a frequent violator of game laws, it is probable that he told the pair in sequence.

264. Recorded from Bernard Johnson, August, 1980, by Tom Barden in Richland Center, Wisconsin. Born in 1910 in Richland County, Johnson farmed in the Bloom City area. His upland southern ancestors were old-time musicians; it is no surprise that Johnson played fiddle for various regional dance bands, including the Kickapoo Troubadours and Smelzer's Hot Shots. See Tom Barden's booklet to accompany Johnson's *It's A Mighty Pretty Waltz*, Ocooch Mountain Records LP.

265. Bernard Johnson, August, 1980. Randolph reports a version in which a stampeding razorback hog runs through the legs of a woman walking to the county fair and carries her into town; see *Sticks in the Knapsack*, pp. 128-129, 166.

266. Floyd Welker, July 22, 1988. A city man in the country is pursued by a bull and bids the same farewell in Masson, *The Best Stories in the World*, pp. 132-133.

267. Jens "Jim" Ingebretson, 1954. For biographical information, see the note for Text 172. The Tom Pratt referred to was born in Barrie, Ontario, in 1858. In 1882, he settled in Washburn County, where he worked in the woods and then ran a "stopping place" (a combination inn and general store) for loggers until shortly before his death in 1928. The next telling is attributed to Pratt, as is Text 161b. Simon Bartosic was a Polish immigrant. Baughman offers several related tall tales under motif X1785, "Lies about stretching or shrinking." X1785(ab) involves a fisherman whose buckskin pants stretch when wet; he cuts off the bottoms, but they shrink when he walks home in the hot sun. X1785(b) involves a man's sweater that stretches so much his wife can get enough yarn from the bottom to make a pair of "wristers" each spring. Ingebretson's version is reprinted from Winton, *Washburn County Historical Collections*, pp. 339-340.

268. Jens "Jim" Ingebretson, 1954. I have not encountered this story elsewhere, though similar tellings are common enough in the Upper Midwest. On August 13, 1979, Pete Trzebiatowski told me:

> I heard one at the burlesque show one time. This girl come out, and she said, "Up here [points to breasts] I'm fat, down here [points to crotch], I'm poor. And that's where you boys got to detour."

Ingebretson's telling is reprinted from Winton, *Washburn County Historical Collections*, pp. 339-340.

269. Thomas O. Church, April, 1987. For biographical information, see the note for Text 159. Green Bay, Wisconsin, is the nearest "big city" for residents of the southwestern Upper Peninsula of Michigan.

270. Recorded from Al Martin, October 12, 1980, by Mark Wagler and Emily Osborn in New Berlin for the Wisconsin Humor Project. A slow talking Ozarker offers the same retort to an inquisitive woman in Vance Randolph, *The Talking Turtle and Other Ozark Folktales* (NYC: Columbia University Press, 1957), pp. 116-117, 207; an Irishman confounds a coroner in Moulton, *2500 Jokes For All Occasions*, #1719.

271. Al Martin, October 12, 1980. Martin told this immediately after the prior example.

272. Recorded from Art Moilanen, July, 1987, by Nick Spitzer at the Smithsonian Institution's Festival of American Folklife, Washington, D.C. A retired logger and tavernkeeper, Moilanen was born in 1917 in Mass City, Ontonogan County, Michigan, where he still resides. He is revered as the region's finest Finnish-American dance musician. See my article, "Reading the 'Newspaper Dress': An Expose of Art Moilanen's Musical Traditions," in Michigan Folklife Reader, ed. C. Kurt Dewhurst and Yvonne Lockwood (East Lansing: Michigan State University Press, 1988), pp. 205-223.

273. Recorded from an unidentified teller, February 9, 1979, by Mark Wagler and Emily Osborn in Gotham, Wisconsin.

274a, 274b. The first telling was recorded from Joseph Doyle, July 30, 1987. For biographical information, see the note for Text 25. The second was recorded from Frank Strukel, August 4, 1978. For biographical information, see the note for Text 110. Leo and Charlie, conjured with a trace of brogue, were neighbors of Doyle who commonly figured in his anecdotes, both true and traveled. Jim Flynn is a legendary "working boss" for maintenance workers or "bullgangers" in open-pit iron mines on Minnesota's Mesabi Range. Frank Strukel worked for Flynn and tells a string of anecdotes about him, including the next. Each is distinguished by mimicry of Flynn's slow monotonous speech and deadpan expression. The region's Scandinavians claim responsibility for round-the-clock booze production on *Stan Boreson Tells Diamond Jim's Favorite Jokes*, side 2, band 4 and in Powers, *The New Uff Da*, p. 6.

275. Frank Strukel, August 4, 1978. Strukel told this immediately following the previous example.

276. Pete Trzebiatowski, June 13, 1978. For biographical information, see the note for Text 20. This telling, which Pete quickly identified as "just a joke," came out of a discussion about the tavernkeeper's need for a supply of jokes to entertain customers. Konkolville was one of several rural taverns Trzebiatowski managed. He frequently adapted jokes to these settings and cast himself in them. For variants on the "robbing Peter to pay Paul" adage, see Joey Adams, *Encyclopedia of Humor* (NYC: Bobbs-Merrill, 1968), p. 40, and Anonymous, *Jumbo Jokepot* (Fort Worth, Texas: S.R.I. Publishing, 1965), p. 17.

277. Pete Trzebiatowski, June 13, 1978. This joke was told immediately after the preceding example. Parallels include the following: Anonymous, *Sexorama* p. 120; Elgart *Over Sixteen*, p. 156; Harold Hart, *The Bawdy Bedside Reader* (NYC: Bell Publishing, 1971), p. 455; Marquard, *212 Spicy Stories*, p. 122; and Wilde, *The Official Sex Maniac's/Virgin's Joke Book*, p. 52.

278. Felix Milanowski, November 12, 1980. A fine Polish-style button accordionist, Milanowski well remembers the Saturday-night barn dances referred to in this telling. In the late 1920s and early 1930s he and his friends would typically leave the parties in the wee hours so they could make it to 5:30 morning mass in Ashland.

279. Pete Trzebiatowski, August 13, 1979. French, Irish, and English immigrants from Canada settled areas to the north and west of Portage County in the late 19th century when Trzebiatowski's parents arrived from Poland. Herbert Halpert cites numerous American versions of this story in Randolph, *The Talking Turtle*, pp. 197-198. Joke-book versions include Cohen, *More Laughing Out Loud*, p. 166; Copeland, *10,000 Jokes, Toasts, and Stories*, #1440; Fuller, *Thesaurus of Anecdotes*, #580; Johnson et al, *Laughter Library*, # 542; Powers, *The New Uff Da*, p. 17, and *Ya, Sure, Ya Betcha*, p. 40.

280. Recorded from Truman Kent, March 15, 1981, by Mark Wagler and Emily Osborn in Richland Center for the Wisconsin Humor Project.

281. Edwin Pearson, July 29, 1987. For biographical information, see the note for Text 65.

282. Recorded from an unidentified male teller, February 9, 1979, by Mark Wagler and Emily Osborn in Gotham, Wisconsin. This and the next three were all from the same teller. This is how the teller described Nels Bennett:

> He had new ones every couple weeks.... He never told lies to hurt anybody.... He and Lizzie, his wife, were very nice people. Good farmers. Nels always dressed in clean overalls. Gave you something every time you stopped. She was a marvelous cook. She would never contradict his stories.

Dogs are still used for farm work and for hunting birds and raccoons in southwestern Wisconsin. Emily Osborn reports more Nels Bennett stories, recorded from Ed Tubbs of Muscoda, in "Richland County Stories To Tickle Your Funny Bone," *Ocooch Mountain News* 4:1-2 (1978), pp. 26-27.

283. Recorded from an unidentified male teller, February 9, 1979, by Mark Wagler and Emily Osborn, Gotham, Wisconsin. This is the second of four tales in the Nels Bennett cycle. Horse teams for farming and logging remain in fairly common use in hilly, wooded southwestern Wisconsin, and horse pulls are an important part of county fairs and other summer rural events. This is related to Baughman motif X1759*(d), "Man or animal takes log out of bark."

284. Recorded from an unidentified male teller, February 9, 1979, by Mark Wagler and Emily Osborn, Gotham, Wisconsin. This is the third of four tales in the Nels Bennett cycle. Baughman cites a variant under motif X1004.1(db), "Hunter grabs stunned deer by antlers; it recovers, tosses him to its back. He escapes by slashing its throat with knife."

285. Recorded from an unidentified male teller, February 9, 1979, by Mark Wagler and Emily Osborn, Gotham, Wisconsin. This is the last of four tales in the Nels Bennett cycle. Rattlesnakes are common in southwestern Wisconsin, especially in the bluffs along the Mississippi River, and the swelling of snake-bit objects is extraordinarily widespread in North American folklore. This is AT Type 1899M, "Snakebite Causes Object to Swell." Baughman provides motif X1204.1(a), "Snake strikes wagon tongue, causing it to swell with various results." Examples are cited from Alberta, Indiana, Missouri, Wyoming, and Wisconsin. In the latter instance, Lake Shore Kearney sets the tale "in the southern part of the state" in *The Hodag* (Madison, Wisconsin: Democrat Printing Company, 1928), pp. 36-38.

Hunters and Fishers

286. Recorded from Ellis Nelson, April 8, 1980, by Mark Wagler, Muscoda, Wisconsin, for the Pine River Valley Folklore Project. Ellis Nelson is a welder, mechanic, gunsmith, and service station operator in Muscoda. His place of business is a local hangout where coffee and doughnuts are free and storytelling is common. In his spare time, Nelson makes fanciful sculptures from scrap metal. See Paul Tichenor, "Nelson's Gas Station in Muscoda," *Ocooch Mountain News* 4:7 (1978), 14-16.

287. Recorded from Paul Traskowski, September 30, 1980, by Mark Wagler and Emily Osborn, Wind Lake, for the Wisconsin Humor Project. Eagle River is a popular resort area in northern Wisconsin. As early as the 1820s, a Vermonter traveling in Wisconsin complained that the "Moscketos beat all I ever met with before." See Willard Keyes, "A Journal of Life in Wisconsin 100 Years Ago," *Wisconsin Magazine of History* 3 (1919-1920), pp. 339-363. Baughman provides motif X1286.1.5(a).

288. Recorded from Mel Bigge, October 12, 1980, by Mark Wagler and Emily Osborn, New Berlin, for the Wisconsin Humor Project. Da Yoopers, a regional band from Ishpeming, Michigan, performs a song, "Chicquito War," about the numerous offspring of a chicken and a mosquito that fly away with the singer's little brother. When their bills pierce his roof, he clenches them and the fowl-insects carry off the housetop. Da Yoopers, *Culture Shock*, You Guys Records, 1987. Another Upper-Midwestern roof-raising example appears in Gage, *Still Another Northwoods Reader*, p. 37

289. Roman David "Bimbo" Alexa, July 18, 1989. For biographical information, see the note for Text 157. Alexa heard this telling and the next from Hank Sploettser, originally from Engadine, Michigan, a World War II veteran and log sawyer in camps, now retired in Crystal Falls, Michigan. Alexa subtly conveys the insect's considerable size in this tale by noting that it was fornicating "flat-footed."

290. Roman David "Bimbo" Alexa, July 18, 1989. Like the previous telling, Alexa heard this from Hank Sploettser.

291. Recorded from Halsey Rinehart, February 9, 1979, by Mark Wagler and Emily Osborn, Gotham, Wisconsin. Born 1917 in Richland County, Wisconsin, Rinehart retired after working as a teacher, a farmer, a storekeeper, an insurance agent, and a county government official. Besides being a noted teller of local anecdotes, he has also been a lay preacher, a painter, and president of his county's historical society. See Thomas Barden, "Putting Flesh on the Bones of the Past: Halsey Rinehart, Artist and Storyteller," *Wisconsin Academy Review* 30:2 (1984), pp. 59-62. Rodney Jenny, to whom the story is attributed, is from Reedsburg in adjacent Sauk County. In a version attributed to Abraham Lincoln, the seized beast is a wild boar; see Moulton, *2500 Jokes For All Occasions*, #2035.

292a, 292b. The first telling was recorded from George Russell, June 17, 1975, at the Russell home, Bruce, Wisconsin. For biographical information, see the note for Text 52. Paul Fournier, the guide of Russell's tale, was born in Kankakee, Illinois, in 1866. He came to Rice Lake, Wisconsin, with an older brother and an ox in 1876. After working in the woods as a logger and teamster, he ran a hardware store before opening the Paul Bunyan Resort on the north end of Rice Lake. "There he regaled the tourists with wild tales of the lumbering era, embroidered in his own witty fashion. He frequently acted as a guide for hunting and fishing parties also," as reported in *Rice Lake Chronotype Centennial Edition* 101:1 (September 11, 1974), section E, p. 13. The second telling was recorded from the co-proprietor of Chet and Ruth's Polish Palace tavern, June 7, 1978, by James P. Leary, at the tavern in Plover, Wisconsin. Chet's telling was the 181st of 182 I recorded that night—the longest and most exuberant joke-telling session I have ever experienced. All but two of the rest were told by Leo Garski, Jon Mason, and Emery Olson, whose humor abounds in this anthology. By the time Chet told his bear story, I had heard too many tales and drunk too much beer to ask for biographical information.

Baughman provides a variant, motif X584.1, "Bear chases man back to camp: he explains that he is bringing it into camp to kill it because he did not want to carry it." The versions of George Russell and Chet are matched in Wyman, *Wisconsin Folklore*, p. 80, and in Stangland, *More Ole and Lena*, p. 23.

293. Oren Tikkanen, March 17, 1984. For biographical information, see the note for Text 26. The terms "one pipe s'otgun" and "two pipe s'otgun" are commonly used by Finnish–Americans in the Upper Peninsula of Michigan for single-barreled and double-barreled weapons. For other examples of this usage, see Dorson, "Dialect Stories of the Upper Peninsula," #80, and Text 122 in this collection.

294. Jon Mason, June 1, 1978. For biographical information, see the note for Text 133. For additional references and a lumber camp version, see note and Text 150.

295. Joseph Doyle, July 30, 1987. For biographical information, see the note for Text 25. The Kings, originally named Roi, were French–Canadians who immigrated from Quebec to northern Wiscon-

sin in the 1870s. Gideon King was evidently a character. His restaurant doubled as a "blind pig" early in this century, and in 1915 King shot a neighbor, Laurence Penzkover. See Alvah T. Axtell, *The First 50 Years, Rice Lake Wisconsin, 1875-1925* (Rice Lake: Chronotype Publications, 1980), p.106. Randolph reports an anecdote in which locals, tired of a newcomer's hunting brags, load his shotgun "with ten drams of black powder and a big handful of turkey-shot." The "gun didn't bust," but the recoil "kicked him head over heels and bruised him up considerable." See *Hot Springs and Hell*, #434.

296. Leo Garski, June 7, 1978. For biographical information, see the note for Text 15. This telling and the next, both by Garski, are indicative of the friendly hoaxing banter that accompanies the annual deer season.

297. Leo Garski, August 14, 1979.

298. Recorded from Mel Bigge, October 12, 1980, by Mark Wagler and Emily Osborn, New Berlin, for the Wisconsin Humor Project. Bigge reckoned he "made up" this one.

299. Emery Olson, June 7, 1978. For biographical information, see the note for Text 77. Olson heard this around 1930. Joke-book versions include Copeland, *10,000 Jokes, Toasts, and Stories*, #6119; Fuller, *Thesaurus of Anecdotes*, #1879; Landon, *Wit and Humor of the Age*, pp. 117-118; Moulton, *2500 Jokes For All Occasions*, #1279; and Powers, *Ya, Sure, Ya Betcha*, p. 44

300. Recorded from Ed Grabowski, August 14, 1979, by James P. Leary in the employees' lounge of the Learning Resource Center of the University of Wisconsin–Stevens Point. Born in Chicago in 1920, Grabowski moved with his family to a cutover farm in Oneida County, Wisconsin, in 1932, amidst the Depression. After military service during World War II, he worked for the A&P grocery chain throughout the Upper Midwest, then in an administrative capacity for the University of Wisconsin—Stevens Point. He retired in 1985. A second-generation Polish–American, Grabowski was fond of "Polack jokes," although he was very particular about how, when, where, why, and by whom they were told.

See my article, "The Polack Joke in a Polish-American Community," especially pp. 29-32. Grabowski favored a performance style in which dialogue, gesture, and just enough background information carried the action to its resolution in a punch line. "Mrs. Sussman," seeking a "Long Island duck," engages in the same dialogue with a butcher; see Wilde, *The Last Official Jewish Joke Book* (NYC: Bantam Books, 1980), p. 37.

301. Recorded from an unidentified female teller, July 24, 1980, by Tom Barden and Mark Wagler at the Stoughton Senior Center for the Wisconsin Humor Project. Kaupanger and Swenson are Stoughton residents. For an Ozark version and other examples from Arkansas and Kentucky, see Randolph, *Hot Springs and Hell*, #257.

302a, 302b. The first telling was recorded from Gust Pietala, July 3, 1987. For biographical information, see the note for Text 155. The second was recorded from Jon Mason, May 6, 1982, at the Hilltop Tavern, Stevens Point, Wisconsin. The "whites" to which Gust Pietala refers are whitefish, native to Lakes Superior and Michigan. Jon Mason and Leo Garski were old hunting and fishing buddies, and, as in this telling and the next, Jon Mason often told "Jon-and-Leo jokes" about their misadventures. Baughman types this variant as 1278A and cites five versions from oral tradition. Joke-book versions include Anderson, *Scandinavian Yokes*, p. 20; Anonymous, *The Minnesota Norwegian's Favorite Jokes*, p. 7; Copeland, *10,000 Jokes, Toasts, and Stories*, #6175; Moulton, *2500 Jokes For All Occasions*, #1938; and Wilde, *The Last Official Italian Joke Book* (Los Angeles: Pinnacle Books, 1978), p. 58.

303. Jon Mason, May 6, 1982. Like Text 302b, this is one of Mason's "Jon-and-Leo jokes" about hunting and fishing with his friend, Leo Garski. The degree to which fish are attracted by particular baits, or by the expert manipulation of a range of lures, is warmly debated by sports fishers. Mason told me, with Garski's concurrence, that this telling was based on an actual incident. It had become a staple in Mason's repertoire, and I recorded a less-detailed version from him on August 14, 1979.

304. Emery Olson, May 6, 1982, at the Hilltop Tavern, Stevens Point, Wisconsin. Olson's telling was followed abruptly by Leo Garski: "The only trouble with it was that it didn't last; you had to teach it to swim." A Polish fish drowns in Clements, *Types of the Polack Joke*, p. 30. Typically, the DNR crosses three of the region's most prized game fish: the Coho salmon (introduced into the Great Lakes from the Pacific Northwest to please sports fishers), the walleye (or walleyed pike), and the muskey (or muskellunge). The resultant "Cowalskey" drowns, an ironic comment on the failure of some of the DNR's efforts.

305. Recorded from Les New, September 30, 1980, by Mark Wagler and Emily Osborn in Wind Lake for the Wisconsin Humor Project. New's telling is set on Wind Lake, Racine County, Wisconsin, where he occasionally traveled to fish with his brother-in-law, Ed Palmer. Although I have not found sources for this particular example, Jan Brunvand offers stories concerning "Clever Animals" in "A Classification For Shaggy Dog Stories," *Journal of American Folklore* 76:299 (1963), pp. 53-54.

Bibliography

Adams, Robert J. *Raconteur and Repertoire: A Study of a Southern Indiana Storyteller and His Material.* Bloomington: Indiana University M.A. thesis in Folklore, 1966.

Adams, Joey. *Encyclopedia of Humor.* NYC: Bobbs-Merrill, 1968.

Anderson, Paul F. *Scandinavian Yokes.* Minneapolis, Minnesota: Eggs Press, 1979.

_____. *Scandimania: A Smorgasbord of Fun.* Minneapolis: Eggs Press, 1985.

Anonymous. *Extra-Sextra Special* New York: Scylla Publishing, 1954.

Anonymous. *500 Best Irish Jokes and Limericks.* New York: Bell Publishing, 1968.

Anonymous. *Jumbo Jokepot.* Fort Worth, Texas: S.R.I. Publishing, 1965.

Anonymous. *Lamour LaMerrier.* Fort Worth, Texas: S.R.I. Publishing, 1965.

Anonymous. *A Lei A Day.* Fort Worth: SRI Publishing, 1966.

Anonymous, *Locker Room Humor.* Chicago: Burd Publishing, 1954.

Anonymous, "Pea Soupers," unpublished manuscript. State Historical Society of Wisconsin, ca. 1937.

Anonymous. *The Minnesota Norwegian's Favorite Jokes.* Guthrie, Minnesota: Gifts O' The Wild, 1985.

Anonymous. *Party Jokes For Swingers Only.* New York: Bee-Line Books, 1967.

Anonymous. *Sexorama.* New York: Derby Press, 1955.

Anonymous. *Toujour Manure.* Fort Worth: S.R.I. Publishing, 1966.

Ashton, J. W. "Some Folk Etymologies for Place Names," *Journal of American Folklore,* 57(1944):222.

Axtell, Alvah T. *The First 50 Years, Rice Lake Wisconsin, 1875-1925.* Rice Lake: Chronotype Publications, 1980.

Baker, Ronald L. *Jokelore, Humorous Folktales From Indiana.* Bloomington: Indiana University Press, 1986.

Bancroft, Caroline. "Cousin Jack Stories From Central City." *Colorado Magazine* 21(1944):2.

_____. "Folklore of the Central City District, Colorado," *California Folklore Quarterly,* 4 (1945).

Barden, Tom. "Wisconsin Humor," *Ocooch Mountain News,* 6(1980):6.

Barden, Thomas. "Putting Flesh on the Bones of the Past: Halsey Rinehart, Artist and Storyteller," *Wisconsin Academy Review,* 30(1984):2.

Barnouw, Victor. *Wisconsin Chippewa Myths And Tales, And Their Relation To Chippewa Life.* Madison: University of Wisconsin Press, 1977.

Bartlett, William M. "The Memoirs of Bruno Vinette," *Wisconsin Magazine of History,* 9 (1925-1926).

Baughman, Ernest. *Type and Motif-Index of the Folktales of England and North America.* The Hague: Mouton & Co., 1966.

Berquist, John. Cassette recording. *Ya Sure, You Bet You.* Half Moon Records, HM 1005, 1985.

Bocafucci, Tommy. *The Italian Joke Book.* New York: Belmont Tower Books, 1975.

Boreson, Stan. Phonograph album. *Stan Boreson Tells Diamond Jim's Favorite Yokes.* Huntington Station, NY: Golden Crest Records, LP CR-31028.

Botkin, Benjamin. *A Treasury of American Anecdotes.* NYC: Bonanza Books, 1957.

Brendle, Rev. Thomas R., and William S. Troxell. *Pennsylvania German Folk Tales, Legends, Once-Upon-A-Time Stories, Maxims, and Sayings.* Norristown, Pennsylvania: Pennsylvania German Society, 1944.

Briggs, Katherine. *A Dictionary of British Folktales*, Part A, Volume 2. Bloomington: Indiana University Press, 1970.

Brown, Charles E. *Cousin Jack Stories: Short Stories of the Cornish Lead Miners of Southwestern Wisconsin.* Madison: Wisconsin Folklore Society, 1940.

_____. *Bunyan Backhouse Yarns.* Madison: Wisconsin Folklore Society, 1945.

Brunvand, Jan. "A Classification For Shaggy Dog Stories," *Journal of American Folklore,* 76(1963):299.

Chappelle, Ethel Elliott. *"The Why of Names." In Washburn County, Wisconsin.* Birchwood, Wisconsin: 1965.

Clements, William. *The Types of the Polack Joke.* Bloomington, Indiana: Folklore Forum Bibliographic and Special Series, No. 3, 1969.

Clode, Edward J. *Jokes For All Occasions.* New York: Grosset and Dunlap, 1921.

Cohen, Myron. *More Laughing Out Loud.* New York: The Citadel Press, 1960.

Copeland, Lewis, and Faye Copeland. *10,000 Jokes, Toasts, and Stories.* New York: Garden City Books, 1939.

Corrigan, George. *Calked Boots and Cant Hooks.* Park Falls, Wisconsin: MacGregor Litho, 1977.

Cray, Ed. "The Rabbi Trickster," *Journal of American Folklore* 78(1964):306.

Da Yoopers. Phonograph record. *Culture Shock*, You Guys Records, JO 81148, 1987.

Dance, Daryl Cumber. *Shuckin' and Jivin', Folklore From Contemporary Black Americans.* Bloomington: Indiana University Press, 1978.

Dorson, Richard M. "Folk Traditions of the Upper Peninsula," *Michigan History,* 31(1947):1.

_____. "Dialect Stories of the Upper Peninsula: A New Form of American Folklore." *Journal of American Folklore* 61(1948):240.

_____. *Bloodstoppers and Bearwalkers, Folk Traditions of the Upper Peninsula.* Cambridge: Harvard University Press, 1952.

_____. *Negro Tales from Pine Bluff, Arkansas, and Calvin, Michigan.* Bloomington: Indiana University Press, 1958.

Dundes, Alan, and Carl R. Pagter. *Work Hard and You Shall Be Rewarded, Urban Folklore From the Paperwork Empire.* Bloomington: Indiana University Press, 1978.

Elgart, J.M. *Over Sixteen.* New York: Grayson Publishing, 1951.

_____. *Furthermore Over Sixteen*, vol. 4. New York: Grayson Publishing, 1955.

_____. *Fifth Over Sixteen.* NYC: Grayson Publishing, 1956.

Erickson, Alfred O. "Scandinavia, Wisconsin," *Norwegian-American Studies and Records,* 15, 1949.

Fauset, Arthur Huff. *Folklore From Nova Scotia.* American Folklore Society Memoir 24, 1931.

Fuller, Edmund. *Thesaurus of Anecdotes.* New York: Crown Publishers, 1942

Gage, Cully. *Still Another Northwoods Reader.* Au Train, Michigan: Avery Color Studios, 1989.

Gard, Robert, and L. G. Sorden. *The Romance of Wisconsin Place Names.* New York: October House, 1968.

_____. and L.G. Sorden. *Wisconsin Lore.* Sauk City, Wisconsin: Stanton and Lee, 1976.

Gardner, Brother Dave. Phonograph album. *Rejoice, Dear Hearts,* ca. 1960.

Green, Rayna. "Magnolias Grow in Dirt, The Bawdy Lore of Southern Women," *The Radical Teacher,* 6 (1977).

Hall, J. Mortimer. *Anecdota Americana, Second Series,* reprinted from the 1934 edition as *503 World's Worst Dirty Jokes.* New York: Bell Publishing, 1982.

_____. *Anecdota Americana.* NYC: Humphrey Adams, 1927.

Halpert, Herbert. *Folktales and Legends from the New Jersey Pinelands,* 2 volumes. Bloomington: Indiana University Ph.D. dissertation in Folklore, 1947.

Hart, Harold. *The Bawdy Bedside Reader.* NYC: Bell Publishing, 1971.

Hoffman, Frank. "Motif Index of Erotic Literature," in *Analytical Survey of Anglo–American Traditional Erotica.* Bowling Green, Ohio: Bowling Green University Popular Press, 1973.

Holbrook, Stewart H. *The American Lumberjack.* New York: Collier Books, 1962

Holmes, Fred L. *Old World Wisconsin, Around Europe in the Badger State.* Madison: 1944.

House, Boyce. *Tall Talk from Texas.* San Antonio: Naylor, 1944.

Johnson, Bernard. Phonograph record. *It's A Mighty Pretty Waltz.* Ocooch Mountain Records, 1983.

Johnson, Aili K. "Lore of the Finnish–American Sauna," *Midwest Folklore,* 1(1951):1.

Johnson, J.H., Jerry Sheridan, and Ruth Lawrence, eds. *The Laughter Library.* Indianapolis: Maxwell Droke, 1936.

Kearney, Lake Shore. *The Hodag.* Madison, Wisconsin: Democrat Printing Company, 1928.

Keyes, Willard. "A Journal of Life in Wisconsin 100 Years Ago," *Wisconsin Magazine of History,* 3 (1919-1920).

Kowalski, Mike. *The Polish Joke Book.* New York: Belmont Tower Books, 1974.

Krotzman, James Michael. *Folktales Found In The St. Croix Valley.* M.A.T. thesis in English, University of Wisconsin–Eau Claire, 1973.

Landon, Melville D. *Wit and Humor of the Age.* Chicago: ca. 1901.

Larson, Agnes M. "On the Trail of the Woodsman," *Minnesota History,* 13(1932):4.

Leary, James P. "Stories and Strategies of the Omaha Stockyard." In *Workers Folklore and the Folklore of Working,* ed. Philip Nusbaum and Catherine Swanson. Bloomington, Indiana: Folklore Forum, 1978.

_____. "George Russell: The Repertoire and Personality of a North Country Storyteller." In *Folklore On Two Continents, Essays in Honor of Linda Degh,* eds. Nikolai Burlakoff and Carl Lindahl. Bloomington, Indiana: Trickster Press, 1980.

_____. "The Polack Joke in a Polish-American Community," *Midwestern Journal of Language and Folklore,* 6(1980):1/2.

_____. "Polish Priests and Tavern Keepers in Portage County, Wisconsin," *Midwestern Journal of Language and Folklore*, 8(1982):1.

_____. "Style in Jocular Communication." *Journal of Folklore Research* 21(1984):1.

_____. "The Favorite Jokes of Max Trzebiatowski." In *Humor and the Individual*, ed. Elliott Oring. Los Angeles: The California Folklore Society, 1984.

_____. "Reading the 'Newspaper Dress': An Expose of Art Moilanen's Musical Traditions." In *Michigan Folklife Reader*, ed. C. Kurt Dewhurst and Yvonne Lockwood. East Lansing: Michigan State University Press, 1988.

Lee, Art. *The Lutefisk Ghetto: Life in a Norwegian–American Town.* Staples, Minnesota: Adventure Publications, 1978.

Legman, Gershon. *Rationale of the Dirty Joke, An Analysis of Sexual Humor.* New York: Grove Press, 1968.

_____. *No Laughing Matter, Rationale of the Dirty Joke: Second Series.* Wharton, New Jersey: Breaking Point, Inc., 1975.

Lewis, Arthur Pope. *Now That Reminds Me.* n.p.: The Caxton Press, 1927.

Lockridge, Norman. *Waggish Tales of the Czechs.* NYC: Candide Press, 1947.

Logan, Ben. The Land Remembers: The Story of a Farm and Its People. NYC: Viking Press, 1975.

Lyons, Jimmy. *The Mirth of a Nation.* New York: Vantage Press, 1953.

Marquard, Ralph L. *212 Spicy Stories.* New York: Hart Publishing, 1976.

Martling, Jackie. *Just Another Dirty Joke Book.* Los Angeles: Pinnacle Books, 1982.

Masson, Thomas L. The Best Stories in the World. New York: Doubleday, Page & Company, 1913.

Meiers, Mildred, and Jack Knapp. *Thesaurus of Humor.* NYC: Crown Publishers, 1940.

Moulton, Powers. *2500 Jokes For All Occasions.* Philadelphia: Circle Books, 1942.

Mullen, Patrick B. *I Heard the Old Fishermen Say: Folklore of the Texas Gulf Coast.* Austin: University of Texas Press, 1978.

Nagy, Olga. "Personality and Community in Klara Gyori's Repertoire." In *Studies in Eastern European Folk Narrative*, ed. Linda Degh. Bloomington, Indiana: Folklore Institute, 1978.

Nelligan, John Emmett. *The Life of a Lumberman.* Madison: State Historical Society of Wisconsin, 1929.

Novak, Ned. *The New Polish Joke Book.* NYC: Nordon Publications, 1977.

Osborn, Emily. "Richland County Stories To Tickle Your Funny Bone," *Ocooch Mountain News*, 4(1978):1-2.

Owens, Jim. *Hillbilly Humor.* NYC: Pocket Books, 1970.

Palm, Harry W. *Lumberjack Days in the St. Croix Valley.* Bayport, Minnesota: Bayport Printing House, 1969.

Patten, William. *Among the Humorists and After Dinner Speakers.* NYC: P.F. Collier & Son, 1909.

Pike, Robert. *Tall Trees, Tough Men.* NYC: W.W. Norton & Co., 1967.

Posner, George. *The World's Best Humor.* Philadelphia: Pennsylvania Publishing Company, 1925.

Powers, Charlene. *The New Uff Da, A Collection of 189½ Norwegian Jokes.* Crosby, North Dakota: The Journal Publishing Company, 1977.

_____. *Ya Sure, Ya Betcha!* Crosby, North Dakota: The Journal Publishing Company, 1981.

_____. *Leapin' Lena.* Crosby, North Dakota: The Journal Publishing Company, 1984.

Pride, Fleetwood. *Fleetwood Pride, 1864–1960: The Autobiography of a Maine Woodsman,* ed. Edward D. Ives and David C. Smith. Orono, Maine: Northeast Folklore Society, 1967.

Puotinen, Heino. *Finglish Fables and Other Humorous Finnish Dialect Tales.* White Pine, Michigan: Privately Printed, 1969.

_____. "The Anatomy of Finglish," *Michigan Academician,* 3(1971):3

Randolph, Vance. *The Talking Turtle and Other Ozark Folktales.* NYC: Columbia University Press, 1957.

_____. *Sticks in the Knapsack.* New York: Columbia University Press, 1958.

_____. *Hot Springs and Hell, And Other Folk Jests and Anecdotes from the Ozarks.* Hatboro, Pennsylvania: Folklore Associates, 1965.

_____. *Pissing in the Snow and Other Ozark Folktales.* Urbana: University of Illinois Press, 1976.

Ranke, Kurt. *European Jests and Anecdotes.* Copenhagen: Rosenkilde and Bagger,1972.

Read, Allen Walker. *Classic American Graffiti: A Glossarial Study of the Low Element in the English Vocabulary.* Waukesha, Wisconsin: Maledicta Press, 1977.

Rice Lake Chronotype, Centennial Edition, 101(1974):1, section G.

Roberts, Leonard. *South From Hell-fer-Sartin'.* Berea, Kentucky: Council of the Southern Mountains, 1964.

Rosholt, Malcolm. *Our County, Our Story, Portage County, Wisconsin.* Stevens Point: Worzalla Publishing, 1959.

Runninger, Jack. *Favorite Jokes of Mountain Folks in Boogar Hollow.* Lindale, Georgia: Country Originals, 1971.

Schermerhorn, James. *Schermerhorn's Stories.* New York: George Sully and Company, 1929.

Smith, H. Allen. *Rude Jokes.* Greenwich, Connecticut: Fawcett Gold Medal Books, 1970.

Sorden, L.G. *Lumberjack Lingo.* Spring Green: Wisconsin House, 1969.

Spalding, Henry D. *Encyclopedia of Black Folklore and Humor.* Middle Village, New York: Jonathan David, 1972.

Stangland, Red. *Norwegian Jokes.* Sioux Falls, South Dakota: Norse Press, 1979.

_____. *Uff Da Stories.* Sioux Falls, South Dakota: Norse Press, 1979.

_____. *Polish and Other Ethnic Jokes.* Sioux Falls, South Dakota: Norse Press, 1980.

_____. *Son of Norwegian Jokes.* Sioux Falls, South Dakota: Norse Press, 1980.

_____. *Ole and Lena Jokes.* Sioux Falls, South Dakota: Norse Press, 1986.

Starr, Mary Agnes. *Pea Soup and Johnny Cake.* Madison, Wisconsin: Red Mountain Publishing, 1981.

Thomas, Gerald. "Newfie Jokes." In *Folklore of Canada,* ed. Edith Fowke. Toronto: McClelland and Stewart Limited, 1976.

Thompson, Stith. *Motif Index of Folk Literature,* 6 vols., rev. ed. Bloomington: Indiana University Press, 1955.

_____. *The Types of the Folktale.* Helsinki: Suomalainen Tiedakatemia, 1961.

Thrush, Paul W. *A Dictionary of Mining, Mineral, and Related Terms.* Washington, D.C.: Department of the Interior, Bureau of Mines, 1968.

Tichenor, Paul. "Nelson's Gas Station in Muscoda," *Ocooch Mountain News,* 4(1978):7.

Vennum, Thomas Jr. "The Ojibwa Begging Dance." In *Music and Context: Essays for John M. Ward,* ed. Anne D. Shapiro. Cambridge, Mass.: Department of Music, Harvard University, 1985.

Vineyard, Catherine Marshall. "The Arkansas Traveler." In *Backwoods To Border,* ed. Mody C. Boatright and Donald Day. Austin and Dallas: 1943.

Wagler, Mark. "Jesse Deets," in *Ocooch Mountain News,* 1(1975).

Wells, Robert. *Daylight in the Swamp: Lumberjacking in the Late 19th Century.* Garden City, New York: Doubleday, 1978.

Welsch, Roger. *Shingling the Fog and Other Plains Lies.* Lincoln: University of Nebraska Press, 1972.

Wentworth, Harold, and Stuart Berg. *Dictionary of American Slang.* New York: Thomas Crowell, 1960.

Wilde, Larry. *The Official Irish Joke Book.* Los Angeles: Pinnacle Books, 1974.

_____. *The Official Religious Jokebook.* Los Angeles: Pinnacle Books, 1976.

_____. *The Last Official Polish Joke Book.* Los Angeles: Pinnacle Books, 1977.

_____. *The Last Official Italian Joke Book.* Los Angeles: Pinnacle Books, 1978.

_____. *The Complete Book of Ethnic Humor* Los Angeles: Pinnacle Books, 1978.

_____. *More of the Official Irish Jokebook.* Los Angeles: Pinnacle Books, 1979.

_____. *The Last Official Jewish Joke Book.* NYC: Bantam Books, 1980.

_____. *The Last Official Irish Joke Book.* New York: Bantam Books, 1983.

Winton, Ward. *Washburn County Historical Collections.* Washburn, Wisconsin: Washburn County Historical Society, 1976.

Wyman, Walker D. *The Lumberjack Frontier.* Lincoln: University of Nebraska Press, 1969.

_____. *Wisconsin Folklore.* Madison: University of Wisconsin–Extension, 1979.

Youngman, Henny. *The Best of Henny Youngman,* Vol. 1. New York: Grammercy Publishing, 1978.

Index of Tellers

The numbers after each name are text numbers, not page numbers. Where biographical information about the teller was available, it may be found in the collection note for the first text cited.

Index of Places Where
Material Was Collected